CW00383732

Horton's Guide to
Britain's Railways
in
Feature Films

Horton's Guide to
Britain's Railways
in
Feature Films

Glyn Horton

• A SILVER LINK BOOK •
from
The NOSTALGIA Collection

© Glyn Horton 2007

All rights reserved. No part of this publication may be reproduced, stored in a retrieval system or transmitted, in any form or by any means, electronic, mechanical, photocopying, recording or otherwise, without prior permission in writing from Silver Link Publishing Ltd.

First published in 2007

British Library Cataloguing in Publication Data

A catalogue record for this book is available from the British Library.

ISBN 978 1 85794 287 3

Silver Link Publishing Ltd
The Trundle
Ringstead Road
Great Addington
Kettering
Northants NN14 4BW

Tel/Fax: 01536 330588
email: sales@nostalgiacollection.com
Website: www.nostalgiacollection.com

Printed and bound in the Czech Republic

Acknowledgements

I wish to thank the many people who helped me in researching and compiling this book and making the work so enjoyable and worthwhile. Thanks are due to Frank Dumbleton and members of the Great Western Society, Paul Holroyd and the Vintage Carriage Trust, Barry Jones, Robin Lush, Ruth Milsom, Andrew Parry, John Tunstill, Martin Welch, the staff of the British Film Institute, the Dean Forest Railway, and Editor Will Adams and everyone at Silver Link Publishing for their assistance.

All effort has been made to trace credits for the film stills and illustrations included. I will be pleased to correct any errors or omissions in future editions, and can be contacted via the publisher.

Contents

Bibliography and sources

Books
Adams, Mark *Movie Locations – A Guide to Britain & Ireland* (Boxtree, 2000)
Burrows, Martin *A to Z of London's transport film facts* (London Transport Museum (visitor notes), 2002)
Gifford, Denis *The British Film Catalogue 1895-1985* (David & Charles, 1986)
Griffith, Edward *The Basingstoke & Alton Light Railway* (E. C. Griffith, 1970)
Huntley, John *Railways on the Screen* (Ian Allan, 1993)
Mitchell, Vic and Smith, Keith *Branch Lines to Longmoor* (Middleton Press, 1987)
Reeves, Tony *The Worldwide Guide to Movie Locations* (Titan)
Walker, John (ed) *Halliwell's Film and Video Guide* (HarperCollins, various years)

Some railway magazines and society journals have been referred to in researching this book. They include various issues of *The Railway Magazine*, *Steam Railway*, *Heritage Railways*, *Severn Valley Railway News*, *Bluebell News*, *The Tenterden Terrier*, *Main Line*, *Moors Line*, *Push and Pull*, *West Somerset Railway Journal*, *Great Western Echo*, *Bulliver* and *The Iron Horse*. Also referred to were film magazines *Sight and Sound* and *Monthly Film Bulletin*.

Video
Steam on 35mm (Vols 1-4) and *Diesels and Electrics on 35mm*, both released by Video 125, are excellent compilations of out-takes from British films.
Trains from the Arc (Vols 1-3), also from Video 125, are also excellent compilations of railway film from the 1890s to the 1920s, and include some story film material.

Websites
The following websites have been useful:
www.britmovie.co.uk
www.reelstreets.com
www.imdb.com

About this book

hy did I decide to write this book? Well, I can't think of any better answer than I'm fascinated by railways and I enjoy a good film! I suppose I have to resort to the cliché that the roots of my interest go back to when I was a lot younger than now. I grew up in the 1970s and '80s, so can't claim to have grown up in a 'golden age of cinema-going' or, for that matter, a golden age of the railway (cutbacks and criticism seemed to have dominated that period), and I grew up seeing films on the television not the cinema. However, I quickly became familiar with the railway scenes beamed into the family living room on what seemed an amazingly regular basis.

And there seemed to be nothing more regular than the Christmas family film. *The Railway Children* always seemed to be on. I would watch *Chitty Chitty Bang Bang* expecting the appearance of the 0-6-0 saddle tank (it took quite a few years before I worked out where it was filmed – for a long time I thought it was some kind of early preserved line), and the grandly titled *Those Magnificent Men in their Flying Machines*, with Terry-Thomas landing his plane on the 'Jones Goods'-hauled passenger train. The summer holidays were just as good. *Murder She Said* would appear one afternoon with its opening views of Paddington, and after repeated showings you knew that when Margaret Rutherford began playing golf near the railway line that a 'D600' series 'Warship' diesel would come whining past. The first time I saw *The Titfield Thunderbolt* it was a revelation – a whole Technicolor film on a railway theme! Who can forget the opening shot of the 'West Country' on the S&D, the view at Bristol Temple Meads and Stanley Holloway and Hugh Griffith driving their '1400' down the streets of Woodstock (OK, it was a lorry, but quite a good disguise I thought). One Saturday morning I got to see *Oh Mr Porter* and loved the quick one-liners and interplay between Hay, Marriott and Moffatt. It's one of those films that treat the railway like one big train-set, together with *The Great St Trinian's Train Robbery*, which came out years later.

So, about ten years ago I decided to write this book. I wanted to find a way of covering as many as possible of the British railway scenes that had appeared in feature films, and to produce an easy-to-use A-Z reference guide that would be there for anyone who had an interest in railways and films. I can't pretend that it's been an altogether easy task – I've had to see an awful lot of films, and that means having to sit through an awful lot of rubbish! But it's been incredibly fascinating and rewarding as well. It's made me realise just how many films have featured a train and, even in our trainspotter-mocking, leaves-on-the-line-sneering media age, just how many film-makers rely on a railway scene. You only have to see children clamber to get on board No 5972 *Olton Hall* in it's 'Harry Potter' guise at some Open Day to note the excitement that cinema transfers to its mechanical stars, and how the railways themselves, particularly the preservation movement, have found it excellent for promotion.

Another thing I should add is just how much of the railway scene the cinema has inadvertently captured over the years. Stations, rolling-stock, staff, posters, coach interior décor, etc, have all appeared, and help to date a film instantly. Of course, certain locomotive types appear with regularity – 'Castles', 'V2s', 'Black Fives', 'Royal Scots', 'Lord Nelsons' and Class 47 diesels – but just occasionally a real rarity will show up – the GWR-owned 'ROD' 2-8-0 in *Kate Plus Ten*, a great shot of 'N15X' rebuild No 2332 at the start of *Waterloo Road*, and one of the North British Class 16s in *The Leather Boys*. Locations have followed similar patterns of regularity – London and the Home Counties are unsurprisingly prominent, but interesting oddities include Abbotsbury, the rare GWR branch backwater in *The Small Back Room*, and Sandsend on the Whitby-Scarborough line in *Holiday Camp*.

Originally I conceived this book to concentrate on British standard gauge in the cinema. However, over the years I have widened the net to include narrow gauge, London Underground, light rail systems and even street trams. I stopped short of someone's suggestion that I include roller-coasters! I have thrown in a couple of titles that feature model railways if they are shown in particular detail – also bearing in mind that many older films often used models for special effects. Many films up to the 1960s used studio sets to recreate carriage interiors, station platforms, etc. The designers tried hard, but usually the sets had a fake, cluttered look. I have only included these films if they also contain actual railway scenes – those whose railways never left the studio set (the Denham studio railway excepted) are omitted. Also, this book centres purely on feature films, so documentaries and short films are not included; all the films are more than about 50 minutes in length. There are, however, some drama-documentaries included, such as *Conquest of the Air*, as they contain dramatised scenes with actors.

This book contains an A-Z listing of films that contain known British railway scenes. Please note the emphasis on 'known'. I have not seen every British film ever made, nor am ever likely to. More frustratingly, there are films that I know contain railway sequences but are unavailable for viewing. However, this list is the most comprehensive compiled so far and certainly contains most of the major railway scenes that have appeared on the big screen since cinema began.

Each entry follows a common format, as follows:

Film title

The title of the film on its initial release. Please bear in mind that some films were re-titled at a later date or when released to foreign countries. Some films are known to have had about three or four different titles.

Country of origin

The country that made the film. As this book deals with British railways on film, clearly the majority of the films are British-made and are listed as 'GB'. American films that include British railway scenes appear as 'US', while other countries appear under their full title. In recent years many films have been made as co-productions by more than one country, and this is indicated accordingly.

Year of release

The year that the film was first released in a cinema. Some non-British films may have been released in their home countries quite some time before release here. Occasionally films are completed, then not released in a cinema until some time after. Some films don't get a cinema release at all and go straight to video. Where this has happened I have given the year of video release.

Film company

The production company that made the film. Some company names are abbreviated:

ABPC	Associated British Pictures
AIP	American International Pictures
ATP	Associated Talking Pictures
BBC	British Broadcasting Corporation
BIP	British Instructional Pictures
CFF	Children's Film Foundation
GFD	General Film Distributors
MGM	Metro Goldwyn Mayer
TCF	Twentieth Century Fox
TCM	Turners Classic Movies
UA	United Artists

In recent years many films have been made by a string of different companies, particularly international co-productions. For reasons of space I have listed the most prolific of the companies involved in the production.

DVD/VHS availability

This indicates if the film has had a legitimate commercial release on home video. If a film has had releases on VHS and DVD formats I have indicated availability as 'DVD', as this is now the dominant format; thus films noted as 'VHS' have only ever had a VHS release. These notes do not necessarily mean that the film is currently available on VHS/DVD, just that it has been released in these formats at some time. It might be possible to find deleted videos on the specialist collectors'/second-hand market.

Director

'Dir' indicates the director of the film.

Principal stars

Two principal stars or players from the film are named.

Synopsis

This gives a brief description of the plot of the film.

Railway details

This is the main section for each film entry, and details the railway scenes found in the film with information regarding locomotive types and (where identifiable) numbers, locations (where known) and other points such as trivia, behind-the-scenes detail, errors, etc.

I've used some cinematic terms here that railway enthusiasts may not be too familiar with:

Stock footage – rather than film a train scene specially, many directors illustrate a train journey in the plot with a piece of stock footage taken from the company's film library. It's therefore common for material shot for earlier films to crop up in films years later (eg *Train of Events*) and it usually leads to some odd continuity.

Back projection – it was common in films made up until the 1970s for railway journey scenes to be filmed in a studio. The view out of the window of the passing scenery was created by erecting a large screen on which stock film from an actual train journey was projected. It was used most commonly for these type of scenes, but sometimes back projection was used for shots such as those involving actors hanging out of doors or windows (eg *The Thirty Nine Steps*) or station sequences.

Phantom ride shots – film of the line ahead taken from the front of a moving train, and also known as cab-view shots. In steam days the cameraman was sometimes perched on the front of the loco, but more often on a flat wagon being propelled.

Well, I hope you enjoy using this book. Happy viewing!

A history of railways in British film

The very first railway films of any kind made in this country date from the late 1890s. With film in its infancy and audiences intrigued to see subject matter of any kind, these films are very basic by today's standards, little more than simple shots of trains passing the cameraman – their whole intention was to 'show off' the film medium and thus depict straightforward scenes of everyday life. The recently discovered Mitchell and Kenyon films of northern street scenes, for example, are very typical of this, and, with railways very much a part of late-Victorian life, it was only natural that they should appeal to early film-makers. Very quickly, however, there was felt a need to give audiences an experience of seeing something they wouldn't normally have the chance to, hence the emergence of 'phantom ride' films. These were early examples of 'cab-ride' views, although obviously with steam locos they involved the cameraman either precariously balanced on the front of the engine as it slowly moved forward or positioned on a flat truck in front of the loco. These became quite popular for a while, examples including *Down Exeter Incline* (1898) and *View From an Engine Front – Shilla Mill Tunnel* (1899), both made on the LSWR in Devon.

However, in November 1899 something happened. Enterprising film-maker George A. Smith, who ran a film business in Hove, Sussex, got hold of the Shilla Mill film and split it in the middle at the point when the train entered the tunnel, then adding a scene filmed at his studio with himself kissing a girl supposedly on the train. Train enters tunnel – kiss in tunnel – train leaves tunnel. Entitled simply *The Kiss in the Tunnel*, it lasts barely a minute, but it is the earliest known film in which the railway is used in a storyline. The railway feature film was born.

This in itself was ground-breaking. However, in the same month the Bamforth company in Yorkshire made an almost exact copy of Smith's film with the same title. But there was one strong difference – whereas the Smith film used 'phantom ride' shots for its train sequence, the Bamforth film uses two lineside shots on either side of the studio 'kiss' scene: a long shot of the train entering Queensbury Tunnel on the Bradford-Halifax line and a shot of a Midland Railway train arriving at Monsal Dale in the Peak Forest. This use of lineside scenes set much more of a precedent of how railways would be included in 'story' films, and is also probably the earliest known example of inaccuracy in a railway film, something that has given the enthusiast a lot of unintentional humour since!

As the new century progressed more and more story films used railways as a plot device, and they became increasingly more sophisticated. *A Railway Tragedy* (1904) used scenes on the LB&SCR interspersed with a crime melodrama, including an excellent (for its time) special-effect shot of a woman being saved from death by an approaching express. *When the Devil Drives* (1907) is an early fantasy/horror yarn featuring scenes on the LNWR in the Llandudno area and great use of trick shots involving models. Noteworthy about this period is the diversity of locations – one was just as likely to see a shot of an LSWR express in the London area as a local train in Yorkshire. At this time the pioneer film companies were relatively spread out across the British Isles, and even though the cameramen didn't want to stray too far from the studio with cumbersome equipment, it still meant a regional diversity of train shots, but this was soon to change. Takeovers occurred, cinemas were bought up, companies closed down – some going back to the still photography business from which they had emerged. The emerging big film companies such as Gaumont and Gainsborough opened studios around London and this meant a lot more railway scenes filmed around the capital and the Home Counties. Some companies, such as Mancunian Films, would later make their base in the North (and film their train sequences there accordingly), but from now on it would be the Home Counties that would dominate.

By the 1920s Britain had a fully fledged film industry making full-length features with the railway playing an important part in them. In 1927 the first version of *The Ghost Train* was filmed, and the following year *Underground* used the London 'tube' as its setting, with much filming at Waterloo. In 1929 some of the most spectacular and exciting railway films to date played to audiences – *High Treason* with its vision of the Channel Tunnel; *The Wrecker*, for which Gainsborough bought a Stirling 4-4-0 and coaching stock so they could film it smashing into a lorry on a level crossing; and *The Flying Scotsman*, with its actors clinging to running boards as they hurtled along the Hertford Loop, and uncoupling No 4472 itself at speed.

The 1930s were probably a golden era for both the film and the railway industries. Cinema audiences were high and the 'quota' law (which dictated that a certain proportion of films shown had to be British-made) meant that film studios were going at full pelt. The 'Big Four' railway companies were at their height of innovation and steam locomotive design. The LNER showed off one of its brand-new 'A4' 'Pacifics' at the start of *Oh Mr Porter* (1937), and talented directors such as Alfred Hitchcock made full use of railway locations for such productions as *Number Seventeen* (1932) and *The Thirty Nine Steps* (1935). Bernard Vorhaus made *The Last Journey* (1936) with the full co-operation of the Great Western, and the film makes full use of depicting crack GWR expresses. Although all of these films use a lot of studio-bound scenes, it is notable that film companies were making more and more of their productions 'on location', typically with the use of real railway locations for such films as *The Ghost Train* (1931) and *Oh Mr Porter* (1937), which practically took over the Limpley Stoke-Camerton and Basingstoke and Alton branch lines respectively. The appearance of these 'location'-based films, together with *The Last Journey*, illustrates the financial confidence of British films in this decade, which culminated with producer Alexander Korda even building a railway for filming purposes in the grounds of Denham studios.

It is worth noting that the siting of London studios at locations such as Islington and

Welwyn resulted in a lot of LNER scenes appearing in films of this period (eg *Number Seventeen, Wedding Rehearsal,* etc). Similarly, studios at locations such as Shepherds Bush, Twickenham and Walton-on-Thames resulted in a frequency of Southern scenes (*The Ghost Camera, Bank Holiday*). However, the popularity of regional stars such as Gracie Fields meant that some provincial railway sequences were also captured, such as in *Sing as we Go* (1934) in Lancashire.

The outbreak of the Second World War had a striking effect on the film studios. Money spent on production was radically reduced; in fact some studios were actually closed down to allow alternative use to aid the war effort. A classic comparison of 1930s and wartime production is to look at the 1941 remake of *The Ghost Train* alongside the 1931 version. The earlier film makes extensive use of real outdoor locations on a country branch line with rolling-stock borrowed from the GWR, whereas the 1941 version has a few stock shots from earlier films, some railway scenes from the 1931 film, and most of the story taking place on the studio floor. It was during the war years that stock footage of trains to illustrate a railway journey became a lot more common in productions (with the attendant rise of inaccuracies and continuity errors), probably due to security and financial restrictions. With the end of the war some of the dormant studios re-opened, particularly Denham and Pinewood, the latter having been fairly little used, but which would become very prolific from this time on. The location of these studios in particular resulted in an increase of location work filmed on the GWR, together with Elstree, which saw an increase of LMR Midland Main Line scenes. The post-war era saw a move towards the realistic social drama film, a good example being Ealing Studios' *It Always Rains on Sundays* (1947), which used urban locations such as the LNER's Temple Mills yard.

Ealing Studios became very successful in the post-war period, and continued so into the 1950s. It was in 1952 that they made one the best-loved railway films, *The Titfield Thunderbolt,* which typifies this era in a number of ways. It illustrates the move towards making a film almost entirely on location, and 'taking over' a branch line again. It is also made in colour – the 1950s saw a significant increase in colour production and the Technicolor photography captures the English countryside perfectly. A topical point is made in that it deals with a line closure; although the Beeching Report was still several years away, many branch lines were already feeling the threat. Ealing's swansong was *The Ladykillers,* made in 1955, which used colour photography to capture the moody, smoky blue-brick background of the King's Cross area.

In terms of railway locations the Denham/Pinewood/Elstree studio dominance saw a lot of railway scenes from the north-west/west area of the Home Counties appear in films during this decade, with the GW&GC Joint line receiving particular coverage. Also, the growth of studios at Shepperton and Twickenham south of the Thames saw an increase in scenes on the Southern (the Shepperton branch itself appeared in a number of productions). A particular line that caught the attention of producers during this period was the Longmoor Military Railway (although a couple of pre-war films had used it). In a secluded part of Hampshire, it was relatively quiet, offered extensive facilities and came with trained personnel who were able to easily 'derail' a locomotive and/or coaches for some action shots (see 1956's *Bhowani Junction*). Not surprisingly, the railway was frequently used by film-makers right up until closure in the early 1970s. Some B-movies from this time also used railways for dramatic effect, such as *The Flying Scot* (1957) and *The Gold Express* (1954).

By the end of the 1950s the big film companies were beginning to feel the effects of their main competitor – television. Cinema audiences were in decline and some studios, such as Ealing, were even closed and adapted for television use. There was a significant move towards making films on location in areas outside London, particularly the North of England, in what became known as the 'kitchen sink' dramas. Gritty and grim, they did allow use of fresh railway locations such as Halifax (*Room at the Top*), Bolton (*A Kind of Loving*) and Nottingham (*Saturday Night and Sunday Morning*). At the other end of the scale, film companies fought back with big-budget action and comedy films that included ever more spectacular railway sequences. So we have Terry-Thomas landing his plane on top of a train in *Those Magnificent Men in their Flying Machines* (1965), the 'crash' scene in *The Wrong Box* (1966), and the madcap chases in *The Great St Trinian's Train Robbery* (1966). The St Trinian's film is significant in that it illustrates the influence on film-makers of the actual Great Train Robbery of 1963. This event had an effect on film stories directly – *Robbery* (1967) – and indirectly – *Crooks in Cloisters* (1963) and *Rotten to the Core* (1965). The massive rise of rock and pop music saw a number of film spin-offs – the best-known of which starred the Beatles in *A Hard Day's Night*, which included a railway sequence filmed on the Minehead branch. Marylebone was also used for a famous scene where they were mobbed by their fans. As London stations became modernised, Marylebone became very popular with film companies as a location as it was relatively untouched for period films, and with the run-down and termination of Great Central line services it was quiet, particularly on Sundays and off-peak periods. The 1960s also began the tradition of film companies using preserved railways as locations, with the opening of the Bluebell Railway. *The Innocents* was the first film to be made there in 1961, and the railway turned up in several films throughout the rest of the decade.

Despite the fight-back, British cinema was seen as being in irreversible decline. Audiences continued to dwindle and many cinemas closed. Poor box office takings at the end of the 1960s resulted in most of the American backers pulling out of British production, and the general decrease in money and enthusiasm resulted in fewer films being made – resulting in fewer railway scenes appearing in the 1970s and '80s. The film industry concentrated on making well-budgeted period films and cheaply made horror and comedies. Indeed, the dominance of television is illustrated by the fact that so many of the comedy productions of this time were spin-offs from successful TV sitcoms. The making of period films saw even greater use of the preservation movement, which benefited from the end of steam on BR. Film-makers who wanted to use a steam train now had no choice but to go to a preserved line. The Bluebell continued to be used, particularly by director Ken Russell for films such as *Lisztomania* (1974) and *Tommy* (1975). EMI filmed *The Railway Children* on the Keighley & Worth Valley Railway in 1970, with the line seeing frequent use culminating with *Yanks* in 1979. The Severn Valley Railway also became popular for film use during the 1970s, being used for a spectacular chase scene in *The Seven Per Cent Solution* and the 1978 remake of *The Thirty Nine Steps*. On British Rail, film-makers continued to use Marylebone (*Mahler* and *Carry on Girls*, both 1974) and particularly South London locations, using the lines around Clapham Junction, which always seemed to turn up in police and crime films at this time (*Villain* of 1971, *All Coppers Are* and *The Offence*, both 1972, and *Sweeney 2* of 1974).

The 1980s were another lean decade for British film, although there was more use of preserved railways. The Bluebell remained very popular with a particularly association with Merchant-Ivory films, such as *A Room with a View* (1985), whereas the Severn Valley line seemed, strangely, to go out of favour. More preserved lines made their debuts on the big screen, such as the Great Central (*Buster*, 1988) and the North Yorkshire Moors (*A Month in the Country*, 1987).

The 1990s saw a reversal in fortune for British films with the setting up of a UK Film Council and the emergence of American and European co-productions, which provided a greater source of money. Channel 4 television set up a film production unit called FilmFour, and the BBC did likewise with BBC Films. Thus in the latter half of the decade there was a noticeable increase in film production. Many films were set in London, and the London Underground became a popular location for filming, for example *Sliding Doors* (1997) and *Elephant Juice* (1999). The Aldwych line, which closed to regular use at this time, was actually retained by London Transport for film use (*Patriot Games* in 1991 and *The Wings of the Dove* in 1997). Elsewhere in the capital the new Docklands Light Railway began to make appearances (*Mad Cows*, 1999). After being run down and threatened with closure for years, Marylebone was finally modernised, which ironically meant that it was no longer any good for films set in the past! The film-makers therefore looked to the second quietest and least transformed station in London – St Pancras. This station had already seen more frequent use in the previous decade, and it became well served by film companies into the Millennium. The decade also saw the setting up of regionalised Film Commissions around the UK, which resulted in greater variety of railway locations, notably Scotland (*Trainspotting*, 1996) and the Isle of Man (*Stiff Upper Lips*, 1997). The use of preserved railways was as frequent as ever and, while the big names remained in demand, it was good to see other railways getting their share of the limelight, namely the Dean Forest Railway (*Darklands*, 1996), East Lancashire Railway (*Let Him Have It*, 1991) and Chinnor and Princes Risborough (*Photographing Fairies*, 1997).

The new Millennium has seen film companies utilising the railway on screen as much as before. By far the dominant image on screens over the last few years has been the 'Hogwarts Express' in the highly successful series of 'Harry Potter' films, with King's Cross station and Glenfinnan Viaduct becoming iconic images around the globe. The 'Harry Potter' phenomenon, and 'Thomas the Tank Engine' before it (*Thomas and the Magic Railroad*, 2000) have placed images of the steam railway before younger audiences to an extent not seen for many years. Certainly this has provided the preservation movement with excellent publicity and a lucrative source of income. The 'Harry Potter' films also illustrate an ever-growing element of many films of recent years – the use of computer-generated imagery (CGI). Thus real shots of trains can be blended into artistic effects brought up by a CGI team, such as the generated views of 1930s Paddington created for the early scenes in *The Chronicles of Narnia* in 2005.

The computerised imagery of modern film-making is definitely a long way from the early short hand-cranked films of the 1900s. But it is important to remember that cinema has always been about entertainment and spectacle. The audiences that wondered at the early short story films such as *A Kiss in the Tunnel* or even the antics of Will Hay at Buggleskelly and the suspense of *The Thirty Nine Steps* are not much different from the audiences that wonder at Harry Potter's Ford Anglia flying over the 'Hogwarts Express'. Railways have been used by cinema across the decades for dramatic and comedic effect, and the fascination shows no sign of abating. To misquote old Harbottle in *Oh Mr Porter*, the next train's not yet gone!

THE ABOMINABLE DR PHIBES
GB 1971 AIP DVD
Dir: Robert Fuest
Joseph Cotten, Vincent Price

A disfigured surgeon seeks revenge on the doctors who failed to save his wife

In one scene Cotten and his on-screen son are playing with an O-gauge layout that includes a model of 'Royal Scot' 4-6-0 No 6100.

ADOLF HITLER – MY PART IN HIS DOWNFALL
GB 1972 UA-Norcon
Dir: Norman Cohen
Jim Dale, Spike Milligan

Dramatisation of Spike Milligan's experiences as a WW2 recruit

Closing scenes feature Horsted Keynes station (posing as 'Aldershot') on the Bluebell Railway, with preserved 'Dukedog' 4-4-0 No 3217 used for station shots and a run-by filmed at Holywell.

THE ADVENTURES OF JANE
GB 1949 Eros
Dirs: Edward G. Whitling, Alf Goulding
Christobel Leighton-Porter, Wally Patch

A film version of the adventures of Jane, famous comic strip character from the Daily Mirror

Features some shots of Brighton station.

AGATHA
GB 1978 Warner
Dir: Michael Apted
Vanessa Redgrave, Dustin Hoffman

A fictionalised story about what happened to Agatha Christie during her real-life disappearance in the 1920s

York station was disguised as 'Harrogate' for the film, much of the filming using the bay platforms at the north end of the station. 'A3' 4-6-2 No 4472 *Flying Scotsman* and 'J72' 0-6-0T *Joem* were both used. No 4472 was given the new identities 4474 and 4480 on opposite sides of the engine, to give the impression that action was taking place on separate occasions with different trains, a level of authenticity quite welcoming in a feature film. Coaching stock came from a number of sources, including Pullman car 'Mary' from the Keighley & Worth Valley Railway.

THE ALF GARNETT SAGA
GB 1972 Columbia
Dir: Bob Kellett
Warren Mitchell, Dandy Nichols

The further adventures of Alf Garnett as he adapts to life on a housing estate

Features some good passing shots of Eastern Region EMUs on the LTS lines: two Class 305 units (including set No 447) and a Class 302 (set No 227).

ALFIE
GB 1966 Paramount DVD
Dir: Lewis Gilbert
Michael Caine, Vivian Merchant

Adventures of a irresponsible Cockney lothario

Features a scene showing the St Pancras station approaches in the background, with a DMU just visible and a Sulzer-engined Type 2 diesel can be heard. In a another scene Caine walks down a street in Brixton; his face is in close-up, which results in the background being out of focus, but a blurred outline of a Class 71 electric passes over a bridge behind him. There is also a brief shot in Waterloo station with SR EMUs in the background.

ALI G INDAHOUSE
GB 2002 UIP/Working Title DVD
Dir: Mark Mylod
Sacha Baron Cohen, Michael Gambon

Ali G stands as an MP and wins

There is a very brief shot of a steam loco on a miniature railway at an unknown location, but possibly in the Staines area.

ALIVE AND KICKING
GB 1958 ABP
Dir: Cyril Frankel
Sybil Thorndyke, Kathleen Harrison

Three old ladies escape from a home and set themselves up in Scotland

Features a 1930s stock shot of a GWR express 4-6-0, probably a 'King'.

ALL COPPERS ARE
GB 1972 Rank VHS
Dir: Sidney Hayers
Nicky Henson, Martin Potter

A crook and a cop both have affairs with the same girl

Most of the film was shot around Battersea and there are considerable railway scenes in the Queenstown Road/Clapham Junction area. Included are SR two-car suburban 4-SUB, 4-COR and South Western express units, together with examples of Class 33 and Class 73, both running light. There is also a chase sequence filmed in one of the coal yards at Battersea with 16-ton mineral and hopper wagons evident.

ALL CREATURES GREAT AND SMALL
GB 1974 EMI DVD
Dir: Claude Whatham
Simon Ward, Anthony Hopkins

The life of a country vet in pre-war Yorkshire

The film opens with a shot of the northern bay platforms in York station with 1930s posters to add period flavour. A couple of parcels vans are visible but no locos.

ALL OR NOTHING
GB 2002 Studio Canal/Thin Man DVD
Dir: Mike Leigh
Timothy Spall, Lesley Manville

A taxi driver's family copes with life on a London housing estate

Stratford station appears in the background of one scene, with a Docklands Light Railway unit and a Class 365 EMU just visible.

THE ALPHABET MURDERS
GB 1965 MGM
Dir: Frank Tashlin
Tony Randall, Robert Morley

Hercule Poirot investigates a series of strange murders

Includes a night scene at Victoria station using BR Mk 1 coaches (no loco visible), a couple of night shots of diesel-hauled expresses and a back-projected shot of a steam-hauled train. As these scenes take place at night, exact loco types cannot be identified.

AMA

GB 1991 Artificial Eye
Dirs: Kwesi Owusu, Kwate Nee-Owoo
Thomas Baptiste, Anima Misa

Fantasy drama about Africans living in London

Features a scene on Hungerford bridge in London with an SR suburban EMU passing.

THE AMAZING QUEST OF ERNEST BLISS
(aka THE AMAZING ADVENTURE)

GB 1936 UA DVD
Dir: Alfred Zeisler
Cary Grant, Mary Brian

A millionaire bets he can be successful without using his wealth

Some shots in the East London area with a local passenger made up of LMS 3rd Class non-corridor stock (loco not seen) and an LNER 'J52' 0-6-0T on a freight. Also seen is a 1920s LT District Line train and a shot of the frontage of LT Stepney Green station.

AN AMERICAN WEREWOLF IN LONDON

GB 1981 Polygram DVD
Dir: John Landis
David Naughton, Jenny Agutter

An American tourist is bitten by a werewolf and becomes one himself

Features a sequence involving the werewolf stalking a commuter on the Underground. These scenes were filmed at Tottenham Court Road station on the Northern Line and used 1972 tube stock. Aldwych station was also used for some scenes.

AMY FOSTER

GB/US/France 1997 Columbia TriStar DVD
Dir: Beeban Kidron
Vincent Perez, Rachel Weisz

In 19th-century Cornwall a shipwrecked Russian marries a local servant girl

Features a railway scene supposedly set in the Ukraine but which was actually filmed on two preserved railways, the Keighley & Worth Valley and the North Yorkshire Moors. Preserved L&YR 'A' Class No 1300 was used, adorned with dummy cow-catcher, large headlight and European-style numberplates (H-17) on cab and tender sides to appear like a vintage Russian loco, and hauling a train of various vans suitably weathered. A signal on the K&WVR had a continental-style arm fitted to add to the effect.

THE ANGRY SILENCE

GB 1960 British Lion DVD
Dir: Guy Green
Richard Attenborough, Pier Angeli

A factory worker suffers at work when he refuses to join a strike

The film's opening features ex-LMS 3MT 2-6-2T No 40010 arriving with a local at Willesden Junction Low Level (Watford lines).

ANNA KARENINA

GB 1948 BL/London Films DVD
Dir: Julien Duvivier
Vivien Leigh, Ralph Richardson

Adaptation of Tolstoy's tragic novel

London Films borrowed two ex-SECR 'B1' Class 4-4-0s Nos 1445 and 1454 for this film to play a couple of pseudo-Russian locos. This involved fitting the locos with massive smokestacks, headlights, built-up tenders and railings around the front-end footplating. Filming took place at night at Tattenham Corner station with some suitably disguised stock. Some studio and model work appears throughout the film but the Tattenham shots appear at certain moments, most clearly in the final scenes where Karenina commits suicide. Indeed, there is a close-up of the smokebox of one of the 'B1s', which really gives the game away.

ANOTHER MAN'S POISON

GB 1951 Douglas Fairbanks Jnr/Daniel
    M. Angel
Dir: Irving Rapper
Bette Davis, Anthony Steel

A novelist poisons her husband and her lover

Features a night scene at an unknown station in the North of England with an Ivatt 2MT 2-6-0 passing.

ANOTHER TIME ANOTHER PLACE

GB 1958 Paramount DVD
Dir: Lewis Allen
Lana Turner, Glynis Johns

An American has an affair with a war correspondent, and after he is killed she sees his widow

Lana Turner takes a trip to Cornwall in the film by train, which is illustrated by a stock shot of 'King' 4-6-0 No 6004 on an express near Teignmouth. Then there are some nice shots of Looe station with a '4500' 2-6-2T in attendance with the branch train. The same location appears at the end of the film with good shots taken on the platform and overlooking from the river.

APPOINTMENT WITH CRIME

GB 1945 British National
Dir: John Harlow
William Hartnell, Robert Beatty

An ex-convict swears revenge on the gang that let him take the rap for the crime

A train robbery sequence is interspersed with the usual varying stock shots of changing locomotives including an ex-LSWR 4-4-0 and a GWR 4-6-0, filmed day for night, therefore making exact identifications difficult. Also, later in the film there is a shot of an LMS 'Compound' 4-4-0 leaving St Pancras with a train.

ARABESQUE

US 1966 Universal DVD
Dir: Stanley Donen
Gregory Peck, Sophia Loren

An Oxford professor finds his life is in danger when he is asked to decipher a hieroglyphic

Some scenes filmed on Waterloo station with a good shot of a Southern Region 4-SUB EMU arriving. The climax was filmed on the famous Crumlin Viaduct on the Pontypool-Neath line in South Wales, shortly before its demolition. Look closely and you can see that the track has already been lifted.

ARTHUR'S DYKE

GB 2001 Evolution Films DVD
Dir: Gerry Poulson
Pauline Quirke, Dennis Waterman

A group of friends reunite to walk Offa's Dyke

'Chepstow' station in the film is actually Abergavenny, with a shot of a Class 158 'Sprinter' DMU arriving.

THE ASPHYX

GB 1972 Glendale
Dir: Peter Newbrook
Robert Stephens, Robert Powell

A scientist separates the spirit of death from the body with tragic results

Features an aerial shot over Clapham Junction with Southern suburban EMUs passing.

THE ASTONISHED HEART

GB 1949 Gainsborough
Dirs: Terence Fisher, Anthony
    Darnborough
Noel Coward, Margaret Leighton

A married psychiatrist has an affair with another woman

A scene in the film mixes footage of Paddington station concourse with studio filming, and there appear to be ex-GWR 4-6-0s in the background.

THE AVENGERS

US 1998 Warner DVD
Dir: Jeremy Chechik
Ralph Fiennes, Uma Thurman

Unsuccessful attempt to update the 1960s TV series with Steed and Miss Peel having to save the world from a mad meteorologist

London's old Kingsway tram subway is used in the film as the entrance to the government's secret headquarters.

B

B MONKEY

GB 1998 Buena Vista/Miramax DVD
Dir: Michael Radford
Asia Argento, Jared Harris

A London schoolteacher begins an affair with an Italian jewel thief

Various shots are included on the London Underground featuring 1972 Northern line stock, Circle/District 'C'-type stock and 1990s-built tube stock. There is also a scene at Waterloo International with a Class 373 Eurostar in evidence.

BACHELOR OF HEARTS

GB 1958 Rank
Dir: Wolf Rilla
Hardy Kruger, Sylvia Syms

A German student goes to Cambridge University

Features a departure scene from London King's Cross with 'blood and custard'-liveried Mk 1 stock (loco not visible), a run-by shot of an ex-LNER 'B17' 4-6-0 and a shot of the frontage of Cambridge station – all in all a good accurate depiction of a London to Cambridge train journey!

BACKGROUND

GB 1953 Group Three
Dir: Daniel Birt
Valerie Hobson, Philip Friend

A couple decide on divorce but worry about the effect on the children

Features a scene at London Victoria station – the departing train engine is not shown, but there appears to be an ex-SR 'King Arthur' 4-6-0 at the stop-blocks.

BANK HOLIDAY

GB 1938 GFD/Gainsborough VHS
Dir: Carol Reed
Margaret Lockwood, Hugh Williams

Adventures of various holidaymakers on a day out to Brighton

This classic film includes a number of railway scenes but disgraces itself by firstly showing the holidaymakers departing for Brighton behind a Gresley 'A1' 'Pacific' leaving King's Cross station! It partly makes up for this later on though, with some scenes at Waterloo station featuring Southern locos. Good shots of 'Schools' 4-4-0 No 938, 'Lord Nelson' 4-6-0 No 956, a Urie 4-6-0, an ex-LSWR 0-4-4T and a distant pre-war SR EMU.

BARNACLE BILL

GB 1957 Ealing
Dir: Charles Frend
Alec Guinness, Irene Browne

An unsuccessful captain takes command of a seaside pier

The pier features a working miniature 4-4-0 steam loco with open seated stock on basic narrow gauge track. Filmed at Hunstanton pier, Norfolk.

THE BATTLE OF THE SEXES
GB 1960 Prometheus DVD
Dir: Charles Crichton
Peter Sellers, Constance Cummings

An American efficiency expert causes upset to a Scottish tweed manufacturer

A rail journey between London and Edinburgh is illustrated by some stock footage of Paddington station, a passing streamlined LMS 'Coronation' 'Pacific' (from *Brief Encounter*) and a distant view of an 'A4' 'Pacific' approaching Edinburgh Waverley.

THE BATTLE OF THE VILLA FLORITA
GB 1964 Warner
Dir: Delmer Daves
Maureen O'Hara, Rossano Brazzi

Two children try to break up their mother's romance with a concert pianist

One good shot of a Class 117 DMU, probably on the Maidenhead-High Wycombe branch, and a scene at Marylebone station featuring Class 115 DMUs.

THE BEAST IN THE CELLAR
GB 1970 Tigon-Leander DVD
Dir: James Kelly
Flora Robson, Beryl Reid

Two elderly spinsters keep their disfigured brother locked up but he goes on the rampage

This horror film features a scene on the Bluebell Railway at Horsted Keynes station; the train loco, however, is too far off to be properly identified.

BEAT GIRL
GB 1960 Renown VHS
Dir: Edward T. Greville
David Farrar, Noelle Adam

An architect's daughter rebels against her father's new wife

Includes a scene of some teenagers playing chicken on a railway line, which includes shots of ex-LMS 'Black Five' 4-6-0s, and a run-by shot of 'Royal Scot' 4-6-0 No 46100 on Bushey troughs (stock footage filmed for *Train of Events*).

BEAUTIFUL CREATURES
GB 2000 Universal DVD
Dir: Bill Eagles
Rachel Weisz, Susan Lynch

A woman kills her boyfriend and her friend helps her dispose of the body

Some of the railway scenes were filmed on the Bluebell Railway featuring maroon Mk 1 stock, as well as the Bo'ness Railway (at Bo'ness station itself) and a lineside shot next to the WCML – no locos are seen.

BEAUTIFUL PEOPLE
GB 1999 Warner/Channel 4 DVD
Dir: Jasmin Dizdar
Charlotte Coleman, Roger Sloman

In London, various examples of ethnic intolerance come to a head

Features some filming around the ECML in North London with Class 313 and Class 365 EMUs seen.

THE BEAUTY JUNGLE
GB 1964 Rank
Dir: Val Guest
Janette Scott, Ian Hendry

A typist enters a beauty contest and becomes Miss Globe but finds life at the top hard

Features a fashion shoot scene taken on Marylebone station platforms.

THE BED SITTING ROOM
GB 1969 UA
Dir: Richard Lester
Ralph Richardson, Spike Milligan

Various survivors of a nuclear war eke out a frugal existence

Part of the plot of this surreal fantasy involves a family living on an London Underground train, the unit involved being 1960 tube stock possibly filmed on the Aldwych branch.

BEDAZZLED
GB 1967 TCF DVD
Dir: Stanley Donen
Peter Cook, Dudley Moore

A cook makes a pact with the Devil

In one scene Cook and Moore are walking close to Subway Junction near Paddington and a 'Hymek' diesel passes on a short parcels train.

BELL BOTTOM GEORGE
GB 1943 Columbia
Dir: Marcel Varnel
George Formby, Ann Firth

A sailor catches a ring of spies

The film climaxes with a car chase that was filmed in and around Fleetwood, and a couple of 1930s Blackpool single-deck trams are seen. Also, in the dockside scenes, some LMS coaches and wagons are visible in the background.

THE BELLES OF ST TRINIAN'S
GB 1954 British Lion DVD
Dir: Frank Launder
Alastair Sim, George Cole

The first film featuring the notorious schoolgirls

Features a shot of Paddington station (from stock footage), a distant shot of a GWR 4-6-0 on an express, and a brief comedy scene filmed at Seer Green station on the GW&GC Joint line.

BELLMAN AND TRUE
GB 1987 HandMade/Euston Films DVD
Dir: Richard Loncraine
Bernard Hill

A computer expert is used by gangsters for a heist

Includes some good scenes filmed at Paddington station at the start of the film with plenty of HSTs on view, including set No 253 051.

THE BELSTONE FOX
GB 1973 Rank DVD
Dir: James Hill
Eric Porter, Rachel Roberts

A fox and a hound grow up together but this leads to tragedy for the humans

One of the most dramatic moments in the film features the fox leading the hunt's hounds onto a railway line, which are then killed by a train. Some good shots of a 'Hymek' on a goods train feature in these scenes, which were filmed on the Minehead branch.

BEND IT LIKE BECKHAM
GB 2002 Kintop/Helgron/Film Council DVD
Dir: Gurinder Chadha
Parminder K Nagra, Keira Knightley

A young Indian girl dreams of becoming a professional footballer

Features scenes at Hounslow Central and Piccadilly Circus LT stations with 1970s Piccadilly Line stock.

BETRAYAL
GB 1983 Horizon
Dir: David Jones
Jeremy Irons, Ben Kingsley

The story of a publisher and his wife who has an affair

Includes a shot of LT 'C'-type stock filmed on the Hammersmith line.

BEYOND THIS PLACE
GB 1959 Renown
Dir: Jack Cardiff
Van Johnson, Vera Miles

An American in London turns detective to clear his wrongly convicted father

Features a scene on a level crossing at night in which Johnson is nearly run down by an unidentified EMU. Location unknown.

BHAJI ON THE BEACH
GB 1993 Channel 4/First Independent
 DVD
Dir: Gurinder Chadha
Kim Vithana, Jimmi Harkishin

A group of Asian women have a day out in Blackpool

This successful comedy bases most of its story in Blackpool, thus a number of Blackpool trams are on camera – a double-deck Balloon, an OMO type and illuminated trams all feature.

BHOWANI JUNCTION
GB 1956 MGM DVD
Dir: George Cukor
Stewart Granger, Ava Gardner

Drama set in India during the last days of the British Raj

Although mostly filmed in Pakistan using that railway's steam locos (including some Beyer-Peacock types), the film features the aftermath of a spectacular crash, which was filmed on the Longmoor Military Railway. 'WD' 2-10-0 No 600 *Gordon* was suitably disguised as an Indian Railways loco, complete with mock-up fittings, and was placed at the bottom of an embankment on the Hollywater Loop section, together with some rolling-stock (including two 12-wheel Caledonian coaches that were sadly destroyed for the filming). Longmoor carved a bit of a niche as a location for recreating train disasters, as the re-railing procedures formed part of the training for Army Reserve Units (see also *The Interrupted Journey*).

THE BIG BLOCKADE
GB 1941 Ealing VHS
Dir: Charles Frend
Michael Redgrave, John Mills

Various Britishers realise the importance of blockading Germany in the war

A propaganda film that includes a scene

meant to represent a German train; however, one close-up of the wheels and splashers of the loco as the train starts clearly reveal them to belong to a GWR 4-6-0, taken from stock footage.

THE BIG MONEY
GB 1956 Rank
Dir: John Paddy Carstairs
Ian Carmichael, Belinda Lee

The son of a family of crooks sets out to prove he can pull off a big heist

Features a run-by shot of two ex-SR 2-BIL EMUs somewhere on the SW Division.

BIGGLES
GB 1986 UIP/Compact
 Yellowbill/Tambarle DVD
Dir: John Hough
Neil Dickson, Alex-Hyde-White

An American executive is transported back to World War One to help an airman

Created from the W. E. Johns stories but updated to include things such as time travel. The 1917 scenes feature a helicopter landing on a flat wagon on a moving train and taking off again. At the time of making the film this stunt had not been attempted before. The scene was filmed on the Nene Valley Railway with the train hauled by preserved Nord DeGlehn 'Compound' 4-6-0 No 3628.

BILLY ELLIOT
GB 2000 UIP/BBC/Working Title DVD
Dir: Stephen Daldry
Jamie Bell, Julie Walters

During the 1984 miners' strike a boy learns ballet instead of boxing

Features a scene on the Jubilee Line extension at Canary Wharf station with 1970s tube stock (despite the fact that the station did not exist until 15 years after the film events took place!).

BILLY LIAR
GB 1963 Vic Films DVD
Dir: John Schlesinger
Tom Courtenay, Julie Christie

An undertaker's clerk lives in a fantasy world that he finds hard to separate from reality

This classic 1960s comedy features a sequence at a railway station that, although set in Bradford, was filmed at Marylebone. No locos are seen although a diesel horn is heard at one point.

BITTER HARVEST
GB 1963 Independent Artists DVD
Dir: Peter Graham Scott
Janet Munro, John Stride

A Welsh girl goes to London and dreams of fame

A lot of the story takes place in a tenement overlooking the WR main line between Paddington and Westbourne Park. Various trains seen passing are hauled by 'Castle' 4-6-0s, '9400' 0-6-0PTs on empty stock movements, a couple of 'Hymeks' and a 'Warship' (believed to be D807). There is also a scene on Paddington station itself with a 'Castle' 4-6-0 visible. Out-takes appear in Video 125's *Steam on 35mm* Vol 4.

BLACK BEAUTY
GB/US 1993 Warner DVD
Dir: Caroline Thompson
David Thewlis, Peter Davison

Adventures of a horse from birth to pasture

Features a scene filmed at Horsted Keynes on the Bluebell Railway. No locos visible.

BLACK JOY
GB 1977 Winkast
Dir: Anthony Simmons
Norman Beaton, Trevor Thomas

A Guyanan immigrant falls in with ne'er-do-wells in Brixton

The film was made on location in Brixton with Brixton LT station frontage and passing BR-built Southern Region suburban EMUs seen.

THE BLACK SHEEP OF WHITEHALL
GB 1941 Ealing VHS
Dirs: Basil Dearden, Will Hay
Will Hay, John Mills

An incompetent teacher beats spies who are keeping a boffin in a nursing home

The journey to the nursing home comprises one of the most mixed-up series of shots seen of a rail journey. First there is general shot of Paddington station, but the train gets under way behind an SR 'L1' 4-4-0 (the number possibly 1753) filmed at Victoria. There are two shots of the train en route taken from stock footage – the familiar track-level shot of a 'Royal Scot' in the Lune Gorge and an LNER 'A5' 4-6-2T entering a tunnel on the GC. Finally the train arrives behind GWR 'Grange' 4-6-0 No 6815, filmed at High Wycombe station. All of the 'Big Four' in one railway journey!

THE BLACK WINDMILL
GB 1974 Universal DVD
Dir: Don Siegel
Michael Caine, Janet Suzman

A secret serviceman's son is kidnapped

Features a scene on the London Underground with 1960 tube stock.

BLACKMAIL
GB 1929 AIP DVD
Dir: Alfred Hitchcock
Anny Ondra, Sara Allgood

A police inspector finds his girl is suspected of murder and he is blackmailed

This Hitchcock thriller features a very brief shot of a London tram passing as Ondra looks out of a window.

THE BLISS OF MRS BLOSSOM
GB 1968 Paramount
Dir: Joe McGrath
Shirley MacLaine, Richard Attenborough

The wife of a bra manufacturer keeps her lover in the attic

The film features a dream sequence in which preserved ex-GWR '6100' 2-6-2T No 6106 appears in full psychedelic livery, complete with swirling coloured patterns and a portrait of a naked woman on the smokebox door! Filming took place at GWS Taplow.

BLOW-UP
GB 1966 MGM DVD
Dir: Michelangelo Antonioni
David Hemmings, Sarah Miles

A London fashion photographer believes he has seen a murder, but is it a fantasy?

Near the opening of this 'Swinging Sixties' drama a green SR two-car suburban EMU is seen passing over a bridge. Filmed at Copeland Road in the Peckham area.

BLUE ICE
US 1992 Guild DVD
Dir: Russell Mulcahy
Michael Caine, Sean Young

A former secret agent in London becomes embroiled with murder and arms smuggling

One of the most exciting scenes in the film (it featured in most of the trailers) involved Caine chasing a murderer onto railway tracks in South London and almost getting hit by a train. What the train is, however, is a bit confusing because as it approaches Caine it is an arcing 4-EPB EMU, but as it passes away it is an SR Class 205-type DEMU.

BLUE JUICE
GB 1995 FilmFour DVD
Dir: Carl Prechezer
Sean Pertwee, Ewan McGregor

The life of the surfers at a Cornish resort

Features a scene at St Erth station on the Cornish main line. No trains are featured.

THE BLUE LAMP
GB 1950 Ealing DVD
Dir: Basil Dearden
Jack Warner, Dirk Bogarde

A respected copper is shot in a bank raid and a manhunt is launched to catch the killer

This classic Ealing drama features a lengthy police chase as its climax, which includes a chase across the LT Central Line tracks just outside White City and a shot of a rake of 1920s tube stock. An unused out-take from this scene is included in the video *Diesel and Electrics on 35mm*.

BLUE MURDER AT ST TRINIAN'S
GB 1957 British Lion DVD
Dir: Frank Launder
Terry-Thomas, George Cole

The awful schoolgirls go to Rome and become involved with jewel thieves

Features a night shot of a passing express hauled by an ex-SR 'Merchant Navy' 'Pacific'.

THE BLUE PETER
GB 1955 British Lion
Dir: Wolf Rilla
Kieron Moore, Greta Gynt

A war hero finds a purpose as a trainer at an adventure school for boys

Includes a good scenic shot of an ex-GWR 'Dukedog' 4-4-0 on the Cambrian Coast line and a shot of Penhelig station.

BLUE SCAR
GB 1948 British Lion
Dir: Jill Craigie
Emrys Jones, Gwyneth Vaughan

A mine manager finds that life in his Welsh village is simpler than the city

Features some good rare shots of Abergwynfi station in South Wales, with GWR '5700' 0-6-0PT No 7798 on the branch train. Also includes a shot outside Paddington station.

BLUEBEARD'S TEN HONEYMOONS
GB 1960 Anglo-Allied
Dir: W. Lee Wilder
George Sanders, Corinne Calvet

An impoverished aristocrat kills women for their money

Set in France, yet includes railway scenes obviously filmed on British Railways. A scene where one of Landru's victims is pushed to her death above a railway yard includes a night scene of an SR 'C' Class 0-6-0 at an unknown SR location, and later in the film there is a night scene believed to have been filmed at Brickett Wood station on the Watford Junction-St Albans Abbey branch with an ex-LMS 4F 0-6-0.

BOB'S WEEKEND
GB 1996 Erinfilm DVD
Dir: Jevon O'Neill
Bruce Jones, Charlotte Jones

A security officer goes to Blackpool after losing his job and learns to start a new life

Includes some shots of Blackpool trams with an open-top Balloon double-decker prominent, and some fleeting shots of standard Balloons.

BORN ROMANTIC
GB 2000 Optimum/BBC DVD
Dir: David Kane
Craig Ferguson, Jane Horrocks

The stories of various people who go to a salsa club

Features a scene on King's Cross station with a GNER-liveried HST prominent, and a distant night shot of a LT tube train, location unknown. Also includes a shot of the frontage of Camden Town Underground station.

THE BOXER
GB/Ireland/US 1997 Universal DVD
Dir: Jim Sheridan
Daniel Day Lewis, Emily Watson

A former IRA prisoner sets up a boxing school for young boys

The final scenes for the film were filmed in the Dublin North Wall area and the container rail yards and wagons are visible. There is also a night scene filmed in the same location with an indistinct view of an Irish 141/181-type diesel on a freightliner.

A BOY A GIRL AND A BIKE
GB 1949 Gainsborough
Dir: Ralph Smart
John McCallum, Honor Blackman

Romantic complications develop in a cycling club.

One of the characters lives in a flat that overlooks a railway (actually a superimposed projection), and in the background of one scene there is a 'Black Five' pulling out on a passenger train. Although the story is set in Yorkshire the railway scene is St Pancras.

THE BOY WHO TURNED YELLOW
GB 1972 CFF VHS
Dir: Michael Powell
Mark Dignam, Robert Eddison

A boy turns yellow after being visited by an alien

Features a scene on the London Underground in which the train the boy is travelling on turns yellow as well as its passengers. Chalk Farm and Hampstead tube stations were used as locations.

BRANDY FOR THE PARSON
GB 1952 Group Three
Dir: John Eldridge
James Donald, Kenneth More

A couple on holiday in the West Country find themselves smuggling brandy into Britain

Features a run-by of an express hauled by an ex-SR 'West Country' 'Pacific', filmed on the main line, possibly between Exeter and Salisbury.

BRANNIGAN
GB 1975 UA DVD
Dir: Douglas Hickox
John Wayne, Richard Attenborough

An American cop goes to London to track down a gangster

Includes a shot of St Pancras station (no trains seen) and a view of the freight lines in East London's dockland.

THE BRASS MONKEY
GB 1948 UA DVD
Dir: Thornton Freeland
Carole Landis, Carroll Levis

A radio singer thwarts an attempt to steal a precious idol

Includes a shot of a boat train leaving an unknown port; no engine is visible but there are Southern coaches.

BREAKFAST ON PLUTO
GB 2006 Pathé DVD
Dir: Neil Jordan
Liam Neeson, Cillian Murphy

An Irish transvestite goes to London to search for his mother

Features a scene on the footbridge in Paddington station with an HST, 'Heathrow Express' EMU and Class 180 'Adelante' unit in the background; there's a shot on board a Class 455 EMU, one on the London Underground at a Piccadilly Line station with 1972 stock, and some views of the Southend Pier tramway.

BREAKING GLASS
GB 1980 GTO VHS
Dir: Brian Gibson
Hazel O'Connor, Phil Daniels

The rise and fall of a pop-singer

Features a couple of surreal scenes filmed on the London Underground on board 1938 tube stock – Finsbury Park station is the location for one shot. Also includes a scene filmed on an unknown BR station with Mk 2C air-conditioned stock.

THE BRIDAL PATH
GB 1959 British Lion
Dir: Frank Launder
Bill Travers, Fiona Clyne

A young Hebridean islander travels to the mainland in search of a wife

This film was shot entirely using Highland locations, so the one railway shot is a Scottish one – an ex-Caledonian 0-4-4T on a branch-line train, probably filmed on the Killin branch.

THE BRIDES OF FU MANCHU
GB 1966 Anglo Amalgamated VHS
Dir: Don Sharp
Christopher Lee, Douglas Wilmer

The 'yellow peril' kidnaps young women to blackmail their influential boyfriends

Features a scene of a train made up of LMS coaches leaving Marylebone station – loco not visible.

BRIDGET JONES'S DIARY
GB/US 2001 Universal/Miramax DVD
Dir: Sharon Maguire
Renee Zellweger, Hugh Grant

A single woman in her 30s looks for love in the wrong places

This very popular romantic hit includes a couple of railway shots – a Connex-liveried Class 319 EMU crossing the Ouse Valley viaduct on the Brighton line and a partially obscured shot of another Class 319 (this time in NSE livery) crossing a bridge in Borough, South London.

BRIEF ENCOUNTER
GB 1945 Rank DVD
Dir: David Lean
Celia Johnson, Trevor Howard

A married woman embarks on a doomed romance with a doctor

A much-celebrated classic film, which perhaps more than any other recreates the sights and sounds of a railway station at night in the steam era. The bulk of the action was filmed at Carnforth, junction for the Cumbrian Coast line on the WCML, and it remains a minor mystery why this location was chosen, considering it was a story set in the Home Counties, and there were so many other locations a lot closer to the film studio. Part of the answer is perhaps the exact needs of David Lean – a station served by main-line expresses and local trains, with a buffet and, in particular, sloping exits to a subway. It was felt that filming the characters running up and down a sloping subway was much more romantic and dramatic than to have them clumping up and down steps! Famously, in one scene a destination board can be seen directing passengers to a train bound for Clapham, Giggleswick and Hellifield.

Carnforth doubled for 'Milford Junction', together with some scenes shot at Watford Junction (which appear during the opening titles), with WCML expresses – locos featured are a couple of unrebuilt 'Royal Scots' and two streamlined 'Duchesses' (one a going-away shot). Many of the shots of the expresses were spoiled by the trains slowing down due to the loco crew's surprise at finding the station lit up by the film crews' lights, and a memo was dispatched telling crews to, if anything, go faster. In the event, during one night many of the expresses had to stop at Carnforth anyway for water, due to the nearby water troughs being frozen solid.

Many of these express shots went into the stock library and frequently turned up in films during the 1950s and '60s (eg *Mandy*, *Escape by Night*, *The Battle of the Sexes*, etc). However, the star of the show was LMS Fowler 2-6-4T No 2429, which hauls the 'local train' that takes Johnson back to 'Ketchworth' every evening. The loco appears three times in the film, and in one scene LMS coach No 25149 is also clearly visible. 'Ketchworth' seems to be very much a studio creation, and in fact a lot of studio work filmed at Denham was blended in with the live action.

BRIEF ENCOUNTER
GB 1974 ITC VHS
Dir: Alan Bridges
Richard Burton, Sophia Loren

A much-maligned remake of the above, updated to the 1970s

This unsuccessful and little-seen version was filmed at Winchester station and at least does contain some nice shots of SR Portsmouth line EMUs, of which set No 7734 is identifiable. A passing mixed freight is also seen, but the loco is not visible.

BRIGHTON ROCK
GB 1947 Associated British DVD
Dir: Roy Boulting
Richard Attenborough, Hermione Baddeley

The teenage leader of a gang marries a girl as an alibi to cover for a murder, but it proves to be his downfall

Features a scene outside Brighton station. A driver's-view EMU run into Brighton was shot for the film but not used – the footage appears in *Diesels and Electrics on 35mm*.

THE BRIGHTON STRANGLER
US 1945 RKO
Dir: Max Nosseck
John Loder, June Duprez

An actor takes on the part of a murderer and finds himself playing it in real life

A Hollywood-made B-movie set in Britain, this includes one stock shot of SR 'King Arthur' 4-6-0 No 748 leaving Waterloo on an express.

BRIMSTONE AND TREACLE
GB 1982 Namara DVD
Dir: Richard Loncraine
Sting, Denholm Elliott

A strange young man has a diabolic effect on a middle-class family

Some views of SR suburban EMUs, including 4-EPBs, filmed in the Southwark area.

BULLDOG JACK
GB 1934 Gaumont VHS
Dir: Walter Forde
Jack Hulbert, Ralph Richardson

A playboy poses as Bulldog Drummond to capture the notorious Morelle gang

The climax of the film features the villain sending off an Underground train containing Hulbert and his colleagues to what seems like certain disaster. As the train careers through station after station, Hulbert climbs onto the roof (!) to get to the driver's cab and brake the train just in time to prevent it colliding with a stationary train in the carriage sidings. Some filming was done at the closed British Museum (or Bloomsbury) station on the Central Line, but the majority of the action was filmed in the studio, involving sets and model work and featuring recreations of 1920s-type tube stock. Some cab-view shots from a real tube train were also used. Some imaginary stations were displayed on the Underground route map on board the train, including Camden Hill, Kensington Park, East Perivale and Western Avenue.

BULLET BOY
GB 2004 BBC Films DVD
Dir: Saul Dibb
Leon Black, Chris Callendar

Life in the black community of East London, with the threat of gun crime

Features a shooting scene filmed at Hackney Downs station in East London with a couple of Class 315 EMUs passing by.

BULLSEYE
US 1990 Castle Premier VHS
Dir: Michael Winner
Michael Caine, Roger Moore

Two con-men are asked to impersonate nuclear scientists

Some scenes in the film involve the 'Orient Express' making a tour of Britain's castles, which, even when we are supposed to be in Scotland, seems to be hauled by a Class 73 electro-diesel normally only seen on the Southern Region. What is more, in some shots it is a named 73, in others an un-named example. These scenes were filmed at London Victoria, various locations on the SR and on the Mid Hants railway, where, although not seen in the film, a Class 47 provided motive power. Also, a scene was filmed in the railway section of the Science Museum, with the stars sitting on board the LT 1924 tube stock exhibit – *Rocket, Caerphilly Castle* and the prototype 'Deltic' are also seen.

BULLSHOT
GB 1983 HandMade DVD
Dir: Dick Clement
Alan Shearman, Diz White

Spoof comedy featuring hero Bullshot Crummond

Some comedy scenes were filmed on the Bluebell Railway utilising trains hauled by preserved 'Schools' Class 4-4-0 No 928 and 'C' Class 0-6-0 No 592.

BUSTER
GB 1988 Vestron DVD
Dir: David Green
Phil Collins, Julie Walters

The life of Great Train Robber Buster Edwards

The early part of the film features a realistic depiction of the Great Train Robbery filmed on the Great Central Railway at Swithland Sidings. Preserved

Class 40 diesel No 40 106 was repainted with a small yellow warning panel and fitted with split-box indicators to represent the actual class member involved, No D326, with the GCR mail train set disguised on one side with flush sides to represent the LMS mail coaches. Loughborough Central became Glasgow Central, with much of the green paintwork becoming Scottish blue – all in all, a well-recreated example of a historical event, with only the GCR's then lack of a four-track section giving the game away.

BUTLEY

GB/US 1973 DVD
Dir: Harold Pinter
Alan Bates, Jessica Tandy

A lecturer has personal problems at a university

Features a scene on the London Underground with 1960 tube stock and Kilburn Park station.

CAGE OF GOLD
GB 1950 Ealing
Dir: Basil Dearden
Jean Simmons, David Farrar

A girl's ex-husband is murdered and she is suspected

Features two express shots hauled by ex-LMS 'Royal Scots', one a rebuilt example and the other No 46100 *Royal Scot* itself filmed on Bushey troughs (stock shot filmed for *Train of Events*). There is also a scene on the London Underground featuring 1920s tube stock.

CALLAN
GB 1974 EMI DVD
Dir: Don Sharp
Edward Woodward, Eric Porter

A former secret agent eliminates enemies of the government

One of the most exciting moments in the film features a car chase that results in the villain's car stalling on a level crossing and being hit by a train. A Class 33/0 diesel and three Mk 1 coaches were used for this sequence, which edited together various run-by shots and at least one camera shot mounted on the side of the loco. The scene was filmed on a single-track section somewhere on the SR, possibly on either the Lydd or Grain branches.

THE CAMERONS
GB 1974 CFF
Dir: Freddie Wilson
Lois Marshall, Joseph McKenna

A group of children thwart crooks in the Far North of Scotland

This children's film features a lot of scenes filmed on the Aberdeen-Inverness line with Forres (as 'Moorland Junction') and Elgin (as 'Rioch') stations both making appearances. There is a lot of footage of Class 120 DMUs, although obviously filmed on different occasions, which explains why in the course of a journey the train is three-car in some scenes and six-car in others. A nice touch is that in one scene one of the child actors is reading a copy of *Trains Illustrated* No 11 with a Class 76 electric on the cover!

CANDLESHOE
GB 1977 Walt Disney VHS
Dir: Norman Tokar
David Niven, Jodie Foster

A butler prevents an attempt to pass off a fake heiress to an English estate

One of the big scenes in this film involves a car chasing a steam train, climaxing with the chauffeur (played by Niven) parking the car on a crossing and stopping the train by hand signal, the buffers of the loco stopping just inches from his chest (a scene not dissimilar from the train-stopping scene in *The Railway Children*). The Severn Valley Railway was chosen for this sequence, using preserved GWR '4500' 2-6-2T No 4566 and chocolate-and-cream stock (filled with extras, including many SVR members). Arley station appears in one shot, with others shots filmed at Trimpley reservoirs, Eardington road bridge and Victoria bridge. The train-stopping scene was filmed at Waterworks Crossing, and although No 4566 was used for most of the filming, the shot of the loco pulling up a foot or so in front of Niven used a full-size mock-up of the front and smokebox of the loco to protect the actor – this mock-up was taken away by the film company after completion of the scene.

A CANTERBURY TALE
GB 1944 Rank DVD
Dirs: Michael Powell, Emeric Pressburger
Eric Portman, Sheila Sim

An insane magistrate is unmasked by a land girl and a soldier

A classic film that features a number of train scenes filmed on the Southern in the Kent area. There's a distant shot of a Maunsell 'Mogul' and a shot of a rebuilt Wainwright 4-4-0 passing Harbledown Junction signal box where the Dover line crossed the Elham Valley railway. The station scenes were filmed at Selling and Canterbury West (which features an arrival behind an 'H' Class 0-4-4T).

THE CAPTIVE HEART
GB 1946 Ealing DVD
Dir: Basil Dearden
Michael Redgrave, Jack Warner

The lives of British POWs at a German camp

One flashback scene of Aston Rowant station on the GWR Watlington branch line with a distant train approaching.

CAPTIVES
GB 1994 Entertainment/BBC VHS
Dir: Angela Pope
Julia Ormond, Tim Roth

A dentist is blackmailed after she begins an affair with a convicted murderer

Includes a shot of LT Southgate station and scenes in South London featuring a Class 455 and SR semi-fast EMUs.

CAREER GIRLS
GB 1997 FilmFour DVD
Dir: Mike Leigh
Katrin Cartlidge, Lynda Steadman

Two ex-students meet again ten years later and see how their lives have changed

Features two scenes at King's Cross station, including an HST set, with power car No 43116 leading, and a departing train of Mk 4 stock with a DVT at the rear (Class 91 not visible).

CARLTON BROWNE OF THE F.O.
GB 1958 British Lion DVD
Dirs: Jeffrey Dell, Roy Boulting
Terry-Thomas, Peter Sellers

Precious mineral deposits are found on a British colony and an incompetent minister is sent to negotiate

Features a comedy scene involving an character painting a white boundary line down the middle of a railway track into a tunnel, then the train emerging with the white stripe up the front of the engine! The loco is 'A1X' 'Terrier' 0-6-0T No 32640, disguised with a cow-catcher and other fittings to represent a loco in the South Seas, and the location is the west end of Midhurst Tunnel on the Midhurst-Pulborough branch, Sussex.

CARRINGTON
GB/France 1995 Polygram DVD
Dir: Christopher Hampton
Emma Thompson, Jonathan Pryce

The story of a woman artist's love affair with the writer Lytton Strachey

The film, which is set at the start of the Second World War, includes a scene filmed on the North Yorkshire Moors Railway at Goathland station with Lambton Tank 0-6-2T No 5 heading the train.

CARRY ON CABBY
GB 1963 Anglo Amalgamated DVD
Dir: Gerald Thomas
Sid James, Hattie Jacques

The neglected wife of a cab driver sets up a rival business with female drivers

One scene is filmed outside Windsor & Eton Central station, a popular location for 1950s and '60s film companies.

CARRY ON GIRLS
GB 1974 Rank DVD
Dir: Gerald Thomas
Sid James, Barbara Windsor

A beauty contest at a seaside resort annoys the Women's Lib movement

Includes a comedy scene at Marylebone station with some Class 115 DMUs used for the filming and in the background.

CARRY ON LOVING
GB 1970 Rank DVD
Dir: Gerald Thomas
Sid James, Kenneth Williams

Comedy misadventures plague a computer dating agency

Near the start of the film there is a shot of a Class 117 DMU departure from Windsor & Eton Central, masquerading as 'Much Snogging on the Green'!

CARRY ON REGARDLESS
GB 1960 Anglo Amalgamated DVD
Dir: Gerald Thomas
Sid James, Kenneth Williams

A group of unemployables form an odd-job agency

The best of the series for railway scenes. There is an amusing parody of the Forth Bridge scene from *The Thirty Nine Steps*, which features Kenneth Connor leaping from the train into a giant puddle! This utilises stock footage from the 1959 version of John Buchan's classic with a couple of shots of 'A4' No 60027, and the same shot of the passing 'A2' 'Pacific' that nearly mows down our hero (a direct shot from the 1959 film). Also included is a scene with Kenneth Williams filmed at Windsor & Eton Central with an arriving green Class 117 DMU.

CARRY ON SERGEANT
GB 1958 Anglo Amalgamated DVD
Dir: Gerald Thomas
Bob Monkhouse, Kenneth Connor

A group of motley army recruits eventually prove their worth

The first 'Carry On' film features a railway journey scene made up of a studio set carriage interior and a stock shot of SR 'Lord Nelson' 4-6-0 No 859.

CASTAWAY
GB 1986 Cannon DVD
Dir: Nicholas Roeg
Amanda Donohue, Oliver Reed

A London girl accepts an offer to marry a man and live with him on a tropical island

Features an interior shot on a LT 'C'-type Circle Line underground train believed to have been filmed at Bayswater station.

CAUGHT IN THE ACT
GB 1996 Midsummer
Dir: Mark Groenstreet
Sara Crowe, Annette Badland

Three girls form a musical group to perform on a talent show

Some good shots taken inside and outside Wymondham station in East Anglia with a couple of Class 158 'Sprinter' DMUs (including No 158 854) featuring.

THE CHAIN
GB 1984 Quintet/Channel 4 DVD
Dir: Jack Gold
Warren Mitchell, Denis Lawson

The stories of seven couples all involved in moving home

The film uses some aerial shots of areas of London and some trains are seen, including an LT train made up of 1970s tube stock, possibly Piccadilly Line; an SR semi-fast 1970s EMU; and a general shot of Old Oak Common carriage yards with a distant Class 47 on a rake of stock.

THE CHALLENGE
GB 1960 John Temple-Smith/Alexandra
Dir: John Gilling
Jayne Mansfield, Anthony Quayle

A lady mobster kidnaps a convict's son to get at stolen loot

The climax of the film features a race against time to prevent the boy being killed by the mobsters throwing him under a train. These scenes were filmed on the Longmoor Military Railway at various lineside locations and at Longmoor Downs station, masquerading under the name 'Fourways'. The main motive power is provided by 'WD' 2-10-0 No 601 *Kitchener*, but one of the railway's 'Austerity' 0-6-0STs also appears. Added to this are some stock shots used throughout the film of various locos including LMS 4-6-0s filmed on the Midland Main Line, a 'Castle' and an 'A1/2' 'Pacific'. There are also some shots filmed on Marylebone station. The video *Steam on 35mm Vol 3* (Video 125) features a number of out-takes from the Longmoor footage.

CHANCE OF A LIFETIME
GB 1950 Pilgrim Pictures
Dir: Bernard Miles
Bernard Miles, Basil Radford

The owner of a factory, frustrated by trade unionism, gives the workers the chance to run it themselves

Features a stock shot of a Southern express hauled by an ex-SR 'King Arthur' 4-6-0, filmed at Esher on the LSWR main line.

CHANNEL CROSSING
GB 1933 Gaumont VHS
Dir: Milton Rosmer
Matheson Lang, Constance Cummings

A millionaire faces ruin and tries to drown his secretary's lover on a cross-Channel ferry

The first 5 minutes feature some good shots of railway scenes in the Dover area. 'Lord Nelson' 4-6-0 No 854 is seen passing the white cliffs on a boat train, then there is a studio-bound coach interior shot, but the back projection features a run along the sea wall passing Dover sheds, with a 'P' Class 0-6-0T, a Maunsell 2-6-0 and an ex-SECR 'F1' 4-4-0 among the locos visible. There is a very good shot taken from the tender of a loco running into Dover Marine station, and on the waterfront itself what appears to be an 'O1' 0-6-0 with some vans. The Calais side, later on in the film, includes some equally good shots of a Nord 'Pacific'.

CHAPLIN
GB 1992 Guild/Studio Canal DVD
Dir: Richard Attenborough
Robert Downey Jr, Dan Aykroyd

The life of Charlie Chaplin

Includes one major scene filmed on Paddington station and some shots on the Bluebell Railway with one of the preserved SR Maunsell 2-6-0s.

CHARIOTS OF FIRE
GB 1981 TCF DVD
Dir: Hugh Hudson
Ben Cross, Ian Charleson

In the 1924 Paris Olympics, a Jew and a Scotsman run for Britain

The triumphant return to Britain after the Olympics was filmed in the north bay platforms at York station (representing London Victoria), with preserved NRM exhibits SECR 'D' Class 4-4-0 No756 and GNR 'C1' 4-4-2 No 251 as stationary locos (with fake smoke effects). The frontage of Taplow station on the GW main line was also used for one scene.

CHARLOTTE GRAY
GB 2002 FilmFour DVD
Dir: Gillian Armstrong
Cate Blanchett, Michael Gambon

A woman is recruited as a spy and is sent to France to join up with the Resistance

Features a number of railway scenes, none of which sadly features Second World War traction. The opening shot is of the preserved 'K1' 2-6-0 No 62005 crossing Glenfinnan Viaduct. On arrival at its destination the train is being hauled by BR Standard 4-6-0 No 73082, filmed at Sheffield Park on the Bluebell Railway. The Bluebell was also used for one of the biggest scenes in the film, the blowing up of a German ammunition train. Standard 9F 2-10-0 No 92240 was the haulage for this (a 1950s design with BR smokebox plate playing a French engine in the 1940s!) complete with a train carrying armoured vehicles and a couple of balsa-wood vans made by the special effects crew. The explosion was filmed between Caseford Bridge and Three Arch Bridge, but the aftermath scenes, after the train has derailed, were filmed using mock-ups at Chertsey.

CHEER BOYS CHEER
GB 1939 ATP
Dir: Walter Forde
Jimmy O'Dea, Nova Pilbeam

A small brewery is threatened with takeover by a larger rival

Includes a brief shot of the platforms of Chiswick Park LT station on the District Line with a couple of 1924 tube trains passing on Piccadilly Line services.

CHILDREN OF MEN
GB/US 2006 Universal DVD
Dir: Alfonso Cuaron
Clive Owen, Michael Caine

In the future human infertility creates anarchy and fear

Includes scenes filmed on the Mid Hants line at Alresford station with a graffiti-embellished Class 117 DMU.

THE CHILTERN HUNDREDS
GB 1949 Rank
Dir: John Paddy Carstairs
Cecil Parker, A. E. Matthews

An earl's son stands as a Labour candidate at an election, while the butler stands as a Tory

Features a very rare shot of the last surviving ex-GWR '2000' Class 0-6-0ST, No 1925, entering Denham station on the GW&GC Joint line. The loco was withdrawn in 1951. This scene appears in the Video 125 video *Steam on 35mm, Vol 3*.

CHITTY CHITTY BANG BANG
GB 1968 UA DVD
Dir: Ken Hughes
Dick Van Dyke, Sally Ann Howes

An inventor creates a flying car with magical properties

This much-loved children's classic features a musical sequence where the car rides alongside a rather wacky-looking GWR train. Filmed on the Hollywater Loop of the Longmoor Military Railway and using Hunslet 'Austerity' 0-6-0ST No 196, the loco has been given a tall dummy chimney and copper-painted dome, with the letters GWR painted on the tanks in decorative style similar to 'Pullman'-type lettering. Add the fact that the loco is hauling Southern coaches and you have a very odd ensemble for a GWR train!

A CHORUS OF DISAPPROVAL
GB 1990 Curzon VHS
Dir: Michael Winner
Jeremy Irons, Anthony Hopkins

A newcomer joins an amateur choir and finds that he gets the attention of the female members

The film opens and closes with shots of Scarborough station. The opening sequence is made up of shots of a Class 150/2 'Sprinter' DMU en route to the resort, Irons sitting in an HST interior, then the train's arrival at the terminus, by which time it appears to have become a Class 142 railbus.

THE CHRONICLES OF NARNIA
US 2005 Walt Disney DVD
Dir: Andrew Adamson
William Moseley, Tilda Swinton

Four evacuated children find a magical world through a wardrobe

Successful and lavish version of the classic children's saga with a good long railway sequence near the start of the film as the children are evacuated from London to the West of England. The scenes at Paddington station reveal the wonders of modern CGI techniques – the overhead view of the platforms amalgamates footage of the station with computer imagery of GWR trains. However, the platform scenes with the actors and the onboard shots were filmed on a sound stage in New Zealand. There is another good computer-generated shot of the GWR express passing through the London suburbs before we get our first shots of a 'real' train – and excellent shots they are too! A GWR passenger train on the Severn Valley Railway behind 'Manor' Class 4-6-0 No 7802 is followed during the title sequence with helicopter shots and close-up views. 'Pewsey' station is actually the SVR's Highley. Incredibly for a very British story, these were the only scenes filmed in Britain. Indeed, the scene where the children are standing on 'Coombe Halt' was filmed in New Zealand.

CHURCHILL – THE HOLLYWOOD YEARS
GB 2004 Pathé DVD
Dir: Peter Richardson
Christian Slater, Leslie Phillips

A secret document reveals that Winston Churchill was in fact an American GI

A spoof drama satirising the Hollywood distortion of war stories, this features extensive scenes filmed on the South Devon and Torbay steam railways, with Buckfastleigh as 'Frothington' and Kingswear as 'Buckingham Palace' stations! The South Devon was used for battle scenes featuring German soldiers both at Buckfastleigh and Bishops Bridge Junction, with stunt sequences using preserved GWR '1600' Class 0-6-0PT No 1638, '2251' Class 0-6-0 No 3205, and '1400' Class 0-4-2T No 1420. '4500' Class 2-6-2T No 4555 appears for the Kingswear scenes, and there's an odd continuity error at one point where Christian Slater jumps on board No 1420 at Bishops Bridge and is later seen driving the loco in the cab of No 4555!

CIRCUS
GB/US 2000 Columbia/FDC DVD
Dir: Rob Walker
John Hannah, Brian Conley

A conman and a crook attempt to outwit one another

A couple of shots of 'Brighton' station feature in this noir-like drama; however, the actual location is Slough, easily recognisable by the ornate station buildings. No trains are featured.

THE CITADEL
GB 1938 MGM
Dir: King Vidor
Robert Donat, Rosalind Russell

An idealistic doctor acts true to his principles in a mining village but changes when he goes to London

The film opens with an actual shot of a South Wales valley branch train – a GWR '5600' 0-6-2T passing by with a local at an unidentified location. The arrival night shot at 'Blaenelly', however, features what looks like an LNER 0-6-0 with a rake of six-wheel ex-GER coaches, location unknown. There are some London trams in the background of one of the London scenes.

THE CLAIRVOYANT
GB 1934 Gainsborough VHS
Dir: Maurice Elvey
Claude Rains, Fay Wray

A fake clairvoyant has a real vision of a mining disaster that comes true

Features a couple of haphazardly constructed shots to illustrate a railway journey – some shots at Dover Marine station, a passing shot on the ECML of a train made up of LNER teak coaches, and a shot of an SR 'King Arthur'.

CLIMBING HIGH
GB 1938 Gaumont
Dir: Carol Reed
Jessie Matthews, Michael Redgrave

A rich man poses as a model to win a girl

One brief shot of a 1920s LT District/Circle Line train, partially obscured by an advertising hoarding.

CLOCKWISE
GB 1986 EMI DVD
Dir: Christopher Morahan
John Cleese, Alison Steadman

A headmaster on his way to a conference is delayed by a series of circumstances

The main railway scene in the film (where Cleese leaves his written speech on a train) was filmed at Hull Paragon, with some good shots on the station

platforms and concourse. Although we don't see the locos hauling the 'Norwich' and 'Plymouth' trains (made up of Mk 1 stock), if you look carefully at the scene where Cleese chases after his wife's car in the station there is a Class 31 and a Class 108 DMU in the background.

CLOCKWORK MICE
GB 1995 Feature Film/Metrodome DVD
Dir: Vadim Jean
Ian Hart, Ruaidhri Conroy

A young teacher tries to put a problem pupil on the straight and narrow

The climax to the film features the boy character jumping on the roof of a train and performing a roof walk while in motion (obviously using a stuntman). These scenes made extensive use of the Mid Hants Railway, with Medstead & Four Marks and Alresford stations both appearing. Two preserved BR Standard 4-6-0s were used, Nos 73080 (for the roof-walk train) and 76017 (for a passing train). Preserved Class 27 and 08 diesels can be seen as the train arrives at Alresford. An interesting note regarding this film is that the boy has an interest in railways and his locker at the school is adorned with photo cuttings of various types, including 'Royal Scots' and a 'Hall', 'Western' Class 20 and Class 47 diesels, and the RTC Class 46 *Ixion*.

CLOSING NUMBERS
GB 1992 Channel 4
Dir: Stephen Whittaker
Jane Asher, Tim Woodward

A couple's relationship is blown apart when the husband contracts AIDs

A couple of scenes of HST run-bys on the Midland Main Line, probably in the Harpenden area. In one shot the leading power car is No 43064.

CLOUDBURST
GB 1951 Exclusive/Hammer
Dir: Francis Searle
Robert Preston, Elizabeth Sellars

A code expert takes revenge on the criminals who killed his wife in a hit-and-run incident

A couple of London trams can be discerned behind the opening titles in a night shot of Westminster Bridge.

THE CLOUDED YELLOW
GB 1950 Sydney Box/Carillon
Dir: Ralph Thomas
Trevor Howard, Jean Simmons

An ex-secret service agent takes a job tending a butterfly collection but this involves him in murder

This Hitchcockian thriller includes a number of railway scenes, which refreshingly depict locations outside the Home Counties area. As well as shots of the London Underground featuring tube train stock, there are shots of Newcastle Central station, featuring an ex-NER Tyneside EMU, and Liverpool Lime Street. The climax of the film is filmed in Liverpool docks with good shots of an EMU on the Liverpool Overhead Railway and steam dock shunters of the 0-4-0 and 0-6-0ST variety, including M&D&HB 0-4-0ST No 4.

COCK O' THE NORTH
GB 1935 Panther-Mitchell
Dir: Oswald Mitchell
George Carney, Marie Lohr

A railwayman is forced to take early retirement through injury and his colleagues stage a charity concert to help him

This little-known musical film seems to have been lost for many years and thus seems even less likely now of being rediscovered. Its importance lies in the fact that then new LNER 'P2' 2-8-2 No 2001 *Cock o' the North* was used as part of the plot, being the loco the railway driver

was rostered to drive before his accident. No other details of other locomotives and locations used are known and, unlike the 1931 version of *The Ghost Train*, no real attempt seems to have been made to find this missing classic.

COCKLESHELL HEROES
GB 1955 Columbia/Warwick DVD
Dir: Jose Ferrer
Jose Ferrer, Trevor Howard

During the Second World War, Marines are trained to travel by canoe into occupied France and attach limpet mines to German shipping

Part of the film centres on the Marines undergoing training, including a cross-country ingenuity exercise in which some of the characters get a lift home by train! Featured are an ex-SR 'S15' 4-6-0 on a heavy freight (on which a couple of characters jump aboard) and an SR pre-war two-car suburban EMU arriving at Chertsey station. Also featured during this long montage sequence are a shot of Shepperton station, 'T9' 4-4-0 No 30729 passing over a level crossing with a short freight, and a passing ex-GER 'F5' 2-4-2T with a local at Custom House station in East London. Note again that although we are in the Second World War the locos are in BR livery and there are British Railways signs at the stations!

COLD COMFORT FARM
GB 1995 BBC DVD
Dir: John Schlesinger
Kate Beckinsale, Eileen Atkins

A London cousin visits a family of misfits on their country farm and changes their lives for the better

Kate Beckinsale's journey from London to the country by train utilised the Kent & East Sussex Railway, with Northiam station posing as 'Beershorn Halt'. Motive power was provided by Manning Wardle 0-6-0ST.

COME ON GEORGE
GB 1936 ATP/Ealing VHS
Dir: Anthony Kimmins
George Formby, Pat Kirkwood

A stableboy rides a racehorse to victory

Features a railway journey that involves Formby walking along the roof of the coaches and diving for cover when they reach a tunnel. A comedy scene precedes this, filmed at what is believed to be Potters Bar station, with LNER 'D3' Class 4-4-0 No 4309 prominent. Then there is a stock shot of an express hauled by a 'Lanky' 'Dreadnought' 4-6-0, believed to have been filmed in the Lune Gorge. The roof-walking scene is a combination of real footage involving a stuntman and film of Formby on a roof mock-up in a studio in front of back projection. Locations are again unknown, but the stunt scenes are filmed on LNER coaches. Finally, there is a shot of a horsebox being unloaded at a cattle siding somewhere on the LNER, with what looks like an 'N5' 0-6-2T shunting in the background.

THE COMEDY MAN
GB 1963 British Lion VHS
Dir: Alvin Rakoff
Kenneth More, Billie Whitelaw

An out-of-work actor finds success as a star of TV commercials

Includes a shot of St Pancras with a split-box Class 45 diesel at the buffer stops with an express, and a Class 27 just peeping in next to it. Also some distant shots filmed overlooking the approaches to Paddington in the Ranelagh Bridge area with an ex-GWR Prairie tank, and, at the film's end, a 'Western' diesel on an up express.

COMFORT AND JOY
GB 1984 EMI/Lake VHS
Dir: Bill Forsyth
Bill Paterson, Eleanor David

A Glasgow DJ gets mixed up in a local ice-cream-seller war

Filmed on location in the Glasgow area, in one shot a split-box Class 37 diesel on a breakdown train can be seen in the background.

THE COMMITMENTS
US 1991 TCF/Beacon DVD
Dir: Alan Parker
Robert Arkins, Michael Aherne

A group of Dublin youths form a soul band

Filmed in and around Dublin, one scene is filmed of the cast on board one of the city's CIE 'Dart' EMUs.

THE COMMON TOUCH
GB 1941 British National
Dir: John Baxter
Greta Gynt, Geoffrey Hibbert

A young man comes home to take over his father's business

Features a stock shot of an express hauled by an ex-LNWR 'Claughton' 4-6-0, filmed in the Lune Gorge.

CONFESSIONS FROM A HOLIDAY CAMP
GB 1977 Columbia DVD
Dir: Norman Cohen
Robin Askwith, Anthony Booth

An entertainments officer at a holiday camp has various sexual adventures

Includes a station shot filmed on the Midland Main Line with a Class 127 DMU in the background, one car numbered M51601.

CONFLICT OF WINGS
GB 1954 Group Three
Dir. John Eldridge
John Gregson, Muriel Pavlow

Villagers attempt to fight the RAF using a bird sanctuary as a firing range

Features a shot of an ex-LNER 'B1' 4-6-0 on a cross-country service filmed somewhere in East Anglia.

CONQUEST OF THE AIR
GB 1937 London Films/Alexander Korda
  DVD
Dir: Zoltan Korda
Laurence Olivier, Franklin Dyall

The story of flight through the ages

Although this drama-documentary concerns itself only with air travel, there is one railway scene – a shot of a Southern Railway train heading away from Waterloo. Although we don't see the engine, there is a good shot of the coaches. Film not released until 1940.

CONSPIRATOR
GB 1949 MGM
Dir: Victor Saville
Robert Taylor, Elizabeth Taylor

A guardsman leads a double life as a military man and a spy

Includes scenes filmed at Holborn Underground station in the Aldwych branch platform with 1920s tube stock. Later in the film there are a couple of shots of GWR '7400' Class 0-6-0PTs hauling branch trains in North Wales, believed to have been filmed on the Bala Junction-Blaenau Ffestiniog branch.

THE CONSTANT GARDENER
GB 2005 Universal/Potboiler/Epsilon
  DVD
Dir: Fernando Meirelles
Ralph Fiennes, Rachel Weisz

A bureaucrat tries to find the truth about his wife's death in Kenya

This acclaimed film features a scene with Fiennes at Waterloo International with a couple of Class 373 Eurostars visible.

COOL IT CAROL
GB 1970 Pete Walker/Miracle VHS
Dir: Pete Walker
Robin Askwith, Janet Lynn

A young couple go to London for excitement

Features some scenes taken at Etchingham station with SR 'Hastings' DEMUs Nos 1034 and 1033. The trip to London is depicted by a shot of SR 4-COR EMU No 3139, and arrival at London features Paddington station!

CORRIDOR OF MIRRORS
GB 1948 Cartier-Romney-Apollo
Dir: Terence Young
Eric Portman, Edana Romney

An art collector believes his mistress is a reincarnation from 400 years before

This supernatural drama features some very 'natural' scenes filmed on a branch line in North Wales, probably the Blaenau Ffestiniog line, with one train hauled by an ex-LNWR 'Cauliflower' 0-6-0 and, at the end the film, some excellent shots of a train hauled by LMS 3P 2-6-2T No 133.

CORRUPTION
GB 1967 Columbia
Dir: Robert Hartford Davis
Peter Cushing, Sue Lloyd

A surgeon kills to restore the beauty of his fiancée

One of the murders takes place on a rail journey and features some shots of pre-war SR EMUs including 2-BIL set No 2633 and a 4-LAV set. Filmed around the South Coast area with scenes at Seaford and Lewes stations.

COTTON QUEEN
GB 1937 Rock Studios
Dirs: Joe Rock, Bernard Vorhaus
Stanley Holloway, Will Fyffe

A mill owner's daughter joins a rival mill without him knowing

Part of the film is set in Blackpool and there are some Blackpool trams on display, including a 1934 boat car type.

COUNT FIVE AND DIE
GB 1957 TCF
Dir: Victor Vicas
Nigel Patrick, Jeffrey Hunter

British intelligence puts out false information to fool the Germans

One scene involves David Kossoff making a rendezvous at an engine shed and yard, believed to be Willesden. A 4F 0-6-0 can be seen moving slowly past, light engine, and some 'Jinties' and Fowler 2-6-4Ts are in the background.

COUNTERBLAST
GB 1948 British National
Dir: Paul Stein
Mervyn Johns, Robert Beatty

A Nazi scientist poses as an Australian to carry out germ warfare tests

This film features a memorable scene in which Johns, intending to release deadly germs on London, travels on the London Underground and imagines seeing one of the passengers turn into a skeleton, causing him to laugh hysterically. These scenes seem to be an amalgam of studio and real shots, with one clearly taken outside Baker Street station. There are also some scenes at Paddington with an express hauled by a GWR 'Hall' 4-6-0 arriving and a shot of a passing express hauled by a 'King'.

THE COURTNEYS OF CURZON STREET
GB 1947 Imperadio
Dir: Herbert Wilcox
Anna Neagle, Michael Wilding

In Victorian England a baronet's son marries a lady's maid

In one scene an O-gauge model railway set is being played with, but the make and type of model are unclear.

CRAZE
GB 1973 EMI VHS
Dir: Freddie Francis
Jack Palance, Diana Dors

A black magic worshipper is compelled to make blood sacrifices to an idol

Palance parks his car outside Taplow station for one scene and boards a DMU formation made up of two Class 123 Inter-City units (is this the only occasion this type has appeared on film?). He arrives at Windsor & Eton Central in a Class 121. His return journey is depicted by a 'Western'-hauled express passing at speed somewhere on the GW main line.

CREEP
GB/Germany 2004 Pathé/Dan Films DVD
Dir: Christopher Smith
Franka Potente, Sean Harris

Travellers on the London Underground are killed by an unseen monster

Horror film set on the London tube, reminiscent in some ways to the 1972 production *Deathline*. Some location work was filmed at Charing Cross Underground station, with the bulk of the film made on the Aldwych branch and station using 1972 tube stock.

CRIMETIME
GB/US/Germany 1995 Channel 4/First Independent
Dir: George Sluizer
Stephen Baldwin, Pete Postlethwaite

An actor appearing as a murderer in a crime reconstruction programme begins to identify with the killer

One of the killer's victims is found in a railway yard, but the location is unclear, though it is probably somewhere in London. BR Mk 1 coaches feature in the background.

CROOKS IN CLOISTERS
GB 1963 ABPC VHS
Dir: Jeremy Summers
Ronald Fraser, Barbara Windsor

Fleeing robbers hide out at a monastery by posing as monks

The film begins with the gang staging a train robbery (daring, considering that this was the same year as the Great Train Robbery). The first shot is of a Class 45 diesel on an express on the Midland Main Line near Elstree Tunnels. The robbery scenes were filmed at Brent Sidings, Cricklewood, using another Class 45, No D140. Out-takes of the Elstree shots featuring Class 45-hauled expresses and a couple of Class 127 DMUs survive and are included in *Diesels and Electrics on 35mm* (Video 125).

CROUPIER
GB 1997 Channel 4/BFI/Little Bird DVD
Dir: Mike Hodges
Clive Owen, Kate Hardie

A novelist becomes a croupier at a casino and uses it for his novel

Some shots were taken inside 1972 tube stock on the London Underground, probably on the Bakerloo Line (in one shot Owen is seen emerging from a subway off Piccadilly Circus station).

THE CRUCIFER OF BLOOD
GB/US 1991 TCM
Dir: Fraser Clarke Heston
Charlton Heston, Edward Fox

Sherlock Holmes investigates mysterious deaths surrounding a secret pact made by soldiers over loot

Features some railway shots filmed at Buckingham Railway Centre, Quainton Road, using trains hauled by the preserved ex-GWR '5700' 0-6-0PT No L89 and one of the railway's ex-industrial 'Austerity' 0-6-0STs.

A CUCKOO IN THE NEST
GB 1933 Gaumont VHS
Dir: Tom Walls
Ralph Lynn, Tom Walls

A newly-wed husband is forced to spend a night with an old flame

Features some scenes filmed at Paddington station (locos not seen). The film was remade in 1954 as *Fast and Loose* (qv).

CUP FEVER
GB 1965 CFF DVD
Dir: David Bracknell
Denis Gilmore, Susan George

A junior football team face many obstacles before winning their league

The film features a shot of the old Manchester United football ground at Old Trafford and a Stanier 2-6-4 tank can be seen emerging from under a bridge in the foreground, running light.

DAD SAVAGE

GB 1997 Polygram DVD
Dir: Betsan Morris Evans
Patrick Stewart, Kevin McKidd

A gangster in Norfolk attempts to find who killed his son and attempted to steal his loot

Includes a quick glimpse of narrow-gauge 0-4-0 steam loco *Pilgrim* with open and closed carriages on the Wells & Walsingham steam railway.

DAKOTA ROAD

GB 1990 Mayfair/FilmFour
Dir: Nick Ward
Charlotte Chatton, Jason Carter

A teenage girl in East Anglia suffers a series of tragedies

The film centres on a number of scenes around Shippea Hill station on the Ely-Norwich line, with shots of the signal box and passing trains, these comprising Class 101 Metro-Cammell DMUs in Network SouthEast and blue/grey liveries and a Class 156 'Sprinter'. There are also a couple of driver-view shots taken from the front of a Met-Cam unit.

DANDY DICK

GB 1935 BIP VHS
Dir: William Beaudine
Will Hay, Nancy Burne

A vicar becomes involved with racehorse doping

Features a shot of LMS Stanier 2-6-4T No 2509 arriving at an unknown station with a local train.

DANGEROUS AFTERNOON

GB 1961 Theatrecraft
Dir: Charles Saunders
Ruth Dunning, Nora Nicholson

An ex-convict runs a home for female ex-convicts and poisons a blackmailer

Includes a semi-distant shot of an SR suburban EMU passing over a level crossing somewhere in South London.

THE DARK MAN

GB 1950 GFD VHS
Dir: Jeffrey Dell
Maxwell Reed, Edward Underdown

After a black-marketeer is murdered, the killer goes after a witness to the crime

The climax of the film was shot around Romney Marsh, with some of the sidings around Dungeness visible in a couple of scenes.

THE DARK ROAD

GB 1947 Hammer/Exclusive
Dir: Alfred J. Goulding
Charles Stuart, Michael Ripper

The rise and fall of a young criminal

Low-budget B-movie using a few locations outside London – some shots at Blackpool with a single-deck Brush car (together with a couple of double-deck buses) and a shot on Manchester Victoria station (no locos seen).

DARKLANDS
GB 1996 Metrodome/Lluniau Lliw Cyf
  VHS
Dir: Julian Richards
Craig Fairbrass, Rowena King

A journalist in South Wales discovers a pagan cult involved in ritual sacrifice

The railway scenes where Fairbrass boards a train that takes him to his fate were filmed on the Dean Forest Railway, with St Mary's Halt and Norchard both being used as night-time locations. One of the railway's preserved Class 108 DMUs was utilised.

DARLING
GB 1965 Anglo-Amalgamated DVD
Dir: John Schlesinger
Julie Christie, Dirk Bogarde

An ambitious young woman balances relationships with various men with a jet-set lifestyle

Features a brief going-away shot of a 'Western' diesel on an express on the WR main line. A number of shots were filmed at this location but remained unused until the release of the video *Diesel and Electrics on 35mm* (Video 125) – these feature approaching shots of another 'Western', a 'Hymek' and a 'Blue Pullman'. The film also includes a scene of Bogarde and Christie having a row at Notting Hill Gate LT station.

DARLING LILI
US 1970 Paramount
Dir: Blake Edwards
Julie Andrews, Rock Hudson

During the First World War an American flyer falls for a female spy

Most of the action for this film is set in France, although a railway scene was

actually filmed in Ireland. In what has to be one of the weirdest cinematic set-ups in railway history, the preserved 'J15' 0-6-0 No 184 was used with a rake of historic rolling-stock (as in *The First Great Train Robbery* in 1979, the film-makers use the principle that old Irish trains resemble *any* old European trains). However, the 'J15' was at the time not steamworthy, so Metro-Vick 'A' Class diesel No A16 was borrowed from the CIE, disguised by the props department as a baggage car and tucked between the 'J15' and the train to provide motive power, complete with steam effects. The bizarre postscript to this story is that the diesel ran on the CIE on normal services on days not required for filming, still disguised as a baggage car! Scenes were filmed at Beauparc, on the Drogheda-Navan line.

A DATE WITH A DREAM
GB 1948 Tempean DVD
Dir: Dicky Leeman
Terry-Thomas, Jean Carson

A wartime concert party reunion leads to a nightclub success

Includes a scene filmed at the street entrance to East Brixton station, South London.

A DAY IN THE DEATH OF JOE EGG
GB 1971 Columbia
Dir: Peter Medak
Alan Bates, Janet Suzman

A teacher and his wife feel unable to cope with their disabled daughter

Near the film's end Alan Bates boards an express at Bristol Temple Meads station, the haulage provided by a Class 45 'Peak' diesel.

THE DAY OF THE TRIFFIDS
GB 1962 Philip Yordan DVD
Dir: Steve Sekely
Howard Keel, Nicole Maurey

Almost everyone in the world is blinded by a meteor shower and alien plants wreck havoc

This famous science-fiction tale includes a memorably nightmarish scene in which an express train full of blinded passengers crashes into the buffer stops at Marylebone station. The speeded-up sequence was shot at Marylebone with a BR Standard 5MT 4-6-0 as motive power. The same shot, this time at normal speed, appears in the video *Steam on 35mm*, Vol 2.

THE DAY THE EARTH CAUGHT FIRE
GB 1961 British Lion DVD
Dir: Val Guest
Edward Judd, Janet Munro

Nuclear tests tilt the earth of its axis and send it spinning towards the sun

This science-fiction drama features a couple of railway shots to illustrate the news spreading throughout the country, one of a train being loaded with papers at an unidentified London station and a stock footage close-up of the motion of an 'A4' 'Pacific' at speed.

A DAY TO REMEMBER
GB 1953 Rank
Dir: Ralph Thomas
Stanley Holloway, Donald Sinden

A pub darts team takes a day trip to France

Features a stock shot of an SR 'King Arthur' 4-6-0 with an express at Esher on the ex-LSWR main line, a shot that had also appeared in *Chance of a Lifetime* (qv).

DEAD CERT
GB 1974 UA/Woodfall
Dir: Tony Richardson
Scott Anthony, Judi Dench

A jockey investigates a series of racing-related deaths

Features a scene in which a rider on horseback almost collides with a train on a level crossing. Filmed on the Southern

Region with an SR semi-fast EMU briefly seen.

DEATH LINE
GB 1972 Rank DVD
Dir: Gary Sherman
Donald Pleasence, Christopher Lee

Cannibals live in abandoned tunnels at a London Underground station and attack travellers

This creepy horror film has now become a cult classic, but might put you off travelling on the tube late at night! A nice macabre touch is that the main cannibal character, who has grown up in the Underground, only knows one sentence, 'Mind the doors!' Some scenes were filmed at Russell Square station on the Piccadilly Line late at night and also at Aldwych station, using 1960 tube stock.

DEATH OF AN ANGEL
GB 1951 Hammer/Exclusive
Dir: Charles Saunders
Jane Baxter, Patrick Barr

Mystery when a doctor's wife is poisoned in an English village

The film opens and closes with views of branch-line 'auto-trains' arriving and departing from Marlow station with ex-GWR '1400' 0-4-2Ts. There is also one distant shot of an 'auto-train' en route along the branch.

DECLINE AND FALL
GB 1968 TCF
Dir: John Krish
Robin Phillips, Donald Wolfit

An Oxford undergraduate is expelled and has various adventures as a teacher and convicted criminal

Although the original novel was written in the 1920s, this adaptation was updated to contemporary times with one shot of an express hauled by a green Class 47 diesel.

DEFENCE OF THE REALM
GB 1985 Rank VHS
Dir: David Drury
Gabriel Byrne, Greta Scacchi

A journalist investigates the link between an MP and a Russian agent

Includes some scenes around the SR in London with locations such as Hungerford Bridge, Southwark and Blackfriars. 4-EPB and suburban two-car sets feature.

THE DEMI-PARADISE
GB 1943 Two Cities VHS
Dir: Anthony Asquith
Laurence Olivier, Margaret Rutherford

At the start of the Second World War, a Russian inventor is sent to observe life in Britain

Features a number of railway shots with footage of passing trains hauled by a Gresley 'A3' 'Pacific' and a GWR 'Castle' 4-6-0, and a scene at Waterloo station with SR 'T9' 4-4-0 No 705 on a service.

DEMOBBED
GB 1945 Butchers/Mancunian
Dir: John E. Blakeley
Norman Evans, Nat Jackley

A group of incompetent ex-servicemen prevent a robbery

One scene takes place on an unknown Southern station with pre-war SR suburban EMUs just visible in the background.

DERBY DAY
GB 1952 British Lion
Dir: Herbert Wilcox
Anna Neagle, Michael Wilding

Various stories surrounding race-goers who journey to the Derby

This drama was filmed at actual racecourse locations and includes some scenes at Tattenham Corner station of arriving race specials made up of SR

EMUs, with 2-NOL and 3-SUB types in evidence.

DEVILS BAIT
GB 1959 Independent Artists
Dir: Peter Graham Scott
Geoffrey Keen, Jane Hylton

A loaf of bread is accidentally contaminated with rat poison and a desperate police search is made to find it

Includes a good shot of ex-GWR '9400' 0-6-0PT No 9422 running light engine and stopping next to a tramp character involved in the story, believed to have been filmed outside Henley-on-Thames.

DICK BARTON SPECIAL AGENT
GB 1949 Exclusive/Hammer DVD
Dir: Alfred J. Goulding
Don Stannard, George Ford

Dick Barton fights a plot to poison Britain's water supply with cholera

This rather ropey B-movie features a scene near the end where a lorry is brought to a halt just before a level crossing. Includes a couple of shots of goods trains, one with an unknown SR loco running tender-first (either an ex-LSWR 4-4-0 or 0-6-0 type) and one with an ex-LMS 4F 0-6-0 on a train of open plank wagons.

DIE ANOTHER DAY
US/GB 2002 MGM/UA/Eon DVD
Dir: Lee Tamahori
Pierce Brosnan, Halle Berry

James Bond fights renegade Korean fighters bent on gaining power through East-West conflict

Bond's secret MI6 headquarters in the film is set in an abandoned London Underground station, referred to as Vauxhall Cross in the story, and with its own connection to the Underground system. This was the first time that the London Underground had featured in the

Bond series, despite the fact that the network has featured in other spy/thriller films (see *The Liquidator* and *Otley*). Aldwych station was used for some scenes, interspersed with scenes shot on a studio set.

DIFFERENT FOR GIRLS
GB 1996 NTFC/BBC/X Pictures VHS
Dir: Richard Spence
Rupert Graves, Steven Mackintosh

A motorcycle courier falls in love with a schoolboy friend who has had a sex-change

Various shots around London feature trains in the background: the Blackfriars/London Bridge area with Class 465 'Networker', slam-door express EMUs and a Class 319, and the Paddington approaches with 'Network Turbo' and Metropolitan 'C'-type Underground stock in evidence.

DIGBY – THE BIGGEST DOG IN THE WORLD
GB 1973 TCF DVD
Dir: Joseph McGrath
Jim Dale, Spike Milligan

A sheepdog eats an experimental chemical and grows to giant size

This popular family film features a memorable scene in which the giant dog lies down on a railway line in front of an approaching train, much to the driver's consternation. However, he gets up just in time to let the train pass through his legs! The train itself is a Cravens Class 105 two-car DMU, probably filmed on the Bedford-Bletchley line.

DINNER AT THE RITZ
GB 1937 New World
Dir: Harold Schuster
Annabella, Paul Lukas

A French girl exposes swindlers who faked her father's suicide

Features what appears to be a studio-shot scene set supposedly in the countryside with back projection including what appears to be a shot of a passing GWR 4-6-0 on an express.

DIRTY DOZEN – THE NEXT MISSION
US 1985 MGM
Dir: Andrew V. McLaglen
Lee Marvin, Ernest Borgnine

A bunch of criminal soldiers are rounded up for a suicide mission

Features some scenes filmed on the Bluebell Railway, with Horsted Keynes used as the location for the boarding of a troop train hauled by preserved SR 'Q' Class No 541, together with scenes filmed on the Nene Valley Railway using a preserved German '64' Class 2-6-2T.

DIRTY PRETTY THINGS
GB 2003 BBC DVD
Dir: Stephen Frears
Chitwetel Ejiofor, Audrey Tautou

A hotel receptionist discovers an illegal organ donor trade

Features a shot early in the film of a Class 319 'Thameslink' EMU crossing a bridge, filmed in South London.

DIRTY WEEKEND
GB 1993 UIP VHS
Dir: Michael Winner
Lia Williams, Rufus Sewell

A woman decides to take revenge on the men who abuse her

Features a couple of shots on Brighton station, including one with departing SR semi-fast EMU set No 1709, together with a shot of an EMU entering Clayton Tunnel on the Brighton line. An interesting, and totally unexpected, aspect of this film is that in a couple of scenes the central character is drinking out of a Railfreight Distribution mug! How this cropped up in the film is anybody's guess.

DISTANT VOICES STILL LIVES

GB 1988 BFI/FilmFour VHS
Dir: Terence Davies
Freda Dowie, Pete Postlethwaite

Life for a working-class family in Liverpool in 1940s and '50s

Includes a scene filmed at Didcot Railway Centre.

THE DIVORCE OF LADY X

GB 1938 London Films VHS
Dir: Tim Whelan
Laurence Olivier, Merle Oberon

A nobleman's daughter poses as a divorce client

Features one shot of the frontage of Victoria station and a brief run-by of a 'Lord Nelson' 4-6-0 on a Southern express.

DOCTOR IN DISTRESS

GB 1963 Rank DVD
Dir: Ralph Thomas
Dirk Bogarde, James Robertson Justice

Dr Simon Sparrow goes back to work at his old hospital

Includes a scene filmed on Windsor & Eton Central station with Bogarde on a departing train hauled by an unseen diesel-hydraulic loco, and a shot of a passing express hauled by a 'Hymek'.

DOCTOR IN TROUBLE

GB 1970 Rank DVD
Dir: Ralph Thomas
Leslie Phillips, Simon Dee

Dr Burke accidentally becomes a stowaway on a cruise ship

Includes a scene at Windsor & Eton Central station (no trains visible).

DR MORELLE – THE CASE OF THE MISSING HEIRESS

GB 1949 Exclusive/Hammer
Dir: Godfrey Grayson
Valentine Dyall, Julia Lang

Film version of the BBC radio series about a doctor-turned-sleuth

Some very good railway scenes appear in what is only a cheaply made B-movie: a nice shot of an express leaving Paddington behind 'Star' Class 4-6-0 No 4048 *Princess Victoria*; two passing shots of 'Castles' on expresses, both in early 'BRITISH RAILWAYS' livery, and a lovely scene of a GWR-liveried '1400' tank with an auto-coach, probably filmed on the Wallingford branch.

DR TERROR'S HOUSE OF HORRORS

GB 1965 Amicus
Dir: Freddie Francis
Peter Cushing, Ursula Howells

A stranger tells the fortunes of five people during a railway journey

Most of the railway scenes, including the final 'station' scene, are studio reconstructions, but there is an old shot of Paddington near the beginning of the film with a ex-GWR 'Hall' 4-6-0.

THE DOGS OF WAR

GB 1980 UA DVD
Dir: John Irvin
Christopher Walken, Tom Berenger

A mercenary becomes involved in a plot to take over a West African state

Features a panoramic shot of Liverpool Street station with a Class 37 diesel visible at the buffer stops.

DON'T GO BREAKING MY HEART

GB 1998 Polygram VHS
Dir: Willi Paterson
Anthony Edwards, Jenny Seagrove

After a hypnosis session a widow inadvertently falls for a sports therapist

Features a scene on 1990s tube stock somewhere on the London Underground, together with shots of the Waterloo & City line's travelator at Bank and the exterior of Hampstead Underground station.

DOUBLE EXPOSURE
GB 1976 Westwind
Dir: William Webb
Anouska Hempel, David Baron

A top photographer falls for the mistress of a wealthy and powerful man

Includes an on-board train scene filmed on the Bluebell Railway.

DRACULA
US 1973 Dan Curtis Productions
Dir: Dan Curtis
Jack Palance, Simon Ward

Count Dracula comes to England and is pursued by Van Helsing

Includes scenes filmed on the Kent & East Sussex Railway.

DRACULA
GB 1979 Universal VHS
Dir: John Badham
Frank Lagella, Laurence Olivier

Lavish remake of the above

Features scenes filmed on the Bluebell Railway.

DREAM ON
GB 1991 Amber
Dir: Amber Production Team
Anna-Marie Gascoigne, Maureen Harold

A mother and daughter struggle on a Newcastle housing estate

Filmed on location on the Meadowell estate, with one shot of a passing Tyne & Wear Metro EMU.

DREAMING
GB 1944 Ealing
Dir: John Baxter
Flanagan and Allen, Hazel Court

A soldier is knocked out by a bump to the head and dreams

The film opens with a studio-bound

railway journey that includes a stock low-angle shot of a 'Royal Scot' 4-6-0 in the Lune Gorge.

THE DRESSER
GB 1983 Columbia/Goldcrest DVD
Dir: Peter Yates
Albert Finney, Tom Courtenay

A larger-than-life Shakespearean actor has a wild last day on tour

This film has a memorable scene in which Finney, playing the Shakespearean actor, stops a departing train he has just missed by booming 'Stop that train!' in the echoing station so loudly that the driver just has to comply! The scene was filmed at York station (posing as Crewe) and uses items from the National Railway Museum – preserved 'Duchess' 'Pacific' No 46229 *Duchess of Hamilton* is the train engine, with 'Black Five' 4-6-0 No 5407 also used. The coaching stock is made up of 12 condemned Mk 1 coaches painted maroon and lettered 'LMS' for the occasion.

DRIVING LESSONS
GB 2006 Content Film/Tartan
Dir: Jeremy Brock
Rupert Grint, Julie Walters

A teenager takes driving lessons from an eccentric actress who teaches him about life

Features a scene near the end of the film outside Hampstead Underground station.

DUAL ALIBI
GB 1947 British National
Dir: Alfred Travers
Herbert Lom, Phyllis Dixey

Twin trapeze artists hatch a murder plot after being swindled out of a fortune

Most of the film is set in Blackpool and there is a brief stock shot of a couple of illuminated trams – a vintage double-decker with 'Daily Express' advertising and a 'sailing yacht' type.

DUSTY ERMINE

GB 1936 Julius Hagen/Twickenham
Dir: Bernard Vorhaus
Jane Baxter, Anthony Bushell

Police pursue counterfeiters to Switzerland

The crooks' journey to the continent from London is illustrated by a good shot of SR 'N' Class 2-6-0 No 1830 leaving Waterloo on a train, together with a very brief 'over the camera' shot of a GWR 4-6-0.

THE EARLY BIRD
GB 1965 Rank DVD
Dir: Robert Asher
Norman Wisdom, Edward Chapman

A small milk company is threatened by takeover

This Norman Wisdom comedy is memorable for a scene in which Wisdom's milk cart is pushed on to a level crossing and destroyed by a passing 'Blue Pullman'. The crossing itself is a studio set (note the painted backdrop behind) with real shots of a WR Pullman set from stock footage cut in.

THE EARTH DIES SCREAMING
GB 1964 Lippert
Dir: Terence Fisher
Dennis Price, Willard Parker

Survivors of Earth battle alien invaders

The pre-credit sequence depicts the aliens killing most of the Earth's inhabitants by gas attack. A train driver slumps at the controls of a steam engine, which is a Southern large-boilered Drummond 4-4-0 judging by the stock footage, and the ensuing crash scene is made up of footage from *The Wrecker* (1929) (qv). We also see a commuter keeling over on the platform of Shepperton station!

EAST IS EAST
GB 1917 Turner Film Company
Dir: Henry Edwards
Henry Edwards, Florence Turner

A poor girl comes into money but finds the high life too difficult

Includes a scene where a family board a London-bound train made up of 1st and 3rd Class SECR four-wheel coaches filmed at a Kentish station, believed to be Horsmonden on the Hawkhurst branch. No loco seen.

EASY MONEY
GB 1948 GFD
Dir: Bernard Knowles
Jack Warner, Mervyn Johns

Four stories about people who have won the football pools

The second story, which features Mervyn Johns, includes a shot of a GWR suburban train leaving Beaconsfield station on the GW&GC Joint line, loco not visible.

THE ECHO MURDERS
GB 1944 Strand
Dir: John Harlow
David Farrar, Kynaston Reeves

Sexton Blake solves a number of murders in Cornwall

Features a couple of shots of GWR mainline expresses on the London-Bristol line, one hauled by a 'King' 4-6-0, the other a distant 'going-away' shot, so the loco cannot be identified. Bizarrely, Blake's journey from Cornwall to London at the end of the film is depicted by a stock shot of an LMS 'Royal Scot' 4-6-0 in the Lune Gorge! There is also a scene with Farrar hailing a taxi in Paddington station.

EDUCATING RITA
GB 1983 Rank DVD
Dir: Lewis Gilbert
Julie Walters, Michael Caine

A hairdresser enrols on an Open University course

Popular comedy-drama featuring a scene filmed at Dublin Heuston station with coaching stock painted into BR blue/grey livery with BR logos and numbers.

80,000 SUSPECTS
GB 1963 Rank
Dir: Val Guest
Richard Johnson, Claire Bloom

The town of Bath is threatened by a smallpox epidemic

Drama-documentary using actual locations. One scene was shot on the platform of Bath Spa station, but no trains are visible.

ELEPHANT JUICE
GB/US 1999 Miramax/FilmFour
Dir: Sam Miller
Emmanuelle Beart, Sean Gallagher

Three couples help their friend find a partner

Various shots taken on the London Underground, mainly the Northern and Central Lines, with 1990s tube stock (car No 92180 is prominent in one shot).

THE ELEPHANT MAN
US 1980 EMI DVD
Dir: David Lynch
John Hurt, Anthony Hopkins

The story of John Merrick who, despite deformity, became a member of society

Includes a scene at Liverpool Street station and a brief stock shot of preserved Ivatt 2-6-0 No 644 near Arley on the Severn Valley Railway taken from the 1978 *The Thirty Nine Steps.*

EMILY
GB 1977 Emily Productions DVD
Dir: Henry Herbert
Koo Stark, Sarah Brackett

A girl's sexual awakening in 1920s England

Features a train at Horsted Keynes and Holywell on the Bluebell Railway hauled by 'A1X' 0-6-0T No 72 *Fenchurch.*

THE END OF THE AFFAIR
GB 1999 Columbia DVD
Dir: Neil Jordan
Ralph Fiennes, Julianne Moore

A writer reflects on his affair with a married woman during the Second World War

Southgate station on the London Underground was used to recreate one wartime scene. There is also a stock colour aerial shot of a WR steam train somewhere in West London.

THE END OF THE LINE
GB 1959 Eros
Dir: Charles Saunders
Barbara Shelley, Alan Baxter

A writer meets an old flame and finds himself involved in a murder plot

Good shot during the opening credits of the 'Golden Arrow' arriving at London Victoria behind a 'Britannia' 'Pacific', followed by various shots of the platforms and station frontage.

AN ENGLISHMAN'S TRIP TO PARIS
GB 1904 Hepworth DVD
Dir: Lewin Fitzhammon
Actors unknown

Adventures of an Englishman journeying to Paris

Includes scenes filmed outside and on the

platforms of Charing Cross station with a rare shot of a departure behind an SECR 'B' Class 4-4-0 fitted with Holden oil-firing equipment and 'D' Class 4-4-0 No 745 in an adjacent platform. There is also a shot of a boat train arriving at Dover Marine behind another 'D' Class loco.

ENIGMA

GB 2001 Broadway/Intermedia/Jagged
   DVD
Dir: Michael Apted
Kate Winslet, Dougray Scott

A decoder at Bletchley Park tries to trace his missing girlfriend, believed to be a spy

All the railway scenes were filmed on the Great Central Railway at Loughborough Central and various lineside locations, one being used for a getaway scene. Rolling-stock was distinctly unusual for a film set in wartime – BR-liveried 'O4' 2-8-0 No 63601 and Mk 1 coaches, albeit with LMS roundels added for the film.

ENGLISH WITHOUT TEARS

GB 1944 GFD/Two Cities
Dir: Harold French
Lilli Palmer, Michael Wilding

During the Second World War a wealthy ATS girl falls for her butler

Features a brief shot of the platforms of Victoria station with an SR tank loco, probably an 'H' Class, visible at the buffer stops on a rake of stock, acting as a banker.

THE ENGLISHMAN WHO WENT UP A HILL BUT CAME DOWN A MOUNTAIN

GB 1995 Buena Vista/Parallax VHS
Dir: Chris Monger
Hugh Grant, Kenneth Griffith

Two English surveyors declare a Welsh mountain to be really a hill, and the villagers decide to act

Features one scene at Arley station on the Severn Valley Railway.

THE ENTERTAINER

GB 1960 British Lion DVD
Dir: Tony Richardson
Laurence Olivier, Joan Plowright

A cynical old entertainer has one last shot at fame

This classic film was mainly filmed in Morecambe, but there are some night shots of Blackpool trams – two Brush single-deck cars and two illuminated types – an old double-decker and a pseudo-'paddle steamer'. Near the start of the film is a scene on a main-line station, believed to be Liverpool Street, but no trains are visible.

ESCAPADE

GB 1955 Pinnacle
Dir: Philip Leacock
John Mills, Alastair Sim

The children of a pacifist steal a plane to fly to Vienna to deliver an anti-war petition

Features a stock shot of unrebuilt 'Royal Scot' 4-6-0 No 46100 on Bushey troughs, filmed for *Train of Events* (1948).

ESCAPE

GB 1948 TCF
Dir: Joseph Mankiewicz
Rex Harrison, Peggy Cummings

A prisoner escapes from Dartmoor but says he's innocent

Features scenes filmed on the Dart Valley line.

ESCAPE BY NIGHT

GB 1953 Eros
Dir: John Gilling
Bonar Colleano, Sid James

A journalist hides out with a crook in order to get a story

The flight of two of the characters near a railway yard is illustrated with a stock shot from *Brief Encounter* of a streamlined 'Duchess' 'Pacific' on an express at Watford Junction.

ESCAPE FROM THE DARK
GB 1976 Walt Disney VHS
Dir: Charles Jarrott
Alastair Sim, Peter Barkworth

Two boys attempt to rescue pit ponies from a slaughterhouse in Yorkshire

A railway scene involving an attempt to load the horses onto wagons was filmed on the Keighley & Worth Valley Railway, so at least the railway shots were in Yorkshire! The actual location was a siding in Oakworth yard, and used preserved Manchester Ship Canal 0-6-0T No 31.

EVERY DAY'S A HOLIDAY
GB 1964 Grand National
Dir: James Hill
John Leyton, Ron Moody

Young people get jobs at a holiday camp so they can enter a talent contest

Features a good shot of Class 305 EMU set No 153 on a Clacton-bound service to illustrate the journey to the camp.

EVERY HOME SHOULD HAVE ONE
GB 1970 British Lion VHS
Dir: James Clark
Marty Feldman, Shelley Berman

An advertising man uses sex to sell porridge

During a comedy chase sequence there is a semi-distant shot of a couple of SR 4-SUB EMUs passing over a bridge somewhere in the South London suburbs.

EVERYTHING IS RHYTHM
GB 1936 Joe Rock VHS
Dir: Alfred Goulding
Harry Roy and his Band, Princess Pearl

A dance band leader falls for a European princess

A montage sequence of the band touring the European states is at one point illustrated by a run-by shot of a very British-looking passenger train made up of Southern rolling-stock; sadly we do not see the locomotive.

EXPOSÉ
GB 1976 Norfolk International DVD
Dir: James Kenelm Clarke
Udo Kier, Fiona Richmond

A writer living at an isolated house is subject to frightening visions

Features some excellent shots of Hatfield Peveril station and the GE main line with passing ER trains – a pair of Class 309 Clacton-line EMUs, a couple of Class 305 outer-suburban units and a Class 47 diesel on an express.

EYE OF THE NEEDLE
GB 1981 UA DVD
Dir: Richard Marquand
Donald Sutherland, Kate Nelligan

In wartime Britain a German spy flees to a Scottish island after being discovered in London

The railway journey to Scotland features some wildly varying and in some cases improbable motive power. Featured locos include a 'Black Five', a 'Britannia' (a post-war design), two Southern locos (a Maunsell 2-6-0 and an 'S15' 4-6-0) and a BR Standard 4-6-0 (another 1951 design!). All shots were filmed on the Mid Hants Railway, with the additional signal box scene filmed at Alresford. The early goods depot scenes in London are believed to have been filmed at Battersea.

FACE

GB 1997 UIP/BBC VHS
Dir: Antonia Bird
Robert Carlyle, Ray Winstone

A group of thieves carry out a robbery, but one of them is a traitor

Features a couple of shots of Underground stations around London, unfortunately unknown. Near the start there is a night shot of a Docklands Light Railway unit.

THE FACE OF FU MANCHU

GB 1965 Anglo-EMI VHS
Dir: Don Sharp
Nigel Green, Christopher Lee

A London crime wave is linked to the mastermind Fu Manchu

During a car chase scene supposedly set in London there is a good shot of the cars passing a Hudswell-Clarke 0-6-0ST on a rake of wagons. The location is actually Dublin, and the line is the tramway that linked the Guinness brewery with Kingsbridge goods yard near Heuston station. The industrial loco belonged to the brewery.

FAHRENHEIT 451

GB 1966 Rank VHS
Dir: Francois Truffaut
Oskar Werner, Julie Christie

In a fascist future books are forbidden and are burned by firemen

In the resistance camp that features in the closing scenes of the film there appears to be an old Southern Railway suburban coach being used as a dwelling – it seems too complete to be a mock-up. The futuristic monorail that appears in the film was a real experimental type located at Chateauneuf-sur-Loire near Orleans in France.

FAIRYTALE – A TRUE STORY

US 1997 Warner DVD
Dir: Charles Sturridge
Paul McGann, Peter O'Toole

In 1917 two girls become famous for apparently taking photos of fairies

Based on a real-life story that took place in Yorkshire, the film uses an accurate location, namely the Keighley & Worth Valley Railway, with shots at Keighley station and along the line. A nice touch was the use of accurate rolling-stock rather than the 'shoot anything in steam' procedure beloved by film producers in the past; preserved Lancashire & Yorkshire Railway 0-6-0 No 1300 was brought in from the East Lancashire Railway.

FALLING FOR YOU

GB 1933 Gainsborough VHS
Dir: Jack Hulbert, Robert Stevenson
Jack Hulbert, Cicely Courtneidge

Two reporters go to Switzerland to trace a missing heiress

Features a scene at Folkestone Harbour with SR 'C' Class 0-6-0 No 1213 visible.

FAMILY LIFE

GB　1971　British Lion　VHS
Dir: Ken Loach
Sandy Ratcliff, Bill Dean

A young girl becomes mentally ill through pressure from her parents

Includes a couple of scenes on the London Underground with 1960 tube stock and a Central Line station.

THE FARMER'S WIFE

GB　1940　Associated British
Dir: Leslie Arliss
Wilfred Lawson, Patricia Roc

A farmer seeks a wife but marries his housekeeper

Features a scene at Cole Green station on the Welwyn-Hertford branch line.

FAST AND LOOSE

GB　1954　GFD　VHS
Dir: Gordon Parry
Brian Reece, Kay Kendall

A husband misses his train and has to spend the night with an old flame

Includes a scene at Paddington station with a departing train leaving Platform 1. An ex-GWR Pannier tank can be seen moving light engine behind a rake of coaches. Later in the film there is a nice shot of an ex-LNER 'L1' 2-6-4T arriving with a local at Denham Golf Club station. Out-takes also turn up in *Steam on 35mm, Vol 3*.

FATHER BROWN

GB　1954　Columbia
Dir: Robert Hamer
Alec Guinness, Peter Finch

A Catholic clergyman pursues a master thief for a priceless church relic

A generally successful attempt to film G. K. Chesterton's character, it includes a scene in which Guinness has to leap on board a departing train at Victoria station. There is a good view of a Southern coach but no locos are seen.

FEAST OF JULY

GB/US　1995　Buena
　　Vista/Touchstone/Merchant Ivory
Dir: Christopher Menaul
Embeth Davidtz, Tom Bell

A woman finds love with a simple-minded youth in Victorian times

Features scenes filmed on the Keighley & Worth Valley Railway.

FELICIA'S JOURNEY

GB/Canada　1999　Icon/Marquis　DVD
Dir: Atom Egoyan
Bob Hoskins, Elaine Cassidy

A pregnant Irish girl comes to England and is befriended by a strange middle-aged man

A great deal of the film was shot in the northern suburbs of Birmingham, and there is one semi-distant shot of a passing 'Centro'-liveried Class 323 EMU.

FERRY CROSS THE MERSEY

GB　1965　UA/Subafilms
Dir: Jeremy Summers
Gerry and the Pacemakers, Eric Barker

A pop band forms for a music competition

Features a 'Keystone Kops'-style comedy sequence with a hearse speeding through the streets of Liverpool and at one point being chased in the docks area by a Class 03 diesel shunter with match wagon. A considerable number of wagons (vans and mineral types) and parcel vans can be seen in the yards.

THE FIEND

GB　1971　World Arts Media
Dir: Robert Hartford-Davis
Ann Todd, Patrick Magee

A religion-obsessed young man becomes a serial killer

Early on in the film there is a fight scene in a garage next to a railway line and a formation of blue SR 4-COR EMUs can be seen passing, somewhere in south-west London.

THE FILE OF THE GOLDEN GOOSE
GB 1969 UA
Dir: Sam Wanamaker
Yul Brynner, Edward Woodward

An American agent works with Scotland Yard to track a criminal gang

Features some good shots filmed at Liverpool Street station with a Class 47 diesel and Class 305 EMUs visible at the buffer stops.

THE FINAL TEST
GB 1953 Rank VHS
Dir: Anthony Asquith
Jack Warner, Robert Morley

A cricketer looks forward to his last game

There is a good shot near the start of the film of SR 'West Country' 'Pacific' No 34048 arriving at Waterloo station with an express.

A FIRE HAS BEEN ARRANGED
GB 1935 Twickenham DVD
Dir: Leslie S. Hiscott
Bud Flanagan, Chesney Allen

After ten years in prison, two ex-bank robbers try to recover their hidden loot

This film features a comedy sequence very reminiscent of stunt scenes much loved by the Hollywood silent comedies. Flanagan and Allen drive their car from a level crossing on to a railway line and into a tunnel. An express follows in behind them and emerges from the other end followed by the car – still going but missing most of its parts! The express is hauled by GWR 'Star' Class 4-6-0 No 4035 in the 'approaching' shot, a '4300' 2-6-0 as it enters the tunnel, and a 'Hall' as it emerges from the other end! The

location for these scenes is unfortunately unknown, but is possibly on the Bath-Westbury line. There is also a shot of the wrecked car being driven through the middle of Bradford-upon-Avon GWR station.

FIRST A GIRL
GB 1935 Gaumont VHS
Dir: Victor Saville
Jessie Matthews, Sonnie Hale

A messenger girl becomes a musical star by pretending to be a female impersonator

Includes a montage sequence involving a theatre tour from Britain to the Continent with brief glimpses of a Gresley 'Pacific', passing and rail-level footplate shots.

THE FIRST GREAT TRAIN ROBBERY
GB 1978 UA DVD
Dir: Michael Crichton
Sean Connery, Donald Sutherland

In 1855 a ruthless crook picks a gang to rob the London-Folkestone express

All the railway scenes for this frequently shown caper film were shot on the CIE. Dublin Heuston was used for all the 'London Bridge' scenes, including a number of atmospheric night shots, and Cork station was used as 'Folkestone Harbour'. All the train journey scenes were filmed at various locations on the CIE system, on both freight and passenger lines, including Moate (as 'Ashford') and the Bray area, with camera shots taken from on board, on the roofs of the carriages and from a helicopter. The choice of Ireland for these scenes was a good one, as the railway locations remarkably resembled 19th-century British travel on the SECR. Featured was preserved 'J15' 0-6-0 No 184, renumbered 134 for the film and fitted with dummy outside frames and brass dome, although sister loco No 186 was also used. The four-wheel coaches were created specially for the film using old underframes from the CIE and wooden bodies created by the film company.

FIVE CHILDREN AND IT

GB 2004 Capitol Films DVD
Dir: John Stephenson
Kenneth Branagh, Tara Fitzgerald

Five evacuated children make friends with a sand fairy

The start of the film features scenes filmed on the Isle of Man Steam Railway with excellent shots of a train hauled by 2-4-0T No 11 seen from the trackside and from a helicopter. Douglas station appears, renamed 'Hampton Wick', whereas interestingly Castletown station appears as itself.

FIVE SECONDS TO SPARE

GB 1999 Scala Wildgaze/WAVE Pictures
    DVD
Dir: Tom Connolly
Max Beesley, Ray Winstone

A young songwriter gets involved with murder

Includes some shots filmed on St Pancras station, one of which features a Midland Mainline-liveried HST, and a couple of shots on the London Underground with District Line 'D' stock.

FLAME

GB 1974 Goodtimes/VPS DVD
Dir: Richard Loncraine
Slade, Tom Conti

A rock group is promoted by a smart advertising executive in the 1960s

Features a scene filmed on the Kent & East Sussex Railway.

THE FLANAGAN BOY

GB 1953 Hammer/Exclusive
Dir: Reginald LeBorg
Tony Wright, Barbara Payton

A boxer falls for a married woman

Features a night shot of a passing express hauled by a GWR 4-6-0 and a scene on Denham station with the tail end of a departing local train seen, but not the loco.

THE FLYING SCOT

GB 1957 Anglo-Amalgamated VHS
Dir: Compton Bennett
Lee Paterson, Kay Callard

A team of crooks attempts a robbery on an overnight express carrying bank-notes

Almost all the action of this little B-movie takes place on an overnight train, although the robbery itself might take some believing! The first robbery sequence is an imagined, planned event, shot interestingly without any dialogue, and involves the robbers gaining access to the loot by occupying a compartment next door and taking the seating and partitions apart. Railway shots that occur during this sequence are:

- a general view of Paddington station, the announcer giving details for a leaving 'London train'!
- ex-GWR 'Hall' 4-6-0 No 6942 leaving Paddington on a Shrewsbury express (three-quarter rear shot)
- three different shots of streamlined 'Duchess' 'Pacifics' at night on expresses (stock shots from *Brief Encounter*)
- an ex-GWR 'King' on an express in a deep cutting, headcode 187
- night shots of WR and LMR expresses, too dark to discern details
- a 'King' arriving at Paddington with an express (the same shot appears in the film version of 6.5 *Special*)

During the actual robbery the same shots are used, but with these extra ones:

- a 'Duchess' on an express overtaking an 8F 2-8-0 on a freight on the LNWR main line
- a 'going-away' shot of an express silhouetted on an embankment, loco unknown

• a different view of an express arriving at Paddington, this time a 'Castle' with headcode 753

All other scenes appear to be studio shots, although the props department have built quite accurate copies of compartment coaches.

THE FLYING SCOTSMAN
GB 1929 Warner/BIP VHS
Dir: Castleton Knight
Moore Marriott, Raymond Milland

An ex-employee tries to wreck the 'Flying Scotsman'

This film is a very early part-talkie – the first half is silent, then, during the train journey, everyone starts talking! LNER 'Pacific' No 4472 *Flying Scotsman* itself was used by the film company for six weeks of filming, with crews using numerous camera positions on the loco, tender and stock. The early railway scenes in the film are as follows:

• an unknown Gresley 'Pacific' passing on an express
• No 4472 entering King's Cross, general station scene
• No 4472 leaves Top Shed light engine with 'C1' 4-4-2 No 4411 in the background and possibly another 'Pacific'
• No 4472 backs down on to a train at King's Cross, with an 'N2' 0-6-2T alongside
• No 4472 leaves with an express
• a number of driver's-view shots of locations (eg Gasworks Tunnel) taken from the front of the loco, and a 'D49' 4-4-0 passes on an express

The rest of the film is taken up by the attempt to wreck the train, which was filmed on the Hertford Loop. The scenes where actors Pauline Johnson and Alec Hurley climb on to the roof and running-boards of the train were filmed between Crews Hill, Cuffley and Bayford – the actors actually did these shots, not stunt

people. Eventually the loco is uncoupled at speed from the train and the coaches are eventually brought to a stand. The entire sequence is a masterpiece of editing and in many ways an early precedent for *The Last Journey* (qv). These scenes use No 4472 and a rake of Gresley stock with no other locos.

FOR FREEDOM
GB 1940 Gainsborough DVD
Dir: Maurice Elvey
Will Fyffe

A news agency scoops the sinking of the Admiral Graf Spee

One scene depicts a group of reporters working on a newsreel about scientific progress, and there are two interesting shots – one of London trams (including a Feltham car) crossing Westminster Bridge at night and a view of Charing Cross station with a collection of pre-war SR suburban EMUs.

FOR QUEEN AND COUNTRY
GB/US 1988 UIP VHS
Dir: Martin Stellman
Denzel Washington, Dorian Healy

A black soldier returns to civilian life in Britain but feels an outcast

Filmed around South London, in one scene a Class 73 electro-diesel passes in the background on a 'Gatwick Express'.

FOR THEM THAT TRESPASS
GB 1948 ABP
Dir: Alberto Cavalcanti
Richard Todd, Joan Dowling

A man is sent to prison for a crime, and years later he sets out to prove his innocence

The real murderer in the story is an engine driver, but apart from a couple of shots of unrebuilt 'Patriot' 4-6-0s most of the locations (the engine sheds and station platforms) are studio sets. There is a dramatic scene filmed in Welwyn

Tunnel on the LNER main line where the murderer is killed by a passing freight train hauled by a 'WD' 2-8-0, although a couple of shots of 'B1s' also appear in these scenes.

FOR THOSE IN PERIL
GB 1943 Ealing VHS
Dir: Charles Crichton
David Farrar, Ralph Michael

A flyer fails to join the RAF so joins the Air Sea Rescue service

Includes a good shot of SR 2-NOL EMU No 1833 arriving at an unknown South Coast station.

FORBIDDEN
GB 1949 British Lion
Dir: George King
Douglass Montgomery, Hazel Court

A fairground worker is suspected of killing his wife

Set on location in Blackpool, there are a couple of shots of trams – a distant one of a Brush single-deck car and a back projection shot of a Balloon type passing behind Ronald Shiner.

FORBIDDEN CARGO
GB 1954 Rank VHS
Dir: Harold French
Nigel Patrick, Jack Warner

A narcotics agent attempts to trap brother and sister drug smugglers

Features a scene filmed on Victoria station, no trains visible.

FORCE TEN FROM NAVARONE
GB 1979 Columbia DVD
Dir: Guy Hamilton
Robert Shaw, Edward Fox

During the Second World War, commandos are sent to blow up a vital bridge in Yugoslavia

Features a scene supposedly set on the Continent but clearly filmed in Britain, as it features a goods yard (in which the commandos smuggle themselves onto a train) incorporating some very British-looking wagons. VBA van No 200425 is prominent, as well as some vans, a bogie-bolster wagon and coal types. Location unknown, but possibly South London.

FOUR IN THE MORNING
GB 1965 West One
Dir: Anthony Simmons
Ann Lynn, Judi Dench

Four different stories set on one night in London

Includes various shots around London, including a few railway shots. There are a few scenes on the District/Circle Lines of the Underground, including shots of Aldgate station, with District 'R'-type and Circle 'C'-type stock. There is also a shot of an SR suburban EMU crossing the Thames.

FOUR SIDED TRIANGLE
GB 1952 Hammer/Exclusive DVD
Dir: Terence Fisher
Stephen Murray, Barbara Payton

A scientist makes a clone of his ex-girlfriend

Includes a few scenes of arriving and departing trains at Marlow station, terminus of the branch from Bourne End; a '1400' 0-4-2T is seen with 'auto-coach' No W33. Later in the film there is a good run-past shot on the LSWR main line of the 'Bournemouth Belle' hauled by unrebuilt 'Merchant Navy' No 35017.

FRAGMENT OF FEAR
GB 1970 Columbia
Dir: Richard C. Sarafian
David Hemmings, Gayle Hunnicutt

A young writer investigates his aunt's murder

Includes a scene in which a man is killed by falling under an Underground train – this scene was filmed on the Waterloo & City Line using one of its Class 487

EMUs. Later in the film there is a shot of a blue 'Warship' diesel on an express in the Severn Tunnel area, as well as a driver's-view shot of a train entering the Severn Tunnel itself.

FRENCH DRESSING
GB 1963 ABP
Dir: Ken Russell
James Booth, Roy Kinnear

A deckchair attendant has an idea to bring a film festival to a seaside resort

Includes a couple of scenes filmed at Herne Bay station, one of which features a departing train made up of Southern coaches. Despite the steam sound effects on the soundtrack the train is actually hauled by a Class 33 diesel, unseen at the front. The complete longer take appears in Video 125's *Diesels and Electrics on 35mm*.

THE FRENCH LIEUTENANT'S WOMAN
GB 1981 UA DVD
Dir: Karel Reisz
Jeremy Irons, Meryl Streep

In 1867 a man falls for the abandoned mistress of a French seaman

The film features two stories that run parallel to each other – one is the story summarised above, the other a contemporary story about actors playing the characters. The 'present-day' story includes a scene at Exeter St David's station using Mk 2 air-conditioned coaches, but no loco visible. The 1867 scenes use Kingswear station (as 'Exeter') on the Paignton & Dartmouth Railway with preserved GWR '1400' Class 0-4-2T No 1450 arriving with a 'London train'. The front of the station was completely repainted and reproduction posters were put on all the billboards to give the impression of a busy 19th-century station. No 1450 was brought in by road from the Dart Valley Railway and given a paint job

for the filming, which took place 'off season' in October 1980.

FRIDAY THE THIRTEENTH
GB 1933 Gainsborough VHS
Dir: Victor Saville
Jessie Matthews, Emlyn Williams

The stories of several people involved in a bus crash

A couple of the characters involved are shown arriving at King's Cross station on an express hauled by Gresley 'Pacific' No 2582.

FRIEDA
GB 1947 Ealing
Dir: Basil Dearden
David Farrar, Mai Zetterling

An RAF officer marries a German girl but she encounters hostility when they return home

Includes a scene filmed at Hartfield station with 'M7' 0-4-4T No 378 on an arriving branch train. There are also a few stock shots of LMS expresses hauled by (in sequence) a 'Claughton', two unrebuilt 'Royal Scots' and a 'Black Five'. The escape scenes set in Germany involve some model work but also a very real-looking 'WD' 'Austerity' tender loco – possibly this was filmed on the Longmoor Military Railway.

THE FRIGHTENED MAN
GB 1952 Eros
Dir: John Gilling
Dermot Walsh, Barbara Murray

An antique dealer tries to do the best for his son but his plans fall apart

Features a scene at Paddington station with an ex-GWR 'Castle' 4-6-0 on an express, and a shot of an ex-LMS de-streamlined 'Duchess' 'Pacific' on an express in the Camden area.

FROM BEYOND THE GRAVE

GB 1973 Amicus
Dir: Kevin Connor
Ian Carmichael, Margaret Leighton

A series of horror stories linked to an old antique shop

A railway journey in the film, on which Carmichael is prey to an invisible monster, is illustrated by a shot of a Class 87 electric loco on an express, the film being made in the year the class was introduced.

FROM RUSSIA WITH LOVE

GB 1963 UA DVD
Dir: Terence Young
Sean Connery, Robert Shaw

James Bond deals with a Russian spy out to kill him and steals a coding machine

A lot of the action in this Bond film occurs on a train heading from Istanbul into Europe on which there is a memorable fight scene between Connery and Shaw. Most of the railway scenes were filmed on the Continent, but amusingly there are a couple of stock shots of British trains slipped in, both featuring LMS 4-6-0s on the West Coast Main Line hauling expresses made up of Mk 1 coaches. Hardly what you would see on the 'Orient Express' crossing the Turkish desert!

THE FROZEN DEAD

GB 1966 Goldstar
Dir: Herbert J. Leder
Dana Andrews, Anna Palk

A scientist attempts to revive Nazi leaders in a English laboratory

Features some scenes filmed at Merton Park station, with a couple of SR suburban two-car EMUs.

THE FULL MONTY

GB/US 1997 TCF DVD
Dir: Peter Cattaneo
Robert Carlyle, Tom Wilkinson

A group of unemployed steelworkers become male strippers

This successful British comedy of the 1990s features a brief shot of a Sheffield super-tram.

FUNNY BONES

GB 1995 Buena Vista DVD
Dir: Peter Chelsom
Oliver Platt, Lee Evans

A failed American comedian goes to Blackpool and discovers his half-brother

Curiously for a film made on location in Blackpool there are no shots of the trams. What we do get, however, is a rendezvous scene that takes place in a railway coach – an old GWR Hawksworth example – which was filmed at Didcot Railway Centre.

Above APPOINTMENT
WITH CRIME (1945):
William Hartnell is trapped by
his hands in the carriage
window at the dramatic end of
the film. *British National*

Right THE BLISS OF
MRS BLOSSOM (1968):
The front end of GWR '61XX'
No 6106 in 'psychedelic' livery
for this Swinging Sixties film.
Great Western Society

Above CLOCKWISE (1986): John Cleese in a scene filmed at Hull Paragon station. *Canal + Image*

Above right THE FIRST GREAT TRAIN
ROBBERY (1979): Donald Sutherland races
towards GS&WR 'J15' No 184 (as No 134)
at Dublin Heuston station. *BFI*

Right FRIEDA (1947): David Farrar,
Mai Zetterling and 'M7' 0-4-4T No 378
at Hartfield station in a scene from
the Ealing film. *BFI*

Above THE GHOST TRAIN (1931): The cast and crew of
the 'lost' production, filmed on the Camerton branch. *BFI*

Below THE GOOD DIE YOUNG (1954): A tense scene from the film, shot on
the Metropolitan/Circle Lines near Barbican on the London Underground. *Romulus*

THE GREAT ST TRINIAN'S TRAIN ROBBERY (1966): A scene from the hectic chase sequence forming the climax of the film, shot on the Longmoor Military Railway. *BFI*

Above GUMSHOE (1971): Fulton Mackay is not amused on the Underground! *Columbia*

Above right THE HOURS (2003):
Southern coaches at Loughborough Central
station, Great Central Railway. *Paul Holroyd*

Right THE HOURS (2003): Loughborough
Central became 'Richmond' station for the film.
The Isle of Wight Southern stock used can be
seen in the background. *Paul Holroyd*

Above THE INCREDIBLE SARAH (1975): Glenda Jackson as legendary actress Sarah Bernhardt poses with 'Manor' Class 4-6-0 No 7808 *Cookham Manor* at 'London' station (actually Didcot Railway Centre). *Great Western Society*

Left THE INCREDIBLE SARAH (1975): Glenda Jackson in a scene from the film, shot at Didcot Railway Centre. *Great Western Society*

G:MT GREENWICH MEAN TIME

GB 1998 Icon/Anvil/GMT
Dir: John Strickland
Alec Newman, Melanie Gutteridge

Members of a London rock group fall out and get involved with gangsters

The opening scenes feature a roof walk on a moving train, a sequence that involved editing between two types of rolling-stock – a rake of Mk 1 coaches and an NSE-liveried Class 115 DMU – which ends with the train entering a tunnel. It was filmed on the Nene Valley Railway, including Wansford Tunnel.

GAIETY GEORGE

GB 1946 Embassy
Dir: George King
Richard Greene, Ann Todd

The life of theatre impresario George Howard in the early 20th century

A montage sequence of Howard's travels features a couple of shots of express trains hauled by GWR 4-6-0s.

GASBAGS

GB 1940 Gainsborough DVD
Dir: Marcel Varnel
The Crazy Gang, Moore Marriott

Airman in Germany return to Britain in a captured secret weapon

Includes a comedy sequence involving the London Underground, which appears to feature model work of a 1938 tube unit.

THE GATHERING STORM

GB 2002 BBC DVD
Dir: John Schlesinger
Albert Finney, Vanessa Redgrave

The life of Winston Churchill during the 1930s before the Second World War

Scenes were filmed at Horsted Keynes on the Bluebell Railway, interestingly not renamed for the film (it was felt that it was quite likely that Churchill would have used the station at the time to visit Harold Macmillan at nearby Birch Grove), with Southern coaches. Although BR Standard 4-6-0 No 75027 provided the motive power, it does not appear in the film, perhaps a good thing as far as historical accuracy is concerned!

THE GAY DOG

GB 1954 Coronet/Eros
Dir: Maurice Elvey
Wilfred Pickles, Petula Clark

A miner trains a racing greyhound

Includes one scene where Pickles walks across a street and in the background there is an ex-GWR '5700' 0-6-0PT shunting some wagons by a gasworks.

GENEVIEVE

GB 1953 Rank DVD
Dir: Henry Cornelius
Kenneth More, Dinah Sheridan

Two couples race each other on the way back from the Brighton car rally

This classic British comedy features a great deal of vintage road scenes, but there is some railway background in one part of the story. The scene where Kenneth More and John Gregson almost have a fight at a road junction next to a pub was filmed close to West Drayton yard, where the Uxbridge and Staines West branches left the WR main line and the road passes under the railway. In some prints shown on television, where the top and bottom of the film have not been cut off by the TV screen, you get a brief glimpse of a large 2-6-2T passing on top of the embankment at the top of the screen – not forgetting, of course, the tram lines that dominate the opening and closing of the film. These were not filmed at Westminster, as the film suggests, but in Lewisham, where the defunct lines still existed at the time.

THE GENTLE GUNMAN

GB 1952 Ealing VHS
Dir: Basil Dearden
John Mills, Dirk Bogarde

Conflict erupts between brothers in an IRA family where one of them believes in peace

Features a suspenseful scene in which a bomb is timed to go off on the London Underground. This was shot on the Aldwych line platform at Holborn station with 1924 tube stock in evidence. To add to the suspense of the scene there are various shots of the station clock counting down to the explosion, with emphasis on its second hand. This is a studio creation, as Underground station clocks did not have second hands.

THE GENTLE SEX

GB 1943 Rank VHS
Dirs: Leslie Howard, Maurice Elvey
Rosamund John, Joan Greenwood

The lives of several girls working in the ATS

A wartime propaganda film featuring various railway shots around the network at the time: SR 'King Arthur' 4-6-0 No 771 leaving Waterloo on a service; an ex-LNWR 7F 0-8-0 on a freight passing over a level crossing, location unknown; and an LNER 'B17' 4-6-0 on a passing express.

GEORDIE

GB 1955 British Lion VHS
Dir: Frank Launder
Bill Travers, Alastair Sim

A weak Scottish boy goes on a bodybuilding course and becomes an Olympic hammer-thrower

Some excellent shots of 'C16' 4-4-2T No 67488 feature in this film on a local train, possibly on the Aberfoyle branch line at Gartmore station. As a bonus, when Bill Travers goes on his Olympic journey he travels by train, and there is an added shot of an ex-LMS 4F 0-6-0 on a boat service entering Tilbury Riverside station.

GEORGY GIRL

GB 1966 Columbia DVD
Dir: Silvio Narizzano
Lynn Redgrave, Alan Bates

An unattractive girl looks after the illegitimate baby of her friend

Alan Bates leaves an Underground station in one scene, Belsize Park on the Northern Line.

GET CARTER

GB 1971 MGM DVD
Dir: Mike Hodges
Michael Caine, Ian Hendry

A gangster goes to Newcastle to avenge his brother's death

This classic underworld film begins with a train journey from London to Newcastle with scenes of Caine on board intercut with shots taken from the cab of the loco on an actual ECML run. Locations identifiable include the Hadley Wood area, Stoke bank, the Doncaster area and Newcastle Central station, with a Cravens DMU and a 'Deltic' passing on southbound services. Later there are scenes around King Edward and High Level Bridges, with the rear end of an express made up of Mk 1 stock and a Class 25 diesel on a freight crossing respectively. The final scenes feature the sidings at North Blyth coal staithes.

GET CRACKING
GB 1942 Columbia
Dir: Marcel Varnel
George Formby, Edward Rigby

George joins the Home Guard

Features one scene by a railway bridge on the ex-GCR line, over which an 'A5' 4-6-2T is passing with a local.

THE GHOST CAMERA
GB 1934 H&S Films VHS
Dir: Bernard Vorhaus
John Mills, Ida Lupino

A chemist investigates a murder that was caught on camera

Part of the investigation leads to a search for clues by a railway line, and there are some good shots of passing SR 3-SUB EMUs on headcode H routes, the location probably south west suburban London.

A GHOST AT MONTE CARLO
GB 1990 Turner Pictures VHS
Dir: John Hough
Sarah Miles, Oliver Reed

A courtesan takes her niece to Monte Carlo to begin a new life

Includes some night scenes filmed at

Horsted Keynes station on the Bluebell Railway, playing the part of Monte Carlo for the film. The 'Chesham' set was used, together with preserved locomotives '0415' 4-4-2T No 488 and 'B4' No 96 *Normandy*, positioned at either end of the train.

THE GHOST SHIP
GB 1952 Anglo-Amalgamated VHS
Dir: Vernon Sewell
Dermot Walsh, Hazel Court

A young couple buy a boat for a holiday but strange things begin to happen

Features some scenes filmed at Fishergate station on the Brighton-Worthing line, with good shots of some 2-BIL EMUs, including set No 2116 and 2-NOL EMU No 1832.

GHOST STORY
GB 1974 Stephen Weeks
Dir: Stephen Weeks
Murray Melvin, Larry Dann

Former college acquaintances spend a weekend at a country house that turns out to be haunted

Early in the film there is a London Underground scene filmed on the Aldwych branch using 1938 tube stock.

THE GHOST TRAIN
GB/Germany 1927 Gainsborough
Dir: Geza M. Bolvary
Guy Newall, Ilse Bois

Passengers are stranded at a Cornish country station where they are told the story of the ghost train

The first, silent, version of this popular story was filmed on the ex-LSWR Hurstbourne-Fullerton line, with Wherwell pretending to be 'Fal Vale' station. No other details are known and the film appears to be lost.

THE GHOST TRAIN

GB 1931 Gainsborough
Dir: Walter Forde
Jack Hulbert, Cicely Courtneidge

Remake of the above

This is the famous 'lost' version, although some reels survive. It is the best-known of a number of missing railway feature films, and one of the many lost British films in general. Probably this is because of the great deal of location work that features in the film, the GWR apparently having provided comprehensive facilities. There are some shots of Paddington and run-by scenes of 'Kings' and 'Castles' as the train makes its way to the West Country, although there is at least one shot where the train appears to be hauled by a 2800 2-8-0 freight loco. Some of this location work was filmed near Box Tunnel on the GWR main line and on the Bristol-Radstock-Frome line. Stills for these scenes reveal the obvious care taken by the GWR to promote a good image – the coaching stock is immaculate. The station of Fal Vale was provided by Camerton, at one end of the lightly used branch to Limpley Stoke. 'Dean Goods' 0-6-0s Nos 2381 and 2441 were both used on the branch line, 2381 being painted white for night scenes under the limited lighting conditions (and it was the ghost train after all!). The end of the film involves the train, actually being used by smugglers, crashing into the river due to a swing-bridge having been left open. This sequence involved model work, some shots of No 2441 and shots of Barmouth Bridge on the Cambrian Coast line – this is one of the reels that has survived.

THE GHOST TRAIN

GB 1941 Gainsborough DVD
Dir: Walter Forde
Arthur Askey, Richard Murdoch

A further remake

This is the best-known version, revamped as a comedy vehicle for Arthur Askey, with Murdoch as the straight man, ie the main character has been split into two parts. Unfortunately it is also the version with the least interesting railway scenes; being made in the middle of wartime, restrictions were clearly placed on the use of locations with most of the action taking place on studio sets (it was shot at Lime Grove Studios). The tunnel is particularly noticeable for this. Nevertheless the film is still enjoyable, with a shot of a 'King' and one of the streamlined 'Castle', No 5005 *Manorbier Castle*, slowing on an express between Dawlish Warren and Dawlish – this is the scene where Askey pulls the communication cord to retrieve his hat and is a stock shot filmed for Ealing's 1939 production *Return to Yesterday* (it appears in Video 125's *Steam on 35mm*). The final crash scenes are basically made up of footage from the 1931 film with brief shots of 'Dean Goods' No 2441 and the Barmouth swing-bridge.

GIDEON'S DAY

GB 1958 Columbia
Dir: John Ford
Jack Hawkins, Dianne Foster

A Scotland Yard inspector has an eventful day

Features a scene filmed on the Aldwych branch of the London Underground with 1924 tube stock.

THE GIRL IN THE NEWS

GB 1940 TCF
Dir: Carol Reed
Margaret Lockwood, Barry K. Barnes

A nurse is framed for the death of her employer

Includes one general view of the interior of Waterloo station; the other shots appear to be studio reconstructions.

THE GIRL IN THE PICTURE
GB 1986 Rank VHS
Dir: Cary Parker
John Gordon Sinclair, Irina Brook

A photographer breaks up with his girlfriend but then has second thoughts

Includes a semi-distant shot of Class 303 'Blue Train' EMUs crossing the Clyde outside Glasgow Central station.

THE GIRL ON THE BOAT
GB 1962 UA/Knightsbridge DVD
Dir: Henry Kaplan
Norman Wisdom, Millicent Martin

P. G. Wodehouse story about love on a transatlantic liner

The docks of 'New York' that feature at the start of the film are actually Southampton docks, and one of the USA 0-6-0T shunters can be seen in the background (built years after the time the story is set!).

THE GIRL ON THE PIER
GB 1953 Apex
Dir: Lance Comfort
Veronica Hurst, Ron Randell

In Brighton a waxworks exhibitor kills a blackmailer

Includes a scene on Victoria station.

GIRL WITH GREEN EYES
GB 1963 UA/Woodfall VHS
Dir: Desmond Davis
Rita Tushingham, Peter Finch

A young girl has an affair with a middle-aged writer

Despite being mainly filmed in Ireland, near the end of the film there are some shots filmed at an unknown station on the London Underground featuring 1960-built tube stock.

THE GLASS CAGE
GB 1955 Exclusive/Hammer
Dir: Montgomery Tully
John Ireland, Honor Blackman

A freak-show promoter solves a murder

Features a scene at Strand (later Charing Cross) Underground station with 1938-built tube stock.

THE GLASS MOUNTAIN
GB 1949 Victoria
Dir: Henry Cass
Michael Denison, Dulcie Gray

A married composer still loves an Italian girl who saved his life during the war

Although mostly set in Italy there is one scene of a British train journey illustrated by a shot of a GWR 4-6-0 passing over a viaduct in the West Country on an express.

THE GO-BETWEEN
GB 1970 EMI DVD
Dir: Joseph Losey
Alan Bates, Julie Christie

A 12-year-old boy carries love-letters between a farmer and his friend's sister living at a stately home

Includes a shot of the frontage of Norwich Thorpe station.

GO KART GO
GB 1965 CFF DVD
Dir: Jan Darnley-Smith
Dennis Waterman, Wilfrid Brambell

Rival gangs compete in a go-kart rally

The go-kart track is located next to a section of the WCML (believed to be the Rugby-Stafford via Birmingham section) and two expresses can be seen passing in the background during the competition – sadly the film is edited in such a way that we don't see the motive power, but one express is made up of Mk 1s, the other a mix of Mk 1s and ex-LNER stock.

GOING OFF BIG TIME
GB 2000 Entertainment/KT
Dir: Jim Doyle
Neil Fitzmaurice, Dominic Carter

The rise of a ruthless gangster in Liverpool

Includes a middle-distance shot of 'Merseyrail' Class 507/508 EMUs passing through the northern suburbs of Liverpool and a shot of the Mersey railway bridge at Runcorn.

THE GOLD EXPRESS
GB 1954 GFD/Gaumont
Dir: Guy Fergusson, Colin Bell
Vernon Gray, Ann Walford

A news reporter foils a planned robbery of gold treasure on board an express train

This little known B-movie is almost completely set around a railway journey, with all the various characters getting involved as the crime develops. Stanmore station, terminus of the LMR's branch from Harrow & Wealdstone, was used for some night shots of the characters getting on the train, with an ex-LMS sleeping-car and Mk 1 parcels van No M1005 being borrowed from BR for this purpose. The various shots of expresses that appear through the course of the film are so varied in terms of continuity that practically every type of LMS passenger loco appears at some point or other! Whereas some shots are stock footage from *Train of Events* (1948) (qv), most of the rest seem to have been taken for the film itself. In order of appearance, they are:
- a 'Princess Royal' 'Pacific' at Euston
- a Jubilee 4-6-0 leaves Euston on an express
- a rebuilt 'Royal Scot' crosses a viaduct (from *Train of Events*)

All the rest of the shots appear to have been taken of expresses on the WCML – there are two more stock shots from *Train of Events*, which feature 'Royal Scots' passing over a level crossing. The rest are contemporary shots – a couple of 'Black Fives', five shots of rebuilt 'Royal Scot'/'Patriot' 4-6-0s and one each of a 'Jubilee', a 'Duchess' 'Pacific' and a 'Britannia'.

GOLDENEYE
US 1995 UIP/United Artists DVD
Dir: Martin Campbell
Pierce Brosnan, Sean Bean

James Bond goes to Russia to search for a criminal intent on destroying the electronic world

One of the many action highlights of this was a sequence where Bond confronts the villain on board a Russian train, which ends up crashing into a tank parked in a tunnel. All the scenes were filmed on the Nene Valley Railway, clearly in favour with the Bond producers after the making of *Octopussy*, and involved the use of preserved Class 20 diesel No 20 188, then owned by Pete Waterman, and a couple of Mk 1 coaches. The loco was heavily disguised to look like a armoured Soviet loco, but ended up looking more like something from a *Mad Max* movie! This involved a stylised battering-ram-style front end, side guards over the bogies, 'red star' emblems and overall black livery. The coaches received the same livery with sideguards, bars along the windows and a roof pod among other modifications. The explosive crash scenes were achieved by pyrotechnic special effects, and new sound was dubbed over the loco scenes so that it sounds nothing like a real Class 20.

THE GOOD COMPANIONS
GB 1932 Gaumont
Dir: Victor Saville
Edmund Gwenn, Jessie Matthews

Various travellers join a performing troupe

As the group travel round the country on a stage tour there are various stock shots of the trains taking them from place to place – in appearance order, the haulage is an ex-LNWR 'Claughton' 4-6-0, a 2P 4-4-0 and a 'Claughton' double-heading, another 'Claughton', and what appears to be a 'Royal Scot' 4-6-0. Earlier in the film there is a shot of an ex-GER 0-6-0 arriving at the island platform of an unknown LNER station, referred to in the film as 'Dotworth'. Also we see the rear of a departing train seemingly made up of LMS push-pull stock filmed at Watford Junction in the St Albans Abbey branch bay.

THE GOOD COMPANIONS
GB 1956 ABP
Dir: J. Lee Thompson
Eric Portman, Celia Johnson

Remake of the above

A great deal of material was shot for this version in Wales, mainly on the Cambrian Coast line and the Dowlais/Rhymney lines in the South Wales valleys. Most of this footage was never used and only saw the light of day when included in Video 125's *Steam on 35mm* video. The shots that did make the final cut are a semi-distant shot of an ex-GWR '5100' 2-6-2T on a passenger train near Bargoed in the Rhymney Valley and a silhouetted shot of a train crossing Barmouth Viaduct.

THE GOOD DIE YOUNG
GB 1954 Remus DVD
Dir: Lewis Gilbert
Laurence Harvey, Richard Basehart

Four crooks form a gang to rob a mail van

Features a scene at Waterloo station with SR 4-SUB EMUs. The robbery chase sequence was filmed in the tunnels on the Metropolitan/Circle Lines of the Underground, including a scene at Barbican station with F stock. Another scene (in which one of the gang members is killed by falling on the electrified line) features District Line 'R'-type stock.

GOOD TIME GIRL
GB 1948 Rank VHS
Dir: David MacDonald
Jean Kent, Dennis Price

A delinquent girl heads down the road to ruin

Includes a scene filmed on Brighton station with Kent boarding a departing SR 6-PUL EMU.

GOODBYE MR CHIPS
GB 1969 MGM VHS
Dir: Herbert Ross
Peter O'Toole, Petula Clark

The life of a schoolmaster at a boy's school

Features a scene filmed at Sherborne station given a 1930s makeover as 'Brookfield' with some old Southern coaches prominent (no loco visible).

THE GOOSE STEPS OUT
GB 1942 Ealing VHS
Dirs: Will Hay, Basil Dearden
Will Hay, Charles Hawtrey

An incompetent teacher is sent into Nazi Germany to steal a secret weapon

The climax of the film features a barnstorming plane ride that includes flying along railway lines – in this case what looks like the ex-LSWR main line – with the plane, through editing, narrowly missing collision with a 'Lord Nelson' 4-6-0.

THE GORBALS STORY
GB 1949 Eros
Dir: David MacKane
Russell Hunter, Betty Henderson

An artist remembers his youth growing up in a Glasgow tenement

Mainly filmed on studio sets, there are some early shots of the Gorbals area with a Glasgow tram visible in one.

GRAND NATIONAL NIGHT
GB 1953 Talisman
Dir: Bob McNaught
Nigel Patrick, Moira Lister

A stable owner accidentally kills his wife but events clear him

The plot makes use of train tickets and journeys, but unfortunately most of the train scenes seem to use models and studio sets. There is one real night scene of Patrick leaving a train on a level crossing; the train is made up of a Southern suburban EMU, rather odd as the story is set near Liverpool!

THE GRASS IS GREENER
GB 1960 Grandon VHS
Dir: Stanley Donen
Cary Grant, Deborah Kerr

The wife of an English Earl falls for an American millionaire

Features a scene where Cary Grant departs for London on a Southern branch-line train. This was filmed at Baynards station with 'M7' 0-4-4T No 30132 as the train loco.

THE GREAT BRITISH TRAIN ROBBERY
Germany 1967 Egon Monk Prodis
Dirs: John Olden, Claus Petter
Horst Tappert, Hans Cossey

A recreation of the 1963 Great Train Robbery

This obscure film was originally made for German television and not released in the UK at the time, although it appeared on late-night TV schedules in the 1990s. Apparently filming in some secrecy, the producers got permission to film on railway territory but did not inform anyone what the film was about! It is known that some filming was done around the Folkestone area, of all places, which probably explains the presence of an SR 4-CEP EMU in the credits sequence. Overall, however, there are quite a few good train scenes – as well as the Southern unit, the film starts with a shot of a Class 45 diesel leaving St Pancras with an express, and there is an SR 4-SUB EMU later in the film. The robbery scene features the most improbable railway journey ever filmed, not to mention the inaccuracy in

recreating the robbery itself. The train shots are as follows:
- the mail train leaves 'Glasgow' – a split-box Class 45 leaving St Pancras on an express
- a passing shot of a Class 40-hauled train
- as above, with two Class 40s double-heading
- back to a single Class 40

The gang then rig up a false signal to stop the train. This scene was filmed in Germany, so the train, when it arrives, is hauled by a DB V200 diesel-hydraulic (complete with a large 'lion and wheel' BR emblem on its side) and Continental coaches! Another point of interest is an earlier scene where the gang are planning the robbery with a model train set that features a Hornby Dublo 'Deltic'.

THE GREAT ROCK 'N' ROLL SWINDLE
GB 1979 Virgin/Kendon Films VHS
Dir: Julien Temple
The Sex Pistols, Malcolm McLaren

A drama-documentary about the rise and fall of the punk rock band The Sex Pistols

Features a number of railway scenes, although once again with dubious continuity. McLaren is seen boarding a departing Class 115 DMU at Marylebone station. There are then some interior shots on board Mk 1 stock and a run-by shot of a Class 86/0 electric on a WCML passenger train. The train arrival scenes were filmed at Northampton, but the shot of McLaren running out of the front of the station was filmed at Chesham on the Metropolitan Line!

THE GREAT ST TRINIAN'S TRAIN ROBBERY
GB 1966 British Lion DVD
Dir: Frank Launder
Frankie Howerd, Dora Bryan

St Trinian's is infiltrated by a gang of train robbers

This is a classic that has become well known to enthusiasts over the years, thanks to frequent television screenings, and is probably the most famous of the many films to feature the Longmoor Military Railway, which closed three years after it was released. The railway scenes dominate the last 20 or so minutes of the film, although there is a train robbery sequence at the start of the film that features a night shot of a 'Royal Scot' 4-6-0 and a scene where the schoolgirls are shown arriving at 'Hamingwell Halt' (actually Oakenhanger station) behind an LMR Hunslet 'Austerity' 0-6-0ST and Southern 'birdcage' stock. For the final chase sequence the crooks' train is a short goods hauled by a Hunslet 'Austerity' 0-6-0ST disguised with side tanks, BR emblems and numbered '68961'. This is seen leaving Oakenhanger and joining the LMR's 'main line'. The schoolgirls give chase by hijacking a waiting local at 'Nutcombe' (actually Longmoor Downs) made up of Hunslet 0-6-0ST No 196 and two BR suburban non-corridor coaches. Curiously, whereas the crooks' engine is disguised by the film-makers, No 196 has just been given BR emblems and numbered '68011'. A couple of girls give chase in a permanent-way pump-trolley, and the schoolmistresses, eager to claim the reward for catching the criminals, find a Wickham petrol trolley in the yard and cram into it. The police arrive at Longmoor Downs and commandeer 'Hampshire' 3H DEMU set No 1102, loaned from BR. The girls manage to couple the box van containing the loot onto their train and a frenzied chase ensues, involving trains being switched on to 'up lines and down lines'. All in all, it remains one of the funniest and fastest-moving chase sequences involving trains. The final scenes, where the crooks are arrested, take place at 'Pudham' (actually Liss station – the BR platforms can be seen in the background). Look out for the comedy scene involving the Wickham and one of the LMR's English Electric 0-6-0 diesel shunters (No 878 – in LMR blue livery but with 'BR' on its sides) on a freight.

THE GREEN COCKATOO
GB 1937 TCF
Dir: William Cameron Menzies
John Mills, Robert Newton

A man takes revenge on the gangsters who killed his brother

Features a couple of good shots of passing GWR expresses at the start and end of the film, both hauled by 'Hall' 4-6-0s. The scenes at 'Victoria' are studio sets. There is also a montage sequence of London scenes, which includes a shot of a tram, No 625.

GREGORY'S TWO GIRLS
GB 1999 FilmFour DVD
Dir: Bill Forsyth
John Gordon Sinclair, Carly McKinnon

A schoolteacher lusts after a schoolgirl while ignoring the love offered by a colleague

The sequel to *Gregory's Girl*, which, unlike the first film, features some railway scenes – a Class 150/2 'Sprinter' passing somewhere in southern Scotland and Class 303 EMUs at a terminus station, possibly Wemyss Bay.

GUILTY?
GB 1956 Grand National
Dir: Edmond Greville
John Justin, Barbara Laage

A solicitor investigates a crime for which an ex-Resistance member has been framed

Features a stock shot of a 'Royal Scot' 4-6-0 on an express, taken in 1945 for *Brief Encounter*.

THE GUINEA PIG
GB 1949 Pilgrim VHS
Dir: Roy Boulting
Richard Attenborough, Robert Flemyng

A poor boy goes to a famous public school as a social experiment

Includes a couple of scenes of arriving school trains at Sherborne station on the SR, one with 'King Arthur' 4-6-0 No 448 and the other with one of the then fairly new Bulleid 'Pacifics', No 21C6.

GUMSHOE
GB 1971 Columbia VHS
Dir: Stephen Frears
Albert Finney, Billie Whitelaw

A Liverpool bingo caller finds himself in the middle of a murder case

Features a scene on Liverpool Lime Street station with Mk 2 stock but no loco visible. There are some on-board shots of Finney on a Liverpool express and a scene on the London Underground with 1960 tube stock.

HALF A SIXPENCE
GB 1967 Paramount
Dir: George Sidney
Tommy Steele, Julia Foster

A draper's assistant inherits a fortune and moves into society

During the title sequence at the start of the film there is a scene depicting the Vale of Rheidol Railway with one of the railway's 2-6-2Ts on a branch train.

HALF-LIGHT
GB/Germany 2006 UIP/Lakeshore DVD
Dir: Craig Rosenburg
Demi Moore, Hans Matheson

After the death of her son a novelist heads for Scotland but is still haunted by him

Some scenes were filmed on the Bodmin & Wenford Railway, with Bodmin General appearing as 'Oban' station. A two-car Class 108 DMU appears as the Oban train, and even more bizarrely it's supposed to be an EMU! (Arc flashes from the unit's 'collector shoes' play a key part in the story.)

THE HALFWAY HOUSE
GB 1944 Ealing
Dir: Basil Dearden
Mervyn Johns, Glynis Johns

A group of travellers take refuge at an isolated inn but there is something odd about the owner and his family

The film opens with a street scene outside Cardiff Castle with one of the city's double-decker trams passing. Later some of the characters arrive at East Anstey station on the Taunton-Barnstaple line, posing as 'Ynysgwyn' for the film, with GWR '4300' Class 2-6-0 No 6364 at the head of the train, as well as shots of Paddington and Bristol Temple Meads stations. Video 125's *Steam on 35mm* Vol 2 features another shot taken for this film, probably at the same location, with a '4500' 2-6-2T, but this scene was not used.

HAMLET
US 1996 Rank/Castle Rock DVD
Dir: Kenneth Branagh
Kenneth Branagh, Derek Jacobi

A version of the Shakespearean play updated to the 1800s

This version of the celebrated play features the characters Rosencrantz and Guildenstern arriving at the Danish court in a narrow-gauge steam train. The locomotive appears to be a highly decorative tank loco in black livery and its design. together with the rudimentary nature of the track, suggests that it might be a well-made studio construction.

A HANDFUL OF DUST
GB 1988 Premier DVD
Dir: Charles Sturridge
James Wilby, Kristin Scott Thomas

An aristocratic wife has an affair with a man-about-town

Features a number of scenes filmed on the Bluebell Railway including Sheffield Park and various lineside locations with good shots of preserved SR 'U' Class 2-6-0 No 1618. There is also a scene filmed on Platform 1 of Paddington station (not featuring rolling-stock).

HANDS OF THE RIPPER
GB 1971 Rank/Hammer DVD
Dir: Peter Sasdy
Angharad Rees, Eric Porter

The daughter of Jack the Ripper grows up a psychotic murderer having seen him kill her mother

Features a scene filmed outside Windsor & Eton Central station.

THE HAPPIEST DAYS OF YOUR LIFE
GB 1950 British Lion VHS
Dir: Frank Launder
Alastair Sim, Margaret Rutherford

A government error causes a girls' school to be billeted on a boys' school

Features a scene in which government inspectors arrive by train at a country station. This was filmed at Liss station on the Longmoor Military Railway, with Hunslet 'Austerity' 0-6-0ST No 75079 as motive power.

HAPPY EVER AFTER
GB 1954 ABP VHS
Dir: Mario Zampi
David Niven, Barry Fitzgerald

In rural Ireland the new squire proves unpopular and the villagers plot to kill him

Features a scene supposedly set at an Irish country station but in fact filmed at Braughing on the Buntingford branch in Essex, with ex-LNER 'J15' 0-6-0 No 65464 on suburban stock, with CIE emblems attached.

THE HAPPY FAMILY
GB 1951 London Independent
   Producers
Dir: Muriel Box
Stanley Holloway, Kathleen Harrison

A family refuses to allow a road to be built through their home for the Festival of Britain

Includes an interesting scene with Holloway at a railway location on the Southern Region with one of the brand-new BR Standard 'Britannia' 'Pacific's (possibly No 70000 itself) and an ex-SR 'E4' 0-6-2T.

HAPPY GO LOVELY
GB 1951 Excelsior DVD
Dir: Bruce Humberstone
David Niven, Vera-Ellen

During the Edinburgh Festival a chorus girl falls for a millionaire

The film features a great deal of location footage in the city and there are therefore some shots of Edinburgh trams.

HAPPY IS THE BRIDE
GB 1957 Panther
Dir: Roy Boulting
Ian Carmichael, Janette Scott

A couple plan a quiet wedding but reckon without the intervention of her parents

Features a stock shot of an LNER 'V2' 2-6-2 on an express on the GN main line, filmed during the war years.

A HARD DAY'S NIGHT
GB 1964 UA DVD
Dir: Richard Lester
The Beatles, Wilfrid Brambell

The Beatles head from Liverpool to London to appear on a TV show

The first Beatles film features a train journey in which the band head from Liverpool to London; at both ends they are, of course, mobbed by fans. However, in reality the band travel nowhere, as in the 'Liverpool' scenes the station is clearly Marylebone in London, and when they arrive in 'London' they are at Marylebone again! This scene uses a high camera angle (to show the fans mobbing the train), which just reveals a BR Sulzer Type 2 at the head of Mk 1 coaches, and a Class 115 DMU can be seen in the background. The actual railway journey scenes were filmed on the Taunton-Minehead branch in Somerset, with the scene of the Beatles running alongside the train filmed in the Crowcombe Heathfield area, although it is reported that the Taunton-Barnstaple line was also used for some shots. A rake of Mk 1 stock was used, and, although no locos are visible for these scenes, it is known that on at least one occasion a 'Hymek' was used, No D7076. The train returned to London after each day's filming, with the band getting off at one of the WR suburban stations, such as West Ealing or Acton Main Line, to avoid the fans. All of the footage for this sequence is on board the train, with no run-by shots, although it is known that a 'Western' was used as motive power for the Taunton-London journey at least. An interesting footnote to this film is that another scene featuring a railway background was shot for it but left on the cutting-room floor (although stills survive) – a music sequence filmed at the abandoned Southern Railway Gatwick Airport station.

HARDCORE
GB 1978 Norfolk DVD
Dir: James Kenelm Clarke
Fiona Richmond, Anthony Steel

The sexual adventures of an actress

Features a scene on the Bluebell Railway at Sheffield Park in which a flimsily dressed Richmond is picked up from the lineside – the loco featured is 'USA' 0-6-0T No 30064.

HARRY POTTER AND THE CHAMBER OF SECRETS
GB/US 2002 Warner DVD
Dir: Chris Columbus
Daniel Radcliffe, Emma Watson

Harry ignores warnings not to return to Hogwarts, where the school is attacked by mysterious forces

The second of the highly successful adaptations of the 'Harry Potter' series includes scenes utilising the same locations that feature in the first film. The big railway scene (which featured in the trailers) was a computer-enhanced sequence in which the main characters swoop over No 5972 on Glenfinnan Viaduct in a Ford Anglia car. As well as the viaduct, King's Cross station was again used, with No 5972 and some GNER-liveried Mk 4 coaches in the background. St Pancras was used for the station exteriors.

HARRY POTTER AND THE GOBLET OF FIRE
GB/US 2005 Warner DVD
Dir: Mike Newell
Daniel Radcliffe, Emma Watson

Harry finds himself a competitor in the Quidditch games and meets an old foe

The fourth in the 'Harry Potter' series features some more scenes of No 5972 on the West Highland line and particularly Glenfinnan Viaduct. There are no scenes at King's Cross, however.

HARRY POTTER AND THE PHILOSOPHER'S STONE
GB/US 2001 Warner DVD
Dir: Chris Columbus
Daniel Radcliffe, Emma Watson

The first 'Harry Potter' story ,in which he is first called to Hogwarts

Anyone who has read the popular children's series knows that the 'Hogwarts Express' that takes Harry from Platform

9¾ at King's Cross station to the wizards' school is the best-known feature in the books. Warner hired preserved 'Hall' Class 4-6-0 No 5972 *Olton Hall* and a rake of Mk 1 stock owned by the West Coast Railway Company for this prestigious role, with the loco retaining its fictional red livery for its appearances in the follow-up stories. No 5972 also became *Hogwarts Castle*, which must have caused apoplexy among GWR purists! Filming with the stock occurred at King's Cross itself (with GNER Mk 4s and Class 91s in the background) and on the West Highland line, principally on Glenfinnan Viaduct. The North Yorkshire Moors Railway was also used, with Goathland appearing as 'Hogsmead' station, filming with No 5972 and stock occurring in September/October 2000.

HARRY POTTER AND THE PRISONER OF AZKABAN

GB/US 2004 Warner DVD
Dir: Alfonso Cuaron
Daniel Radcliffe, Emma Watson

In his third year at Hogwarts, Harry learns that an escaped murderer is coming after him

Features more shots filmed on the West Highland line and Glenfinnan Viaduct with No 5972. Sadly filming was disrupted when the train was vandalised between shots, and filming at Glenfinnan was delayed for a day when No 5972 started lineside fires on the dry vegetation. In the event the scenes that appear in the film take place during a night journey. There are also, as in the other films, shots taken at King's Cross, although No 5972 is only visible in the background. In an earlier part of the film, Harry's lodgings in London are close to a suburban line, probably filmed in Borough, with a Connex-liveried slam-door EMU passing.

HATTER'S CASTLE

GB 1941 Paramount
Dir: Lance Comfort
Robert Newton, Deborah Kerr

The rise and fall of a tyrannical hatter in Victorian times

A couple of the characters are killed off in the famous Tay Bridge disaster of 1879. This was recreated with models of the bridge and train in a special large tank built at Highbury Studios with six wind machines providing the storm.

HAUNTED

GB/US 1995 Entertainment/Lumière
  VHS
Dir: Lewis Gilbert
Aidan Quinn, Kate Beckinsale

A sceptic of psychic phenomena is invited to stay at a haunted house

Includes some good scenes filmed on the Bluebell Railway, at Sheffield Park (as 'Edbrook') and Horsted Keynes (as 'Cambridge'), with preserved 'S15' 4-6-0 No 847 heavily featured at both locations and at Waterworks bridge.

A HEAD IN THE CLOUDS

US/GB/Spain/Canada 2004
  Sony/Remstar/Dakota DVD
Dir: John Duigan
Charlize Theron, Penelope Cruz

Three women in Paris find themselves caught up the events of Nazi occupation

Includes one wartime scene set in a French marshalling yard where the Resistance blow up a German munitions train. This was actually filmed at Sheffield Park on the Bluebell Railway, with heavily disguised BR Standard 2-6-4T No 80151 together with a snowplough painted in camouflage colours and fitted with a machine-gun nest. Filming took place in May 2003.

HEART
GB 1998 Feature Film/Granada VHS
Dir: Charles McDougall
Christopher Eccleston, Saskia Reeves

A woman becomes obsessed with the man who has been given her dead son's heart in a transplant operation

Features a number of contemporary railway shots filmed around the Lancashire/Merseyside area, with aerial shots of Class 158 'Sprinter' units and an EWS-liveried Class 37 on stock, some night shots of a passing HST, and interiors of a first-generation DMU.

THE HEART WITHIN
GB 1957 Penington Eady Productions VHS
Dir: David Eady
David Hemmings, Clifford Evans

A young boy helps a black man wrongly accused of murder

Features some scenes of arriving boat trains at Waterloo, one composed of 'blood and custard'-liveried Mk 1s, and another of SR stock, probably taken from newsreel. No locos are seen.

HEARTLANDS
GB 2003 Miramax/DNA/Revolution DVD
Dir: Damien O'Donnell
Michael Sheen, Mark Addy

A member of a darts team loses his wife to the captain and sets off by bike to Blackpool to find her

Includes some pretty extensive scenes on the Blackpool seafront, so a number of trams feature – Brush-built single-deck cars, a Millennium Balloon car and a Centenary car.

HEAVENS ABOVE
GB 1963 British Lion DVD
Dir: John Boulting
Peter Sellers, Cecil Parker

A parson applies his proletarian views to a northern village and soon the entire country is in uproar

Features a scene outside Shepperton station at the start of the film, though no locos or trains are visible. Later there is also one night shot of an LMR steam-hauled express, but the loco is unidentifiable.

HEDD WYNN
Wales 1992 S4C
Dir: Paul Turner
Huw Garmon, Sue Roderick

A Welsh farmer becomes a poet during the First World War and wins a prize posthumously

Some scenes depicting the main character leaving Wales for the front were filmed on the Llangollen Railway, including one scene at Llangollen station itself. The loco featured is preserved LMS 'Jinty' No 7298, which ran under its own number, and No 7470 hauling BR non-corridor stock.

HELL DRIVERS
GB 1957 Rank DVD
Dir: C. Raker Endfield
Stanley Baker, Patrick McGoohan

An ex-con joins a haulage company using death-trap lorries

Includes a scene filmed at an unknown station on the GW&GC Joint line with a train hauled by ex-LMS Fairburn 2-6-4T No 42253.

HENNESSEY
GB 1975 AIP VHS
Dir: Don Sharp
Rod Steiger, Richard Johnson

An ex-IRA man plots to blow up the Houses of Parliament

During a battle scene on a street in Belfast, actually filmed in a West London suburb, a blue suburban DMU can be seen passing in the background. Also includes a scene filmed on the concourse of Waterloo station.

HERE COMES THE SUN
GB 1945 John Baxter VHS
Dir: John Baxter
Bud Flanagan, Chesney Allen

A tipster breaks jail to prove he was framed by a newspaper owner

Features some scenes of a railway journey to Blackpool with shots of an ex-L&YR 'Dreadnought' 4-6-0 and a Fowler 2-6-4T on LMS excursions, and a shot of LMS 'Compound' 4-4-0 No 1185 arriving with a special at Blackpool Central station.

THE HEROES OF TELEMARK
GB 1965 Rank DVD
Dir: Anthony Mann
Kirk Douglas, Michael Redgrave

Norwegian Resistance workers set out to destroy a Nazi heavy water plant

Mainly good scenes of Norwegian tank locos, but there is one shot of a British train near the start, although of dubious accuracy for a Second World War film – an express hauled by a streamlined Bulleid 'Pacific'.

HIDE AND SEEK
GB 1972 CFF DVD
Dir: David Eady
Peter Newby, Gary Kemp

A boy escapes from Approved School in search of his father

Features an aerial shot of Deptford in the early scenes of the film, and a pair of SR 4-EPB EMUs are seen passing.

HIGH HEELS AND LOW LIFES
GB 2001 Touchstone DVD
Dir: Mel Smith
Minnie Driver, Mary McCormack

Two women witness a robbery and try to blackmail the gangsters involved

Includes a railway sequence filmed on the Mid Hants Railway, with Alresford station doubling for Victoria, Three Bridges and Haywards Heath. Preserved Class 33/1 No 33 109 was used with a rake of Mk 2 stock, all bar one painted into colours similar to the First Great Western livery (the odd one was left as NSE). The real London Victoria was used for some shots on its concourse. Another interesting scene was filmed on the platforms of the abandoned Shoreditch station on the closed Dalston Junction-Broad Street line.

HIGH HOPES
GB 1988 Palace/FilmFour DVD
Dir: Mike Leigh
Philip Davis, Ruth Sheen

A family gathers to celebrate their mother's birthday

Features one scene on top of a flat overlooking St Pancras station, with HSTs visible.

HIGH TREASON
GB 1929 Gaumont
Dir: Maurice Elvey
Benita Hume, Basil Gill

Saboteurs try to start a war between Europe and America

An early science-fiction film about life in the future, which is of interest in that it depicts a terrorist attack on a London-Paris express passing through the Channel Tunnel. Most of this sequence involves studio filming (to depict the interior of the coaches, which still seem very 1920s in style!) and model shots to depict trains entering and passing through the tunnel. The entrance features two bores for up and down lines and a giant sign above, interestingly similar to projected designs in the 1960s and, of course, to how the actual tunnel would eventually look. The trains are made up of centre-cab diesel or electric locos on rakes of stock. There are also some aerial scenes of a future London, again using models, which include an elevated urban railway with trains again made up of diesel or electric locos and stock. All in all, a very interesting and unique record of how the future of Britain's railways was seen by film-makers in the 1920s.

HIGH TREASON
GB 1951 GFD VHS
Dir: Roy Boulting
Liam Redmond, Andre Morrell

Saboteurs plan to destroy British power stations

The saboteurs infiltrate Battersea power station by hiding on board a coal train hauled by an Andrew Barclay 0-4-0ST, although it's unclear whether these scenes were actually filmed in Battersea.

HIGHLY DANGEROUS
GB 1950 Rank
Dir: Roy Baker
Margaret Lockwood, Dane Clark

A lady scientist agrees to act as a spy in a Balkan country

Features a scene outside a GWR railway station, believed to be Denham on the GW&GC Joint line, with an express hauled by a GWR 4-6-0 passing in the background.

THE HI-JACKERS
GB 1963 Butchers
Dir: Jim O'Connolly
Anthony Booth, Jacqueline Ellis

A driver and his girlfriend track down the gang who stole his lorry

Features some good shots filmed on Southall station on the WR main line with Class 117 DMUs passing through.

HINDLE WAKES
GB 1927 Gaumont DVD
Dir: Maurice Elvey
Estelle Brody, John Stuart

A Lancashire mill-girl causes scandal when she spends a week away with the mill-owner's son

The first silent version of this famous play includes a great deal of location work in Lancashire and Blackpool, with a view of an LMS 'Compound' 4-4-0 entering a tunnel with an express and some shots of early 'toast-rack' Blackpool trams. Note: the 1931 version does not include any railway scenes.

HINDLE WAKES
GB 1952 Monarch
Dir: Arthur Crabtree
Lisa Daniely, Brian Worth

Remake of the above

This version features some excellent railway scenes, depicting mill-workers on their way for holidays in Blackpool – first there is a shot inside a main-line station, not identifiable, with waiting trains hauled by Ivatt 2MT 2-6-0s. A passenger service leaves behind ex-LMS Stanier 2-6-4T No 42481, followed by a stock shot of GWR coaches passing somewhere in the West! There are some scenes in Blackpool showing crowds disembarking from trains at Central station and shots of Blackpool trams. Finally, the lead characters make a brief journey to Llandudno and there is a good shot of them climbing the Orme in Great Orme Railway tramcar No 4.

THE HISTORY OF MR POLLY
GB 1948 GFD DVD
Dir: Anthony Pelissier
John Mills, Sally Ann Howes

A draper's assistant decides to make a new life

Features a shot of a passing GWR branch-line train hauled by a '1400' 0-4-2T, probably on the Marlow branch.

HOFFMAN
GB 1970 ABP VHS
Dir: Alkin Rakoff
Peter Sellers, Sinead Cusack

A middle-aged man blackmails a typist into staying with him for a weekend

The film opens with some good shots inside King's Cross station. A couple of Class 31s are seen – one at the buffer stops, another running light down the platform.

HOLIDAY CAMP
GB 1947 GFD VHS
Dir: Ken Annakin
Jack Warner, Kathleen Harrison

Life at a summer holiday camp, where a murderer is on the prowl

Holidaymakers are seen arriving at the rarely filmed Sandsend station on the Scarborough-Whitby line behind LNER 'A8' Class 4-6-2T No 9881. This shot also appears in *Steam on 35mm Vol 3*.

HOLIDAYS WITH PAY
GB 1949 Mancunian
Dir: John E. Blakeley
Frank Randle, Tessie O'Shea

Various mishaps of a Northern family on holiday

Includes some scenes filmed in the Isle of Man featuring a Manx Electric Railway unit with trailer No 62 at Douglas Derby Castle station and one of the horse-drawn trams, No 40. There are also some distant shots of Blackpool trams in the mainland scenes.

THE HOLLY AND THE IVY
GB 1952 British Lion VHS
Dir: George More O'Ferrall
Ralph Richardson, Celia Johnson

A turbulent Christmas at a Norfolk country rectory

Some scenes were filmed at Liverpool Street station with an 'N7' Class 0-6-2T

visible, and a stock shot of 'B17' 4-6-0 No 2848 passing with an express filmed in LNER days. Some studio model shots also appear.

HOME AT SEVEN
GB 1952 British Lion VHS
Dir: Ralph Richardson
Ralph Richardson, Margaret Leighton

An office clerk suffers amnesia and finds he might be involved in a murder

Some good shots during the opening sequence of the film show LT Metropolitan Line stock, believed to have been filmed at Baker Street station.

HONEST
GB/France 2000 Pathé DVD
Dir: David A. Stewart
All Saints, James Cosmo

In the 1960s a group of female thieves commit crimes disguised as men

Includes some getaway scenes filmed on the London Underground with 1972-built tube stock, believed to have been filmed at Aldwych.

HOPE AND GLORY
GB 1987 Columbia/Goldcrest VHS
Dir: John Boorman
Sarah Miles, Ian Bannen

Adventures of a small boy and his family in wartime London

Set in the Second World War, the film features a wartime evacuation scene recreated at Marylebone station with preserved SR 'King Arthur' 4-6-0 No 777 *Sir Lamiel* in evidence. Another scene was shot at Horsted Keynes station on the Bluebell Railway, acting as the location for a romantic scene in a movie that the family see in a cinema in the film.

HORROR HOSPITAL
GB 1972 Noteworthy
Dir: Antony Balch
Michael Gough, Robin Askwith

A songwriter goes to a health hotel run by a mysterious doctor

A typical 1970s horror film that includes some good railway scenes depicting the journey from London to the health spa. It starts off with some shots on Waterloo station with 4-EPB sets and 4-CIG unit No 7382. The journey itself features the usual odd continuity expected of film-makers – a stock shot of a 'Western' diesel on an express; a passing green Class 40 with a Class 24 heading in the opposite direction on a freight (this shot was filmed in the 1960s and also appears in Video 125's *Diesels and Electrics on 35mm* – apparently originally shot for a Great Train Robbery film); and finally a couple of SR 2-EPB EMU sets (including set No 5789) at Merton Park station, renamed 'Brittlehurst' for the film.

HOT MILLIONS
US 1968 MGM
Dir: Eric Till
Peter Ustinov, Maggie Smith

A confidence trickster makes millions out of fake companies

Features some scenes filmed with Ustinov at Paddington station and two very brief shots of passing trains – one hauled by a 'Warship' diesel and the other a 'Blue Pullman'.

THE HOURS
US/GB Miramax DVD
Dir: Stephen Daldry
Nicole Kidman, Julianne Moore

Episodes in the lives of three women, including the writer Virginia Woolf

One scene features Woolf, played by Kidman, on the platform of 'Richmond' station, actually Loughborough Central on the Great Central Railway. The locomotive could not be more geographically or historically inaccurate – ex-LNER 'O4' Class 2-8-0 No 63601 in

BR black livery on a rake of historic Southern coaches.

THE HOUSE ACROSS THE LAKE
GB 1954 Exclusive/Hammer
Dir: Ken Hughes
Alex Nicol, Hillary Brooke

A writer becomes involved with a romantic triangle and murder

B-movie drama set in the Lake District with the main character missing a London-bound train made up of a pre-war SR EMU! This scene was filmed at Windsor & Eton Riverside station. Also featured is a stock shot of a 'Black Five' 4-6-0 on a passenger train on one of the Highland lines, probably taken for *I Know Where I'm Going* (1945) (qv).

HOW TO GET AHEAD IN ADVERTISING
GB 1989 Virgin/HandMade VHS
Dir: Bruce Robinson
Richard E. Grant, Rachel Ward

A rebellious advertising man grows a boil that turns into another head

Features a comedy scene on board a commuter train made up of Mk 2 coaches in Network SouthEast livery (including No 17095) and an unknown NSE station. The loco is not visible.

HOWARDS END
GB 1992 Merchant Ivory/FilmFour DVD
Dir: James Ivory
Anthony Hopkins, Vanessa Redgrave

The fortunes of two middle-class families overlap

A number of railway scenes feature in this film. The preserved SR 2-BIL EMU unit appears in a scene shot at St Pancras station (a nice change from the usual preserved steam locos brought out for these period films). There are also some shots of a train journey filmed on the Severn Valley Railway with GWR 'City'

Class 4-4-0 No 3440 *City of Truro* – Victoria Bridge and Bewdley station both appear.

THE HUMAN FACTOR
GB 1979 Rank
Dir: Otto Preminger
Nicol Williamson, Richard Attenborough

A spy in the Foreign Office allows a colleague to be suspected as a mole

Features a shot of a commuter train arriving at Berkhamsted station on the WCML made up of a Class 310 EMU (driving car No 76200).

HUNTED
GB 1952 GFD VHS
Dir: Charles Crichton
Dirk Bogarde, Jon Whiteley

A boy latches onto a runaway murderer

Features a scene where Bogarde and Whiteley leap on board a freight train while on the run, filmed on the Burslem loop-line in the Stoke-on-Trent area with a 4F 0-6-0 as the motive power.

THE HYPNOTIST
GB 1957 Anglo-Amalgamated
Dir: Montgomery Tulley
Paul Carpenter, Patricia Roc

A psychiatrist hypnotises a plane crash victim into killing his wife

Features a scene filmed on Waterloo station.

I

I CAPTURE THE CASTLE
GB 2003 BBC/Momentum DVD
Dir: Tim Fywell
Romola Gavai, Bill Nighy

A teenage girl and her eccentric family survive in a castle in the 1930s

Includes some railway scenes filmed on the Isle of Man Steam Railway at Port St Mary station with 0-6-0T No 15 *Caledonia* in charge of a rake of period-liveried stock. Filming took place overnight in the early hours with the stock kept at Port Erin during the day.

I.D.
GB/Germany 1995 Polygram/BBC DVD
Dir: Philip Davis
Reece Dinsdale, Richard Graham

A policeman working under cover to expose football hooligans becomes one of them

Features a scene filmed on Sheffield Midland station of football supporters alighting from an HST.

I KNOW WHERE I'M GOING
GB 1945 GFD
Dirs: Michael Powell, Emeric Pressburger
Wendy Hiller, Roger Livesey

An independent woman travels to the Hebrides to marry a wealthy old man

This classic film features a rather surreal studio-bound train journey from London to Scotland (in one scene the station master's top hat transforms into an engine chimney!). Everything settles down by the time we are in Scotland, however, and we get one good shot of a 'Black Five' on a train on the West Highland line.

I MET A MURDERER
GB 1939 Grand National
Dir: Roy Kellino
James Mason, Pamela Kellino

A murderer on the run gets involved with a girl novelist

Includes a scene with Mason outside a GWR country station, believed to be Cookham.

I SEE A DARK STRANGER
GB 1945 GFD VHS
Dir: Frank Launder
Deborah Kerr, Trevor Howard

An IRA member comes to England to spy for the Germans

Deborah Kerr's journey to and from Ireland is depicted by a couple of railway journeys, mainly using studio reconstructions of carriage interiors. There is one shot of a British train with a GWR 'Star' 4-6-0 arriving with a passenger service at the curved platforms of Bristol Temple Meads. The 'Irish' scenes were unusually filmed on the Isle of Man, with both the electric and steam railways making appearances. There is a nice shot of Manx Electric Railway car

No 26, and Union Mills on the now closed Peel branch of the steam railway appears as 'Ballysomewhere' with a pair of unidentified 2-4-0Ts on the train.

I SEE ICE
GB 1938 ATP VHS
Dir: Anthony Kimmins
George Formby, Kay Walsh

A photographer's assistant gets into trouble

This comedy features a train journey from Manchester to London, with the stations and carriage interiors being studio sets. Most of real footage is pretty accurate for an LMS journey, although the motive power alters quite a bit. We see an ex-L&YR 2-4-2T and a 'Royal Scot' 4-6-0, and if you keep your eyes peeled on the back projection screen in the interior scenes an engine shed with a Stanier 2-6-4T standing outside shoots past. When Formby pulls the emergency cord there is a good shot of 'Jubilee' 4-6-0 No 5553 *Canada* making a stop filmed specially for the production. Quite a lot of footage was taken for this scene, and this appears in Video 125's *Steam on 35mm* video, as well as being used as stock footage for later films (eg *The Love Match* [qv]). There is an accurate shot of Euston station; indeed, the only non-LMS blip during the journey occurs during a shunting scene when we see a couple of LNER Gresley coaches.

I WANT WHAT I WANT
GB 1971 Marayan
Dir: John Dexter
Anne Heywood, Paul Rogers

A man has a sex-change operation

Features a scene filmed on Windsor & Eton Riverside station with an SR 4-EPB EMU in the background.

I WAS MONTY'S DOUBLE
GB 1958 Film Traders VHS
Dir: John Guillermin
M. E. Clifton-James, John Mills

An actor is hired to imitate Montgomery to confuse the Nazis

Features a scene filmed at Liverpool Street station of Mills arriving on a train hauled by a 'B17' 4-6-0. A complete out-take of the shot appears in *Steam on 35mm Vol 2*, and reveals the loco as No 61606 *Audley End* in mock-up LNER livery.

IF ONLY
GB/France/Spain/Canada/Luxembourg
   1998 Pathé
Dir: Maria Ripoll
Penelope Cruz, Douglas Henshall

An actor who loses a women after confessing to an affair gets a second chance

Features a scene outside the entrance to Maida Vale Underground station.

I'LL NEVER FORGET WHATSISNAME
GB 1967 Universal
Dir: Michael Winner
Oliver Reed, Orson Welles

An advertising executive rebels against society

This satire features a surreal advertising film shot on the Bluebell Railway, with a lady tied to the track as in the old 'Perils of Pauline' westerns. Bluebell Halt was painted in white to appear as a 'ghost' station, with preserved NLR 0-6-0T No 2650 and the 'Chesham' rake painted similarly as a 'ghost train'.

I'LL SLEEP WHEN I'M DEAD
GB 2003 Momentum DVD
Dir: Mike Hodges
Clive Owen, Jonathan Rhys Meyers

An ex-gangster returns to London to discover the truth behind his brother's death

Includes a shot of a Class 319 'Thameslink' EMU crossing a bridge in South London.

IMPACT

GB 1963 Butchers
Dir: Peter Maxwell
Conrad Philips, George Pastell

A nightclub owner blackmails an investigative reporter

Features a scene filmed at Brickett Wood station on the Watford Junction-St Albans Abbey branch with a Class 108 DMU arriving.

THE IMPORTANCE OF BEING EARNEST

GB 2002 Miramax/Ealing DVD
Dir: Oliver Parker
Colin Firth, Rupert Everett

Two friends use the same pseudonym, which creates confusion

Includes a scene filmed at Horsted Keynes (as 'London Victoria') on the Bluebell Railway; preserved SECR 'O1' Class No 65, complete with 'Metropolitan Railway' transfers on its tender, poses as the loco in charge of a train from Brighton. A nice touch for these scenes was having former BR Chairman Sir Peter Parker play a station porter helping Judi Dench get off the train!

IN FADING LIGHT

GB 1991 Amber DVD
Dir: Murray Martin
Joe Caffrey, Maureen Harold

A fishing crew are joined by the skipper's daughter, which creates sexual tension

Includes a scene on Newcastle Central station with a departing train; although the loco is not visible we see Mk 2 Regional Railways-liveried stock, and a shot of a Tyne & Wear Metro unit at North Shields station.

IN WHICH WE SERVE

GB 1942 Rank DVD
Dirs: Noel Coward, David Lean
Noel Coward, John Mills

Survivors from a sunken destroyer recall their life at sea

This classic war film includes a couple of shots of GWR expresses, one hauled by 'King' No 6008 and one by a 'Castle' 4-6-0.

INADMISSIBLE EVIDENCE

GB 1968 Paramount
Dir: Anthony Page
Nicol Williamson, Jill Bennett

A philandering solicitor is close to a nervous breakdown

Includes some scenes of Williamson making a journey by train into London and boarding a rake of 4-EPB EMUs at an unknown station, passing 4-SUBs and 2-BILs en route, and finally some shots of Waterloo. Later in the film there is a shot on the London Underground with 1960 tube stock.

THE INCREDIBLE SARAH

GB 1976 Readers Digest VHS
Dir: Richard Fleischer
Glenda Jackson, Daniel Massey

The life of French actress Sarah Bernhardt

'London' station in the film (unusually no particular terminus is specified) is actually the engine shed at Didcot Railway Centre, with wooden platforms added by the film company. Victorian GWR coaches four-wheeler No 975 and clerestory No 1941 were lettered as Dover boat train stock and there are some good shots of 'Manor' No 7808 *Cookham Manor* with LC&D lettering.

INDISCREET

GB 1958 Grandon
Dir: Stanley Donen
Cary Grant, Ingrid Bergman

An American diplomat in London falls for an actress

Includes a shot filmed at the entrance to London Euston station.

THE INFORMERS

GB 1963 Rank VHS
Dir: Ken Annakin
Nigel Patrick, Colin Blakely

The brother of a murder victim seeks revenge

There are some good shots filmed on Liverpool Street station with maroon Mk 1 coaches, but we don't see any locomotives.

THE INN OF THE SIXTH HAPPINESS

GB 1958 Twentieth Century Fox DVD
Dir: Mark Robson
Ingrid Bergman, Robert Donat

An English missionary's experiences in China

This famous classic includes quite a few good railway scenes. The British scenes were filmed at Liverpool Street station and include a good shot of an arriving passenger train hauled by 'N7' 0-6-2T No 69665. The railway in China is depicted using the faithful old Longmoor Military Railway. Bergman's arrival seems to be filmed in Longmoor yard with a mock-up station and one of the railway's 'USA' 0-6-0Ts disguised as a Chinese loco.

THE INNOCENT SLEEP

GB 1995 Starlight/Timedial VHS
Dir: Scott Mitchell
Rupert Graves, Annabella Sciorra

A tramp witnesses a murder involving a senior policeman

Features a night shot filmed in South London with a passing Class 319 EMU.

THE INNOCENTS

GB 1961 Twentieth Century Fox DVD
Dir: Jack Clayton
Deborah Kerr, Pamela Franklin

A governess at a lonely house suspects that her charges are possessed by the dead

Includes a nice shot of a train arriving at Horsted Keynes station on the Bluebell Railway with SR 'birdcage' coaches but no loco (out of shot). This is believed to be the first occasion when a feature film was shot on the Bluebell, or indeed on any preserved standard gauge line.

INSPECTOR HORNLEIGH GOES TO IT

GB 1940 Twentieth Century Fox
Dir: Walter Forde
Gordon Harker, Alastair Sim

Detectives track down a fifth-columnist

The last of the Inspector Hornleigh films includes the most railway scenes as the traitor makes his getaway on a mail train pursued by the detective. Probably due to wartime restrictions most of the action takes place in the studio, with a few stock run-by shots added. Most of these appear to have been obtained from the famous GPO documentary *Night Mail* (1936). There's a good shot of LMS 'Patriot' 4-6-0 No 5513 arriving at Crewe with a mail, while the rest are a couple of night shots of passing LMS 4-6-0s and a Continental loco.

INSPECTOR HORNLEIGH ON HOLIDAY

GB 1939 Twentieth Century Fox
Dir: Walter Forde
Gordon Harker, Alastair Sim

Detectives solve a murder at a seaside hotel

Features a shot of a passing LMS express hauled by a 'Claughton' 4-6-0 on the WCML.

THE INTERNECINE PROJECT

GB 1974 Maclean and Co
Dir: Ken Hughes
James Coburn, Lee Grant

A professor works for a politician to exterminate people who would spoil his career

Includes a scene filmed on the concourse of Marylebone station.

THE INTERRUPTED JOURNEY

GB 1949 Valiant
Dir: Daniel Birt
Richard Todd, Valerie Hobson

An author runs off with another man's wife and causes tragedy

An integral part of the plot has the eloping couple head off by train with the author having second thoughts on the ensuing journey. Eager to make his escape, he pulls the communication cord and flees from the train across fields to his nearby home. However, as the train is being examined another express ploughs into the back of it. The author then finds himself being pursued by the Railway Inspectorate. Most of the train scenes were filmed in the studio (the crash scene uses models), but the crash aftermath scenes with views of the wreckage were filmed over a few nights on the Longmoor Military Railway using a couple of ambulance coaches painted up on one side for the cameras and the LMR's resident 'Dean Goods' 0-6-0.

INTIMACY

France/GB 2001 Studio Canal/Azor Films
    DVD
Dir: Patrice Chereau
Mark Rylance, Kerry Fox

A man has a wordless and loveless affair with a mysterious woman

Features a scene on the London Underground with Northern Line 1996 tube stock, believed to be at Camden Town station, together with a shot of a passing Class 455 EMU in South London (leading car No 77750).

THE IPCRESS FILE

GB 1965 Rank DVD
Dir: Sidney J. Furie
Michael Caine, Nigel Green

An intelligence man attempts to trace a missing scientist

This famous spy film features a scene where the scientist disappears from a train leaving London. This was filmed at Marylebone station with a steam-hauled loco (possibly a 'Black Five' – not clear due to editing) hauling maroon Mk 1 stock.

THE IRON MAIDEN

GB 1962 Anglo-Amalgamated VHS
Dir: Gerald Thomas
Michael Craig, Alan Hale Jnr

An aircraft designer's main passion is his traction engine

A film very much for traction engine fans (made by the same team that made the 'Carry On' films, it has been unofficially named 'Carry On Genevieve'), it also features some good shots of a Handley Page Victor bomber. These scenes were filmed at Radlett aerodrome, and in the background of one shot there's a clear view of a pair of Class 127 DMUs passing on the Midland Main Line.

ISN'T LIFE WONDERFUL?

GB 1952 ABP
Dir: Harold French
Donald Wolfit, Cecil Parker

A drunken uncle manages to reconcile a lovers' quarrel

Includes a rare shot of an ex-GWR '4500' 2-6-2T on the Princetown branch on Dartmoor (closed 1956) and some familiar shots of a train arriving at Cole Green station on the Welwyn-Hertford branch (loco not seen).

IT ALWAYS RAINS ON SUNDAY

GB 1947 Ealing DVD
Dir: Robert Hamer
Googie Withers, John McCallum

An escaped convict takes refuge in a lover's house in East London

This famous Ealing drama set in the post-war East End has a good night chase sequence filmed in Temple Mills yard, Stratford, although the railway dominates the background throughout the film. Earlier in the film there is a shot of LMS Stanier 2-6-0 No 2974 passing over a level crossing with a freight, location unknown. The chase scene is the climax of the film, with convict McCallum pursued by police led by a pre-Dixon Jack Warner, and there then follows a superbly edited and choreographed cat-and-mouse sequence narrowly avoiding freight trains and shunted wagons. The best bit is McCallum emerging from under a line of wagons and only just missing being mown down by a 'J39' 0-6-0. The worst bit, by today's standards, is some comically inept model work in the scene where McCallum and Warner find themselves in open wagons in a train being pushed over the hump siding. As the wagons roll down the other side into their separate sidings we see a couple of model trucks with very obvious 'stick' figures in them supposedly representing the actors. There are, however, plenty of locos on view, the stars of the show being 'J69' 0-6-0Ts Nos 9607 and 8591, which are seen propelling wagons about. There are also other 'J69s', a 'J52' and an Oerlikon EMU visible in the film. The wagons themselves are a fascinating collection of period pieces such as the open 'Bowson, Cinderford' private owner type out of which McCallum jumps in one shot, and the NE brake-vans.

IT HAPPENED HERE
GB 1963 UA/Kevin Brownlow/Andrew
   Mollo DVD
Dirs: Kevin Brownlow, Andrew Mollo
Sebastian Shaw, Pauline Murray

Events that could have occurred if Britain had been invaded by Germany in 1940

Includes a scene filmed on the old Euston station platforms just before rebuilding, but with no trains visible, a shot of a departing train at an unknown location, with a close-up of a 'B1' 4-6-0, and a scene filmed at Edgware station on the Underground with German soldiers boarding a 1938-stock tube train.

IT SHOULDN'T HAPPEN TO A VET
GB 1976 EMI DVD
Dir: Eric Till
John Alderton, Colin Blakely

Adventures of Yorkshire vet James Herriot before the Second World War

Some good scenes filmed at Oakworth station on the Keighley & Worth Valley Railway with preserved LMS 4F 0-6-0 No 3924.

IT'S A GRAND LIFE
GB 1953 Mancunian DVD
Dir: John E. Blakeley
Frank Randle, Diana Dors

An army private plays cupid

Includes a couple of railway shots filmed in the ex-LMS North West area. During the opening credits there are short local trains passing behind a 2P 4-4-0 and a 2-6-4T, and a shadowy, obscured shot of a local train arriving at a station behind a small LMS tank. Later in the film there is a shot of an express behind a 'Jubilee' 4-6-0.

IT'S A GREAT DAY!
GB 1956 Butchers
Dir: John Warrington
Ruth Dunning, Edward Evans

A film version of the popular TV soap The Grove Family

Includes a shot of an LT 'R'-type train somewhere on the overground section of the District Line.

IT'S THAT MAN AGAIN
GB 1942 GFD VHS
Dir: Walter Forde
Tommy Handley, Jack Train

Film version of the popular wartime ITMA radio show

This film features a railway journey as Handley heads for London to help rescue a bombed-out theatre. This is basically made up of Handley sitting in a studio mock-up of a corridor carriage with back projection of passing scenery through the window. Oddly the scenery is passing right to left at the start of the scene, but after the Mrs Mopp character has appeared it's moving left to right, so halfway through the train has suddenly reversed direction! No locomotives appear for this sequence, but a fascinating collection of bygone rolling-stock passes by – various LMS wagons, vans, open planks, a four-wheel bolster, a brake-van and a coach can be seen in the yards.

J

JACK & SARAH
GB/France 1995 Polygram DVD
Dir: Tim Sullivan
Richard E. Grant, Samantha Mathis

After his wife dies a lawyer brings up their daughter alone

Includes some scenes filmed in the London docklands with Docklands Light Railway units.

JACQUELINE
GB 1956 Rank VHS
Dir: Roy Baker
John Gregson, Kathleen Ryan

Life for a family near the Belfast shipyards

Filmed on location, there is one good shot of one of the shipyard's 0-6-0 saddle tanks.

JEANNIE
GB 1941 GFD
Dir: Harold French
Barbara Mullen, Michael Redgrave

A Scots girl comes into money and heads for Europe

Mullen's trip from Scotland to France is depicted by a shot of SR 'King Arthur' 4-6-0 No 771 arriving at Dover Marine station.

JIGSAW
GB 1962 British Lion
Dir: Val Guest
Jack Warner, Ronald Lewis

Brighton police track down a murderer

This murder mystery was filmed almost entirely in and around Brighton and Hove and uses the local railway atmosphere. Near the start there is a close-up of the front of 'E4' 0-6-2T No 32474 and a shot near Brighton of a passing train hauled by a BR Standard 2-6-4T. There are also scenes filmed at Brighton and Lewes stations.

THE JIGSAW MAN
GB 1984 J&M DVD
Dir: Terence Young
Michael Caine, Laurence Olivier

A British traitor in Moscow returns home as a double agent

Features a shot outside an unknown station on the South Western Division of the Southern Region with a Bournemouth/Portsmouth line express EMU passing in the background.

JOANNA
GB 1968 TCF
Dir: Mike Sarne
Genevieve Waite, Donald Sutherland

Adventures of a girl art student in Swinging London

The opening of this film features the main character's arrival at Paddington station behind a 'Western' diesel. There is also a clear shot of a 'Hymek' with a Class 22 and a DMU just visible. The ending features a big song-and-dance scene on the platforms of Paddington with plenty of Mk 1 coaches and a 'Western' arriving on a train clearly visible in the background.

JOEY BOY
GB 1965 British Lion VHS
Dir: Frank Launder
Harry H. Corbett, Stanley Baxter

A group of petty crooks join the Army

Features a night shot of a passing steam-hauled express, possibly of LMS origin.

JOHN AND JULIE
GB 1955 Group Three
Dir: William Fairchild
Colin Gibson, Leslie Dudley

Two children run away from home to see the 1953 Coronation

This colourful, outdoor film about the Coronation includes some excellent Eastmancolor railway scenes. Near the start there is a good shot of SR 'West Country' 'Pacific' No 34019 leaving Southampton Ocean Terminal with a boat train. The children's flight takes them to Greenford station (with a distant view of the main-line platforms and an 'A3' 'Pacific' on a GC-line express passing) and their own train is hauled by an 'A3'. Amusingly, John identifies the train loco as a 'County', whereas the ticket inspector says it's a 'King' – they're both wrong! The scenes where they are questioned for travelling without tickets were filmed at High Wycombe station. Finally there is a shot of an SR 'Lord Nelson' 4-6-0 arriving with an express at Waterloo.

THE JOKERS
GB 1966 Universal
Dir: Michael Winner
Michael Crawford, Oliver Reed

Two brothers plan to borrow and replace the Crown Jewels

This Swinging London film features some good shots of Waterloo station with a view of the motive power then frequently seen there – a 'Warship', Class 33 and Class 73 are all visible at the buffer stops.

THE JONAH MAN
GB 1904 Gaumont DVD
Dir: Cecil M. Hepworth
Actors unknown

A man finds all modes of transport he uses suddenly disappearing

This early trick film features scenes at Walton-on-Thames station with a train made up of LSWR suburban coaches and a passing express hauled by a Drummond 4-4-0.

JOURNEY TOGETHER
GB 1945 RAF Film Unit VHS
Dir: John Boulting
Richard Attenborough, Edward G.
   Robinson

Trainee pilots receive instruction before their first bombing missions

Features a shot of a passing LNER express hauled by a 'V2' 2-6-2, believed to have been filmed on the Great Central line.

JUDE
GB 1996 Polygram/BBC DVD
Dir: Michael Winterbottom
Christopher Eccleston, Kate Winslet

A rural labourer dreams of becoming a teacher

Features a period train filmed on the Keighley & Worth Valley Railway with coaches from the Vintage Carriages Trust and LMS 'Jinty' 0-6-0 No 47329.

JUGGERNAUT
GB 1974 United Artists
Dir: Richard Lester
Richard Harris, David Hemmings

A mad bomber threatens to blow up a liner

Features a scene on Waterloo station.

JUMPING FOR JOY
GB 1955 Rank VHS
Dir: John Paddy Carstairs
Frankie Howerd, Stanley Holloway

A track attendant acquires a greyhound to win him races

One of the quirks of this comedy is having Stanley Holloway living in an old railway carriage (shades of Titfield!), which a group of crooks sabotages by propelling it onto a main line where it is demolished by an express. Most of these scenes seem to use models and studio sets, but a few real shots of an ex-GWR coach are included – No W2342W. A real shot of a GW-line express is also slotted in, hauled by a 'King'.

JUST ASK FOR DIAMOND
GB 1988 TCF/CFTVF
Dir: Stephen Bayly
Colin Dale, Saeed Jaffrey

A boy detective finds himself up against a gang of crooks

Includes a scene filmed on St Pancras station with an HST in the background.

KATE PLUS TEN

GB 1938 Wainwright
Dir: Reginald Denham
Jack Hulbert, Genevieve Tobin

A police inspector trails the female leader of a bullion gang

This unfairly neglected film features some excellent railway scenes in its final half-hour as the gang steal the train for its gold bullion van. The scene in which the gold is offloaded from the ship was filmed at Brentford Docks at night, and Churchward's saloon coach with a '5700' 0-6-0PT attached can be seen. The railway chase scenes were filmed on the Limpley Stoke-Camerton branch and the Westbury-Bath line (the scene of the train smashing through mock-up level crossing gates was filmed at Freshford), and the level crossing where Hulbert stops the loco to block the crooks is actually outside Camerton station itself. The main star of all these scenes is GWR '4300' Class 2-6-0 No 4364, but look out for a couple of rarities as the police swarm out of a train at Limpley Stoke station. The train pulls in with a 'Bulldog' 4-4-0 on the front, itself an unexpected type to crop up in a movie; however, as the police head down the station ramp a continuity error reveals how the scenes were filmed on separate nights as the train loco has now become one of the GWR-acquired Robinson 2-8-0s! Photos of these are uncommon, let alone one of them turning up in a cinema film.

KEEP THE ASPIDISTRA FLYING

GB 1997 First Independent VHS
Dir: Robert Bierman
Richard E. Grant, Helena Bonham Carter

A copywriter gives up his job to become a poet

Features a scene at St Pancras station, but no trains are involved.

KEEPING MUM

GB 2005 Entertainment DVD
Dir: Niall Johnson
Maggie Smith, Rowan Atkinson

A housekeeper helps a vicar's family by murderous means

Some good scenic shots at the start were filmed on the North Yorkshire Moors Railway with a train hauled by 'Black Five' 4-6-0 No 45407 and an arrest scene at Pickering station.

KES

GB 1969 UA DVD
Dir. Ken Loach
David Bradley, Colin Welland

In the industrial North a boy learns about life through the fate of his pet bird

Filmed on location around Barnsley, there is a shot in one of the collieries in the area with an 'Austerity' 0-6-0ST prominent in the yard.

KHARTOUM
GB 1966 UA VHS
Dir: Basil Dearden
Charlton Heston, Laurence Olivier

The last years of General Gordon

Gordon's meeting with Gladstone was filmed on the Bluebell Railway at Horsted Keynes, with preserved NLR 0-6-0T No 2650 and the 'Chesham' stock. Also includes a scene on Marylebone station.

KILLING DAD
GB 1989 Palace/Scottish TV VHS
Dir: Michael Austin
Richard E. Grant, Denholm Elliott

When an errant father returns to his family his son decides to kill him

There are plenty of railway shots here, but with very dodgy authenticity and continuity. Grant boards a Class 315 EMU for Southend at King's Cross station (!) as his mother bids him goodbye. From one angle she is in the suburban station and there is another Class 315 at an adjacent platform, but then the scene almost immediately changes to her standing in the main-line station with an HST behind her. While Grant is en route to Southend we see shots of Southern Region Class 455 units (no wires!), while the interior shots are of a 'Pacer' DMU. However, the Southend scenes feature some good views of the pier tramway.

A KIND OF LOVING
GB 1962 Anglo-Amalgamated DVD
Dir: John Schlesinger
Alan Bates, June Ritchie

A young Northerner is forced into marriage and living with his mother-in-law

This classic drama, filmed around North West England, features one night scene at a station, possibly Blackburn, with a 'Black Five' entering with a train.

KING RALPH
US 1991 UIP DVD
Dir: David S. Ward
John Goodman, Peter O'Toole

After the Royal Family are electrocuted an American becomes King of England

Features a good shot of a 'Royal Train' arriving at St Pancras station hauled by an Inter-City-liveried Class 47 diesel with royal crests added under the cab windows.

A KISS IN THE TUNNEL
GB 1900 Bamforth DVD
Dir: Unknown
Actors unknown

A young man kisses a girl on a train journey

One of the very first surviving story films to feature a railway element. An unidentified tank engine hauls a train into Queensberry Tunnel on the GNR Bradford-Halifax line and a Midland Johnson 4-4-0 leaves at the other end, arriving at Monsal Dale station on the Peak Forest main line. This film appears in Video 125's *Trains from the Arc*.

A KISS IN THE TUNNEL
GB 1900 George Albert Smith DVD
Dir: George Albert Smith
George Albert Smith, Mrs George Albert Smith

An almost exact copy of the Bamforth film

In this version the railway shots are made up of 'phantom ride' footage from an earlier Hepworth film passing through Shilla Mill Tunnel on the LSWR Devon main line; this is therefore also the first story film to use stock railway footage. As we approach the tunnel an LSWR 0-4-4T dashes past in the opposite direction with a passenger; after the kiss has taken place we emerge from the other end of the tunnel. This film also appears in Video 125's *Trains from the Arc*.

THE LADYKILLERS (1955): A classic image from a classic Ealing comedy – Alec Guinness, Danny Green and Cecil Parker (deceased!) take a trip across the top of Copenhagen Tunnels. *Canal + Image*

Above THE LAST JOURNEY (1936): Filming at Paddington station – note the large crowd on Platform 1 on the right watching the proceedings. *BFI*

Left THE LAST JOURNEY (1936): A cameraman films 'Castle' Class No 5022 passing him at Bramley on the Reading-Basingstoke line during the making of the film. *BFI*

Above right MEETINGS WITH REMARKABLE MEN (1979): The railway works scene, filmed at Didcot Railway Centre. *Great Western Society*

Right MEETINGS WITH REMARKABLE MEN (1979): The locomotive frames belong to No 5051 *Earl Bathurst*. *Great Western Society*

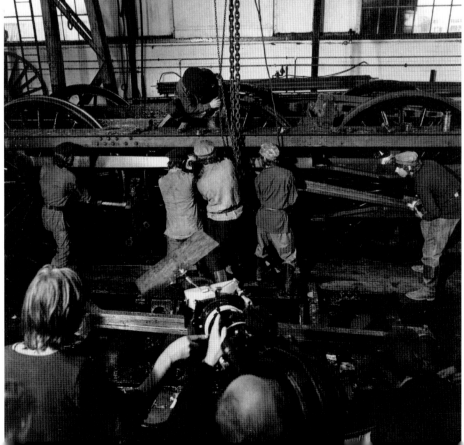

OH MR PORTER (1937): A camera crew are balanced precariously from the cab of an LSWR 'X2' 4-4-0 during the making of this classic comedy on the Basingstoke & Alton Light Railway. *BFI*

Right ONE OF OUR
DINOSAURS IS MISSING
(1975): Star Derek Nimmo
poses with GWR '4300' Class
No 5322 at Marylebone
station. *Great Western Society*

Below ONE OF OUR
DINOSAURS IS MISSING
(1975): Film extras and
No 5322 at Marylebone.
Great Western Society

THE PASSWORD IS COURAGE (1962): Wrecked Fowler 2-6-4T No 42325 and wagons in the spectacular crash scene – the loco was not repaired! Dirk Bogarde is in the foreground. *MGM*

Above THE PRIVATE LIFE OF SHERLOCK HOLMES (1970):
Lancashire & Yorkshire Railway 0-6-0 No 957 is ready for filming in 'L&NWR' apple-green livery
on the Keighley & Worth Valley Railway. *Robin Lush*

Below THE RAILWAY CHILDREN (1970): Filming the 'presentation' scene at Oakworth,
with lavishly decorated GWR '5700' 0-6-0PT No 5775 in the platform. *Robin Lush*

Above ROBBERY (1967): Stanley Baker is interviewed on set with Class 40 No D318 awaiting its moment of fame in the background. *BFI*

Left ROBBERY (1967): Action! The robbers attack the loco crew. *BFI*

KNOCK ON WOOD
US 1954 Paramount
Dir: Norman Panama, Melvin Frank
Danny Kaye, Mai Zetterling

Stolen plans are left in a ventriloquist's dummy

Includes a scene on Waterloo station with a 4-SUB EMU visible.

KNIGHT WITHOUT ARMOUR
GB 1937 London Films VHS
Dir: Jacques Feyder
Robert Donat, Marlene Dietrich

A countess is helped to escape from the Russian Revolution by a British translator

A film by the legendary producer Alexander Korda, this was the production for which a railway was specially built in the grounds of Denham Studios, with two ex-LNER 'J15' 0-6-0s, Nos 7835 and 7541, purchased by London Films and mocked up to look like Russian locomotives together with some stock. The Denham scenes are most easily identifiable in the closing minutes, although some earlier shots were filmed on the Longmoor Military Railway. The 'J15s', which are also briefly visible in *South Riding* (1937), survived at Denham during the war and were later sold to the MoD.

L

LADY GODIVA RIDES AGAIN
GB 1951 British Lion
Dir: Frank Launder
Pauline Stroud, Diana Dors

A small town girl's rise and fall as a movie star

Features a number of railway scenes. First there is a platform shot of a deserted main-line station, sadly unknown, intended to depict typical Sunday train services! Later there is a scene of an SR train arriving at another station hauled by 'L1' Class 4-4-0 No 31754, and a departure scene from Marylebone station with no loco visible but good shots of some nice Gresley coaches.

THE LADY VANISHES
GB 1938 Gaumont British/Gainsborough
   DVD
Dir: Alfred Hitchcock
Margaret Lockwood, Michael Redgrave

An old lady disappears on a Switzerland-London express and two Brits investigate

In this classic Hitchcock thriller the action takes place on an express crossing central Europe. Most of this consists of studio sets, stock footage of Continental railways and some dodgy model shots, but there is one good shot filmed in the United Kingdom near the end of the film – an SR 'Schools' 4-4-0 arriving with a boat train at Victoria station.

THE LADY WITH THE LAMP
GB 1951 British Lion VHS
Dir: Herbert Wilcox
Anna Neagle, Michael Wilding

The life of Florence Nightingale

Nightingale's return to Britain features some excellent shots of the preserved Liverpool & Manchester Railway 0-4-2 *Lion* arriving at Cole Green station on the Welwyn-Hertford line (which closed that year), with a rake of replica L&M 1st Class four-wheelers. Interestingly *Lion* had also featured in *Victoria the Great* (1937) (qv), another Wilcox/Neagle film, so perhaps they decided to use it again for old time's sake! In any case, this is the loco getting more film work a year away from its 'Titfield' stardom.

THE LADYKILLERS
GB 1955 Ealing DVD
Dir: Alexander Mackendrick
Alec Guinness, Katie Johnson

A gang of robbers use an old lady's house as cover, but she outwits them

This famous classic from Ealing Studios ranks alongside *The Titfield Thunderbolt* as its most famous railway-located film. However, whereas 'Titfield' epitomises the rural branch line, 'Ladykillers' is soaked in the atmosphere of smoky tunnels, goods yards and the built-up approaches to a main-line station. Also, unlike 'Titfield' the railway only plays a backdrop to most of the film, but dominates the proceedings for the last half-hour. Most of the details of the film have become well-known over the years – Mrs Wilberforce's house was created specially for the film above the mouth of Copenhagen Tunnel, and the freight trains that the gang fall into are on the goods lines that run out of King's Cross yard. Filming of these scenes took place on Sundays and used two rakes of mineral wagons hauled by Top Shed 'V2s' (Nos 60814 and 60821 are known to have been used). The signal that hits Alec Guinness on the head was specially set up for the film at the mouth of the tunnel, although the actual scene used was filmed with a replica signal in the studio. Other locomotives glimpsed in the area throughout the film are a 'J52', an 'A1' 'Pacific' and an ex-LMS 'Jinty' 0-6-0 crossing over on the North London line with a freight. In addition there are some very good shots of King's Cross itself, including 'L1' 2-6-4T No 67800 passing under Guinness on the footbridge while he is pretending to be a trainspotter. Ealing filmed a large amount of train footage around the tunnels with very little of it making the final cut – this 'bonus' footage (featuring passing 'Pacifics', 'V2s', 'N2s', etc) appears in Video 125's *Steam on 35mm* Vols 1 and 2.

LAMB

GB 1986 Cannon VHS
Dir: Colin Gregg
Liam Neeson, Hugh O'Conor

A young priest absconds with a boy from a harsh Irish reform school

Includes a scene on the concourse of Euston station and a scene at Warren Street station on the London Underground with 1972 tube stock.

THE LANDGIRLS

GB/France 1997 FilmFour DVD
Dir: David Leland
Catherine McCormack, Rachel Weisz

Events in the lives of three land girls in the Second World War

Features some good shots filmed on the West Somerset Railway, with Crowcombe Heathfield station acting as 'Bamford'. Locomotives appearing in the scenes are '5700' 0-6-0PT No 7760 and '4500' 2-6-2T No 4561.

LASSIE

GB/USA/Ireland/France 2005
  Entertainment/Firstsight Films DVD
Dir: Charles Sturridge
Peter O'Toole, Samantha Morton

A poor mining family are forced to sell their dog to a Lord

In this update of the classic animal story, a journey to Scotland features a couple of railway shots using stock material – a 'Duchess' 'Pacific' on an express crossing a viaduct and an 'over the camera' shot of a rebuilt Bulleid 'Pacific'.

THE LAST ADVENTURERS

GB 1937 Conway
Dir: Roy Kellino
Niall MacGinnis, Linden Travers

Lives of men aboard a fishing trawler

Mostly filmed on location around Grimsby and the North Sea, it includes a good shot of a fish train leaving what is believed to be Grimsby docks behind LNER 'K3' Class 2-6-0 No 206.

THE LAST JOURNEY

GB 1936 Twickenham VHS
Dir: Bernard Vorhaus
Godfrey Tearle, Hugh Williams

The driver of an express train goes mad with jealousy and plans to kill all in his charge

This little classic lay in obscurity for many years but frequent showings at transport film screenings and critical re-evaluation of Bernard Vorhaus's work have led to it becoming seen as one of the most exciting and technically well-made railway films of the 1930s. It takes wholesale liberties with its depiction of common railway practice, comically uses speeded-up camerawork on occasion, and the scene where a signalman diverts a goods train into a loop moments before it can be hit by the pursuing express just has to be seen to be believed! But it is absolutely brilliant, one of the best quota-quickie films you are likely to see from this period. The GWR offered full use of facilities to Twickenham Studios during its making, and the railway scenes completely dominate the entire film. Paddington obviously features heavily for the first section, with good shots of its approaches and Ranelagh Bridge loco yard. Once the express is on its way to 'Mulchester', it soon becomes clear that something is wrong as it rushes through booked stops – these scenes were filmed at West Ealing and Slough stations. Much of the action then takes place on the Reading-Basingstoke line, filmed over a number of Sundays, and it is here that the goods train scenes were filmed. Reading was unable to supply the same locomotives and wagons over every weekend of filming, which is why the motive power visibly changes four times. First it is a '5700' 0-6-0PT, then a '4300' 2-6-0, followed by a '2800' 2-8-0 and finally a '2251' 0-6-0. Later in the film there is some footage taken from the front of a train heading along the Dawlish sea wall and the final climax features a rare location – Plymouth Millbay station.

Other locomotives that can be seen in the film include 'Star' 4-6-0 No 4020, 'Hall' Class No 4953, 'Castles' Nos 5004, 5012, 5013 and 5022, and 'King' 4-6-0 No 6004, together with '5700' 0-6-0PTs at Paddington on empty coaching stock duties.

THE LAST PAGE
GB 1952 Exclusive/Hammer
Dir: Terence Fisher
George Brent, Diana Dors

A bookseller is framed for the death of a bookseller

Features a scene filmed on Windsor & Eton Riverside station with an SR pre-war EMU visible.

THE LAST YELLOW
GB 1999 Capitol/BBC DVD
Dir: Julian Farino
Mark Addy, Charlie Creed-Miles

A misfit and his hired gun head for London to exact revenge on the man who crippled his brother

Includes a scene on the London Underground with Circle Line 'C'-type stock.

LATE NIGHT SHOPPING
GB 2001 FilmFour DVD
Dir: Saul Metzstein
Luke de Woolfson, James Lance

A young night-shift worker cannot tell if his girlfriend still lives with him

Features some scenes filmed at Glasgow Central (Low Level) station on the underground section of the Glasgow suburban lines with a couple of Class 303 EMUs, including No 303 088.

THE LAVENDER HILL MOB
GB 1951 Ealing DVD
Dir: Charles Crichton
Alec Guinness, Stanley Holloway

A bank clerk conceives a bullion robbery with an artist

A classic Ealing comedy with a deservedly high reputation. The film includes a shot of a London tram, but the scene with Holloway and Guinness on the London tube is a studio re-creation.

LET HIM HAVE IT 101

LAW AND DISORDER
GB 1958 British Lion
Dir: Charles Crichton
Michael Redgrave, Robert Morley

A crook desperately attempts to prevent his son from learning of his career

Near the end of the film there are some good shots involving Redgrave filmed on Windsor & Eton Central station platforms with 'Hall' 4-6-0 No 5935 departing.

LAXDALE HALL
GB 1952 Group Three
Dir: John Eldridge
Raymond Huntley, Ronald Squire

MPs are sent to investigate a Scottish island that pays no road tax

The journey north from London is depicted using some stock shots from *Brief Encounter* – night shots of expresses hauled by a 'Royal Scot' and a streamlined 'Duchess'.

THE LEATHER BOYS
GB 1963 British Lion VHS
Dir: Sidney J. Furie
Colin Campbell, Rita Tushingham

A young motorcyclist marries but gets disillusioned with his wife

Features a scene overlooking the LSWR main line near Nine Elms with a rebuilt 'West Country' 'Pacific' passing with an express. Much rarer, however, are the scenes near the end of the film where Colin Campbell and Dudley Sutton leave a pub in Silvertown, East London. Across the road is a railway yard where a mixed freight is passing hauled by one of the short-lived North British Class 16 diesels – a class hard to find in photographs let alone a major feature film!

LEFT RIGHT AND CENTRE
GB 1959 Vale/Launder and Gilliat VHS
Dir: Sidney Gilliat
Ian Carmichael, Alastair Sim

A TV personality becomes a Tory candidate at a by-election

Ian Carmichael takes a journey to his constituency at the start of the film. He leaves London by train from Marylebone station (loco not visible) and en route the back projection through the Mk 1 window briefly shows them passing a yard with a Stanier 2-6-4T in attendance. The arrival scenes were filmed at Windsor & Eton Central with a 'Hall' 4-6-0 at the head of the train. In an adjacent platform there is a rake of GWR suburban stock with a '9400' 0-6-0PT at the front.

THE LEGEND OF HELL HOUSE
GB 1973 TCF DVD
Dir: John Hough
Roddy McDowell, Clive Revill

Four people stay at a haunted house that has killed previous investigators

An effective horror film that near the start includes a scene with McDowell on an unknown ER station, possibly in the Lea Valley, with a departing Class 305 EMU.

LEON THE PIG FARMER
GB 1992 Electric VHS
Dirs: Vadim Jean, Gary Sinyor
Mark Frankel, Brian Glover

A Jewish estate agent discovers that his real father is a pig farmer

Features shots around Battersea in South London with some EMUs – a Class 319 and 4-CEP/4-BIG slam-door types. Frankel's scenes visiting his father in Yorkshire include train arrivals at Clapham station, on the Carnforth-Settle 'Little North Western' line with Class 142 'Pacer' units Nos 142 084 and 142 018.

LET HIM HAVE IT
GB 1991 First Independent/British Screen DVD
Dir: Peter Medak
Christopher Eccleston, Paul Reynolds

The real-life story of Derek Bentley, who was executed for a crime committed by another

Features scenes filmed on the East Lancashire Railway near Bury engine sheds with BR Standard 4MT No 76079 on a train. Another preserved Standard 5MT can be seen on shed in the background.

LET'S BE HAPPY
GB 1957 ABP
Dir: Henry Levin
Vera-Ellen, Tony Martin

An American girl inherits a fortune and goes to Scotland

The Scottish scenes include a shot of an Edinburgh tram passing in the background and a scene on a boat below the Forth railway bridge.

LET'S GET LAID
GB 1978 Norfolk International DVD
Dir: James Kenelm Clarke
Robin Askwith, Fiona Richmond

A dim-witted soldier acquires a secret weapon and is pursued by police and spies

Some railway scenes were filmed on the Bluebell Railway, with internal shots taken on board some preserved Bulleid coaches. A couple of shots were filmed at Marylebone, and three stock shots of WR expresses were filmed in the 1950s – two with 'Castles' (one of which is No 5060) and a 'Hall' 4-6-0.

LIBEL
GB 1959 MGM
Dir: Anthony Asquith
Dirk Bogarde, Olivia de Havilland

A baronet is accused of being an impostor

Part of the film is made up of flashbacks to incidents in occupied France during the Second World War, although as Bogarde and company slip through a goods yard the wagons are obviously BR

standard mineral types from the 1950s, with some wooden-bodied types mingled in. Sadly, the location is unknown.

LIEUTENANT DARING AND THE PLANS OF THE MINEFIELD
GB 1911 British and Colonial DVD
Dir: Dave Aylott
Percy Moran, Charles Raymond

Lt Daring foils spies who have taken secret plans

One of a series of popular films in the early silent days. The spies make their escape by train from Charing Cross with a good shot of them boarding an SECR 1st Class carriage. As the train pulls out an 'F1' Class 4-4-0 is revealed with an 0-4-4T behind. There is a shot of a train passing behind a 'D' Class 4-4-0, another 4-4-0 on a train near Folkestone and a scene at Folkestone Harbour station with the rear end of a coach visible. The railway scenes feature in Video 125's production *Trains from the Arc.*

THE LIFE AND DEATH OF COLONEL BLIMP
GB 1943 GFD/Archers DVD
Dirs: Michael Powell, Emeric Pressburger
Roger Livesey, Deborah Kerr

A soldier survives three wars and has affairs with three women

In this famous wartime drama some of the railway scenes are obviously studio interiors, but there is one shot of a GWR 'King' 4-6-0 on a passing express.

LIFE AT THE TOP
GB 1965 Columbia
Dir: Ted Kotcheff
Laurence Harvey, Jean Simmons

Sequel to Room at the Top (qv) ten years on

The Yorkshire scenes feature rare shots of Ilkley station before it was rationalised. No locos are seen but there are good views of maroon-liveried BR Mk 1 coaches on the now closed through platforms.

LIKE IT IS
GB 1997 Channel 4 Films DVD
Dir: Paul Oremland
Steve Bell, Roger Daltrey

A boxer has a gay relationship with a young record producer

Some scenes are filmed in Blackpool and feature a number of passing trams – some double-deck Balloons, vintage Bolton Transport No 66 and the illuminated Rocketship tram. Later in the film there is a scene on board an EMU, probably a Class 455.

LINK
GB 1985 EMI/Cannon VHS
Dir: Richard Franklin
Terence Stamp, Elisabeth Shue

A scientist educates chimpanzees but one becomes malevolent

Elisabeth Shue's journey to the scientist's house where the main story takes place is depicted by a scenic view of a passing HST, location unknown.

THE LIQUIDATOR
GB 1965 MGM VHS
Dir: Jack Cardiff
Rod Taylor, Trevor Howard

An ex-war hero is enlisted by the secret service as an assassin

Includes a scene involving an assassin pushing someone under a train at a London Underground station. This was actually filmed at Bank station on the then BR-owned Waterloo & City Line, and there are a couple of shots of the line's Class 487 EMUs.

LISZTOMANIA
GB 1975 Warner VHS
Dir: Ken Russell
Roger Daltrey, Sara Kestelman

A fantasia based on the life of Franz Liszt

Features a surreal scene where a grand piano is left on a railway line and destroyed by a passing train. Filmed on the Bluebell Railway on Freshfield Bank, a dummy fibreglass piano was used and the locomotive is preserved 'A1X' 'Terrier' No 72 Fenchurch.

LOCH NESS
GB 1995 Polygram DVD
Dir: John Henderson
Ted Danson, Joely Richardson

An American scientist goes to Loch Ness to debunk the myth of the monster

Danson's journey back to London by train features a shot of a Class 87-hauled express on the WCML.

LONDINIUM
US/GB 2001 Sunlight DVD
Dir: Mike Binder
Colin Firth, Mariel Hemingway

Lives of a group of London friends over a number of years

Includes some scenes filmed on Waterloo station with a variety of units visible, including Class 455s, Class 159s and express slam-door stock (coach No 62184 can be seen).

LONDON BELONGS TO ME
GB 1948 GFD DVD
Dir: Sidney Gilliat
Alastair Sim, Richard Attenborough

When a young man is arrested on a murder charge his friends rally to help him

Features a great many shots of London locations with some trams making appearances.

LONDON KILLS ME
GB 1992 Rank VHS
Dir: Hanif Kureishi
Justin Chadwick, Steven Mackintosh

A drug pusher can take a job as a waiter so long as he gets a certain pair of shoes

Includes some railway scenes filmed on the Southern Region around South London, mainly with SR slam-door express stock, including set No 1762.

LONDON MELODY
GB 1937 GFD
Dir: Herbert Wilcox
Anna Neagle, Tullio Carminati

A diplomat falls for a dancer

Features a shot of a passing SR express hauled by a 'Lord Nelson' 4-6-0, and a tram appears in the London scenes.

LONDON TO BRIGHTON
GB 2006 Vertigo/Steel Mill Pictures DVD
Dir: Paul Andrew Williams
Georgia Groome, Lorraine Stanley

A prostitute and a young girl flee to Brighton after killing a client

This gritty thriller features some scenes filmed at Victoria, Waterloo and Brighton stations, with Class 455 EMU No 455 808 and a shot of a Class 319 unit en route to Brighton. The train interior scenes were filmed in Mk 1 stock on the Bluebell Railway.

THE LONELINESS OF THE LONG DISTANCE RUNNER
GB 1962 British Lion DVD
Dir: Tony Richardson
Tom Courtenay, Michael Redgrave

A Borstal boy thinks back on his life while in a race

One scene depicts Courtenay and his friends talking on a hillside above a railway viaduct, and a BR Standard 2-6-4T passes by with a local passenger train. Also featured is a night scene with a train at a railway station. Both these scenes are believed to have been filmed in Nottingham but precise locations are unknown.

THE LONG ARM
GB 1956 Ealing VHS
Dir: Charles Frend
Jack Hawkins, Dorothy Alison

A Scotland Yard superintendent investigates a series of robberies

Involves some railway scenes including a night journey sequence filmed on the WR, partly at Paddington. There is also a good daytime shot later in the film of a 'Britannia' 'Pacific' bringing an express down Camden bank into Euston station. An alternate shot at the same location with a 'Duchess'-hauled express appears on Video 125's *Steam on 35mm* video, as well as a scene of a 'Castle' bringing a passenger train into Chester General station, which somehow didn't make the final cut.

THE LONG GOOD FRIDAY
GB 1980 Black Lion DVD
Dir: John Mackenzie
Bob Hoskins, Helen Mirren

A gangland boss faces reprisals from the competition

Features a scene filmed on Platform 8 at Paddington station of a coffin being offloaded from a train. A Class 47 diesel is at the helm with the parcels van involved being No 81432. Another Class 47 is visible behind, as well as a Class 117 DMU.

THE LONG MEMORY
GB 1952 Rank
Dir: Robert Hamer
John Mills, Elizabeth Sellars

An ex-con framed for murder plots revenge but uncovers a fresh crime

Features scenes filmed on Waterloo station.

LOOK BACK IN ANGER
GB 1959 ABP VHS
Dir: Tony Richardson
Richard Burton, Claire Bloom

An angry young man with a grudge against life has an affair with his wife's best friend

An adaptation of the famous John Osborne play, which started the realist 'kitchen-sink' film cycle, this film makes a great deal of use of actual suburban locations and has some railway sequences. One daytime scene depicts Burton standing on Willesden Junction (Low Level) station – the main-line platforms, which closed three years after the film's release – with a rake of maroon Mk 1s departing. The most vivid and atmospheric scenes are, however, reserved for the final minutes as Burton and Bloom part at a busy railway station at night, very likely also Willesden Junction, with some excellent shots of 'Black Five' 4-6-0 No 45027 on Bloom's train. In fact the 5MT is very much the scene-stealer! The smoke, steam, night photography and departing lovers make these scenes seem like a sourer version of *Brief Encounter*.

LOOK UP AND LAUGH
GB 1935 ATP VHS
Dir: Basil Dean
Gracie Fields, Douglas Wakefield

Market stallholders defy a chain store

Features a sequence where Gracie Fields is aloft over the town in an old biplane. At one point they are flying along a single-track railway line and narrowly miss a GWR large 2-6-2T on a local. Shot with a combination of studio filming and back projection, the location of the line is unknown.

LOST
GB 1955 Rank
Dir: Guy Green
David Farrar, David Knight

A child is stolen and the police trail for evidence

This realistic crime drama uses a lot of outdoor locations, including a railway scene filmed by South Croydon Junction signal box with passing SR 4-EPB EMUs.

LOVE ACTUALLY
GB 2003 Universal/Working Title DVD
Dir: Richard Curtis
Colin Firth, Bill Nighy

Various stories of love in the weeks before Christmas

Includes a scene filmed on the escalators of Canary Wharf Underground station, Jubilee Line.

LOVE + HATE
GB 2006 BBC Films DVD
Dir: Dominic Savage
Samina Awan, Dean Andrews

A racist white boy falls for a Muslim girl

The film was shot entirely in Blackburn and there are some good shots of the station near the end with Class 150 'Sprinter' unit No 150 147 and a couple of Class 142s, including No 142 064.

LOVE LIFE AND LAUGHTER
GB 1934 ATP VHS
Dir: Maurice Elvey
Gracie Fields, John Loder

A prince falls for a film actress

Features a shot of a boat train arriving at London Victoria station behind 'Lord Nelson' 4-6-0 No 861.

THE LOVE LOTTERY
GB 1953 Ealing
Dir: Charles Crichton
David Niven, Peggy Cummins

A British film star is persuaded to offer himself in a lottery

Features a couple of shots of passing express trains – one hauled by a de-streamlined 'Duchess' 'Pacific' (still with sloping smokebox) and one by a GWR 4-6-0.

THE LOVE MATCH
GB 1955 British Lion DVD
Dir: David Paltenghi
Arthur Askey, Thora Hird

A train driver's love of his football team lands him in trouble

This rather neglected comedy is set in Lancashire, and Askey plays a train driver. it is quite refreshing for its time in that it uses a lot of railway filming in an area normally overlooked by film-makers. The opening scenes feature Askey and fireman Glenn Melvin (who wrote the story) racing their freight train home so they can make the match in time. This utilises a lot of 'phantom ride' shots, including entering a smoke-filled tunnel, passing a station and a signal box. The freight is made up of an ex-LMS 4F 0-6-0 with a rake of mixed wagons – a speeded-up shot repeated three times. The shed scenes were filmed at Newton Heath depot, Manchester, with a fine shot of 4F No 44543 on the turntable. Note the tool van No 395097 behind, and that Askey is adopting the wrong method of working the turntable – pulling the lever rather than pushing. Then Askey and Melvin board a motorbike and ride through the yard and shed – there are three 8F 2-8-0s in the yard in the background, one of which is No 48365, and a 'WD' 2-8-0 is visible inside the depot. When Askey and Melvin sneak into the back of the football ground via the railway line a 2P 4-4-0 passes on a passenger train in the background. The precise location of this scene is unknown.

Not all the film was shot in Lancashire, however, as in one scene – when Askey and Melvin go out to look at Shirley Eaton's boyfriend's van – a GWR signal box and signals can be seen in the background with an ex-GWR tender loco passing! Probably this was filmed somewhere in West London.

A couple more shed scenes feature later on. At their home shed No 44543 is visible once again, with a Stanier 2-6-4T and a 'WD' 2-8-0. At 'Milford Junction' (probably also filmed at Newton Heath) there is the back end of a 'Crab' 2-6-0 and a departmental coach visible.

The climax of the film is when Askey, desperate to get to a match on which he has bet money, ties an 'explosives' sheet over one of the wagons of his freight so as to get a clear run since signalmen will think his train is a dangerous runaway. No 44543 is again the loco, and there are a number of repeated passing shots on a line somewhere in Lancashire, with a shot of a 'Black Five' on a passenger entering a tunnel also included. This sequence does include a some stock shots – 'Jubilee' No 5553 doing its emergency stop from *I See Ice* and a 'Black Five' leaving Euston. The final shots of the 4F arriving behind the stand of the football stadium by a signal box were filmed at Burnden Park, then home of Bolton Wanderers FC.

Having been told by management that he will never drive a train again, Askey soon proves them wrong – in the final scene he grins at the audience while driving a miniature train. This is made up of a standard Bassett-Lowke steam loco with two open carriages and is believed to have been filmed in a public park in St Helens.

If all this sounds enjoyable, that's because it is! It's a funny film, with Askey in top form and some great railway scenes from the North of England in the mid-1950s. If it whets your appetite, there is collection of unused shots of the 4F, together with other locos, on Video 125's *Steam on 35mm* Vols 1 and 2.

LOVE ON THE DOLE
GB 1941 British National VHS
Dir: John Baxter
Deborah Kerr, Clifford Evans

Life among cotton-workers in a Lancashire mill town between the wars

Features some railway scenes filmed around Lancashire – LMS 'Compound' 4-4-0 No 1195 on a passenger train, Blackpool Central station, and some industrial scenes with a private 0-6-0ST.

LOVE ON WHEELS
GB 1932 Gainsborough VHS
Dir: Victor Saville
Jack Hulbert, Edmund Gwenn

A department store assistant tries to improve the company's publicity

A montage sequence near the start of the film includes a scene at Waterloo station with an SR 3-SUB EMU and a 0-4-4T near the camera. Also featured are some shots of London 'Metropolitan' trams.

THE LOVE RACE
GB 1931 BIP
Dir: Lupino Lane, Pat Morton
Stanley Lupino, Jack Hobbs

A car magnate's son wins the Schroeder Cup and his girl

Includes a scene filmed at Redbourn station on the Harpenden-Hemel Hempstead branch.

LOVE STORY
GB 1944 GFD VHS
Dir: Leslie Arliss
Margaret Lockwood, Stewart Granger

In Cornwall a half-blind airman falls for an ailing pianist

This famous wartime weepy uses a lot of Cornish locations, including the famous open-air theatre near Land's End. There is one railway shot – an overall view from the hillside of St Ives station with a '4500' 2-6-2T and train in the platform, but the 'departure' scene takes place in the studio.

THE LOVERS
GB 1972 British Lion
Dir: Herbert Wise
Richard Beckinsale, Paula Wilcox

Ups and downs in the relationship of a Manchester couple

One scene in the film is shot in the booking hall and concourse of Manchester Victoria station – no actual trains are seen.

THE LOVES OF JOANNA GODDEN
GB 1947 Ealing
Dir: Charles Frend
Googie Withers, John McCallum

On Romney Marsh a woman farmer has three men in her life

This Ealing drama was filmed mainly on location on Romney Marsh with a couple of shots of the New Romney branch line from Appledore. Interestingly a locomotive was borrowed from the Kent & East Sussex Railway for filming, 'A1X' 'Terrier' No 3, lettered 'SE&CR' (some coaches were also requested from the K&ESR but these proved unsuitable so a couple of ex-SECR coaches owned by the Southern were used). There are two shots – one of the train en route along the branch, and one of it arriving at Lydd Town (with a good view of No 3). Some of this material also appears in *Steam on 35mm* Vol 2.

LUCKY JIM
GB 1957 British Lion DVD
Dir: John Boulting
Ian Carmichael, Hugh Griffith

Mishaps of a lecturer at a provincial university

Carmichael races to a railway station at the climax of the film, believed to have been filmed at Cowley on the West Drayton-Uxbridge branch, with a '4500' 2-6-2T arriving. The departure shots, however, are at an unknown location.

THE LUCKY NUMBER
GB 1932 Gainsborough VHS
Dir: Anthony Asquith
Clifford Molleson, Gordon Harker

A man uses his lottery ticket to pay for drinks but then finds it's a winner

Features some LMS lineside scenes of trains hauled by a 'Royal Scot' 4-6-0 and a 'Compound' 4-4-0.

LUNCH HOUR
GB 1962 Eyeline
Dir: James Hill
Robert Stephens, Shirley Anne Field

An executive has an affair with a female colleague

Includes a brief shot on the London Underground with a District Line R stock train leaving a station on the Circle Line, possibly Paddington. Also features a scene with Shirley Anne Field on board a suburban DMU, probably on the Marylebone route – no exterior shots appear.

M

THE MACKINTOSH MAN
GB 1973 Warner VHS
Dir: John Huston
Paul Newman, James Mason

A government agent is sent to prison to contact a criminal gang

Features a scene on the Waterloo & City Line with a Class 487 unit, and a night stock shot of a green Class 127 DMU arriving at an unknown Midland Main Line station, destination Bedford.

MCVICAR
GB 1980 The Who Films DVD
Dir: Tom Clegg
Roger Daltrey, Adam Faith

The true story of escaped convict John McVicar

Includes a couple of railway shots during the scenes when McVicar is on the run. In a night shot he makes his way down a single track and narrowly avoids a Plasser track machine, location unknown. Later on he makes a den behind an advertising hoarding next to a railway bridge on the WR main line, with a Class 50 diesel passing with Mk 2 stock. Also includes a shot of the frontage of St Pancras station.

MAD ABOUT MEN
GB 1954 GFD
Dir: Ralph Thomas
Glynis Johns, Donald Sinden

Sequel to Miranda (qv), further adventures of the mermaid

Some good colour shots of Paddington feature near the start of the film as Glynis Johns begins her journey to Cornwall. The train starts out behind a 'King' 4-6-0, then changes to a Fairburn 2-6-4T as we see that the express has transformed into a local stopper entering Seer Green station. At least the final train shot is actually in Cornwall – a nice lineside view of a '4500' 2-6-2T with train on the Looe branch.

MAD COWS
GB 1999 Entertainment/Capitol DVD
Dir: Sara Sugarman
Anna Friel, Joanna Lumley

An Australian woman breaks out of jail to stop her baby being adopted

Features a scene on the Docklands Light Railway with one of its two-car units at 'Isle of Dogs' station.

MAD DOGS
GB 2002 Roaring Mice Films DVD
Dir: Ahmed A. Jamal
Paul Barber, Jonathan Pryce

A schizophrenic is haunted by beings telling him the world will end

The film includes many shots filmed on the London Underground mainly with 1990s tube stock but some 1972 examples. Station locations include Elephant and Castle, Embankment, Charing Cross, Leicester Square and the Waterloo & City Line platforms at Bank. There are also scenes on the concourse of Charing Cross Network Rail station and a ghostly scene at Aldwych.

MAD DOGS AND ENGLISHMEN
GB 1995 Entertainment/Movie Screen VHS
Dir: Henry Cole
Elizabeth Hurley, C. Thomas Howell

An aristocratic drug addict is pursued by a corrupt cop

Features a shot overlooking the LTS lines in East London with a pair of Class 312 EMUs passing, and a shot of the front of Sloane Square Underground station.

MADE
GB 1972 EMI VHS
Dir: John Mackenzie
Carol White, Roy Harper

A single mother has affairs with a priest and a rock star

Gritty drama that features a railway journey supposedly heading for Brighton but actually filmed on the WR. A rake of Mk 1s was used for filming, and although the motive power is not seen there is a very brief shot of a 'Western' Class 52 diesel heading past with an express in the opposite direction. The station the train passes through is believed to be Thatcham on the Berks & Hants line. There is also a scene filmed outside the front of Brighton station.

MADE IN HEAVEN
GB 1952 Rank
Dir: John Paddy Carstairs
David Tomlinson, Petula Clark

Married couples compete for the Dunmow Flitch

Features a scene at an unknown SR station with an SR 2-NOL EMU No 1854.

THE MAGIC CHRISTIAN
GB 1970 Commonwealth United DVD
Dir: Joseph McGrath
Peter Sellers, Ringo Starr

The richest man in the world shows how people will do anything for money

This surreal satire contains a good railway sequence filmed on the Twyford-Henley-on-Thames branch of the WR with a Class 47 diesel on a rake of Mk 1 coaches (aboard which Sellers has a boardroom in the film). There is a surreal sequence on board the train during which some stock shots of a 'Blue Pullman' are slotted in. The scene where Sellers buys a hotdog was filmed on Henley station and the station where he and Ringo Starr disembark is Wargrave, en route to Twyford.

THE MAGNET
GB 1950 Ealing DVD
Dir: Charles Frend
William Fox, Stephen Murray

A boy steals a magnet and unexpectedly becomes a hero

Shot on location in Liverpool, this film features some rare shots of the long-closed Liverpool Overhead Railway with some of the refurbished units. There is also a shot of a Liverpool tram.

THE MAGNIFICENT SEVEN DEADLY SINS
GB 1972 Tigon DVD
Dir: Graham Stark
Leslie Phillips, Bruce Forsyth

A collection of comedy sketches based on the seven deadly sins

Includes a sketch set on the London Underground, with a shot of 1960 tube stock arriving at a station, possibly Aldwych.

THE MAGNIFICENT TWO
GB 1967 Rank DVD
Dir: Cliff Owen
Eric Morecambe, Ernie Wise

A travelling salesman in Latin America is persuaded to pose as a rebel leader

The opening scenes depict Morecambe and Wise travelling on a Latin American train. Actually it's a thinly disguised 'WD' Hunslet 'Austerity' 0-6-0ST with dummy headlight and cow-catcher hauling 'birdcage' coaches on the Longmoor Military Railway. There's a clever attempt to superimpose a mountain backcloth in one distant shot of the train. The station where the comedians get off is Oakhanger on the northern section of the LMR.

MAHLER
GB 1974 Goodtimes Enterprises VHS
Dir: Ken Russell
Robert Powell, Georgina Hale

The life of composer Gustav Mahler

Most of the film is made up of flashbacks with a framing story of Mahler making a railway journey across Bavaria to Vienna. Most of these scenes were filmed on the Bluebell Railway and made use of Sheffield Park and Horsted Keynes stations with the railway's preserved BR Standard 4-6-0 No 75027 in evidence (hardly an Austrian loco from the 1920s!). Normal Bluebell services were operated over a couple of filming days and visitors must have been surprised to see Horsted Keynes masquerading as places such as 'Lambach' and 'Vocklabruck'. Even odder, the final scenes use Marylebone station with a rake of blue-liveried Class 115 DMUs in an adjacent platform.

MAN ABOUT THE HOUSE
GB 1974 EMI/Hammer DVD
Dir: John Robins
Richard O'Sullivan, Paula Wilcox

Tenants and their landlords join forces to prevent their terrace being redeveloped

The big-screen version of the successful TV series includes a shot outside Maida Vale Underground station (Bakerloo Line).

MAN AT THE TOP
GB 1973 Hammer VHS
Dir: Mike Vardy
Kenneth Haigh, Nanette Newman

An executive finds his firm is marketing an unsafe drug

In this further sequel to *Room at the Top* (qv) there is a sequence filmed from a car on the M1 motorway near Mill Hill and a pair of Class 25 diesels on a freight pass by on the adjacent Midland Main Line.

MAN DETAINED
GB 1961 Anglo-Amalgamated
Dir: Robert Tronson
Bernard Archard, Elvi Hale

The police track down a London crook

Lively Edgar Wallace mystery featuring a climax where the villain is pursued through a railway freight yard and is killed by a train. Filmed somewhere in South London on the Southern Region, the deadly locomotive appears to be a 'C' Class 0-6-0 and there are a lot of mineral, plank and covered wagons on display, as well as some Southern parcels vans. In an earlier scene in a garage scrapyard a GWR signal box can be seen on an embankment in the background, believed to be Chelsea & Fulham box on the West London line.

THE MAN FROM MOROCCO
GB 1944 ABP
Dir: Max Greene
Anton Walbrook, Margaretta Scott

Captured members of an international brigade are sent to work to build a Sahara railway for the Germans

The Sahara railway building scenes were filmed somewhere on the GWR with a disguised '5700' 0-6-0PT on what is supposed to be a construction train. The loco is numbered '906' and has the lettering 'ETAT' on its tank-sides for the film. Like *Undercover* (qv), there is some surprisingly involved location filming for a wartime production.

MAN FROM TANGIER
GB 1957 Butchers
Dir: Lance Comfort
Robert Hutton, Lisa Gastoni

A pilot becomes entangled with gangs looking for valuable plates

Features a scene on London Victoria station.

THE MAN IN THE MIRROR
GB 1936 JH Productions
Dir: Maurice Elvey
Edward Everett Horton, Alastair Sim

A timid man's reflection steps out of the mirror and helps him

Features a brief rare shot of an ex-LB&SCR 'B4' Class 4-4-0 on a passing express on the SR.

MAN IN THE MOON
GB 1961 Allied Film Makers
Dir: Basil Dearden
Kenneth More, Shirley Anne Field

An super-fit civilian is chosen as the first British astronaut

Features some good shots filmed at Denham station on the GW&GC Joint line with Fairburn 2-6-4Ts on local trains and ex-GWR 'Kings' on passing expresses.

THE MAN IN THE ROAD
GB 1957 Gibraltar
Dir: Lance Comfort
Derek Farr, Ella Raines

An amnesiac scientist is tricked by communists

Includes a good view of Seer Green station on the GW&GC Joint line with a Fairburn 2-6-4T on a local stopper and a GC-line express behind an 'A3' 4-6-2.

THE MAN IN THE WHITE SUIT
GB 1951 Ealing DVD
Dir: Alexander Mackendrick
Alec Guinness, Joan Greenwood

A scientist invents a suit that cannot be destroyed or get dirty

This classic Ealing comedy features a railway scene during the chase sequence near the end. Guinness attempts to buy a ticket at a station and heads over the footbridge when his pursuers arrive. This was filmed at Brimsdown station in the Lea Valley with an ex-LNER 'B1' 4-6-0 in the platform. The opening scene shows a panoramic view of a factory with railway yards and no fewer than five industrial 0-4-0STs visible.

THE MAN WHO CHANGED HIS MIND
GB 1936 Gainsborough
Dir: Robert Stevenson
Boris Karloff, Anna Lee

A scientist experiments with brain transplants

This early horror film features a night shot of an express hauled by an ex-GCR passenger loco, with top-feed apparatus.

THE MAN WHO NEVER WAS
GB 1956 Sumar
Dir: Ronald Neame
Clifton Webb, Stephen Boyd

In 1943 the British secret service fool the Germans by using a dead man with false documents

Includes a scene at Paddington station, but with no locos visible.

THE MAN WHO WOULDN'T TALK
GB 1957 British Lion
Dir: Herbert Wilcox
Anthony Quayle, Anna Neagle

A QC has to defend a man on a murder charge who cannot reveal top secret information

Features a scene involving a secret meeting on the Circle/District Line platforms of Victoria Underground station with some good shots of District Line R stock trains.

MANDY
GB 1952 Ealing VHS
Dir: Alexander Mackendrick
Mandy Miller, Jack Hawkins

A deaf and mute girl is sent to a special school

This famous post-war Ealing drama includes a shot of Euston station as well as stock footage of an express hauled by a 'Royal Scot' 4-6-0 from *Brief Encounter* (qv), part of the Watford Junction footage.

MANTRAP
GB 1953 Exclusive/Hammer
Dir: Terence Fisher
Paul Henreid, Kieron Moore

A doctor tries to help a man wrongly accused of murder

Features a chase scene through a goods yard with some open plank wagons, and a scene outside St Johns Wood Underground station.

MARTHA MEET FRANK, DANIEL & LAURENCE
GB 1998 FilmFour DVD
Dir: Nick Hamm
Monica Potter, Rufus Sewell

Three men fall for the same American woman

Filmed using London locations, there are a couple of railway shots: one of a pair of Docklands Light Railway units crossing a bridge, and a very distant shot of a Freightliner crossing the Thames near Chelsea hauled by a Class 47.

THE MATCH
GB/US/Ireland 1999 Polygram/
   Propaganda/Irish Dreamtime DVD
Dir: Mick Davis
Max Beesley, Isla Blair

Two pub football teams meet for their 100th match with the losers agreeing to close their business

Features a shot of a GNER-liveried HST arriving at a station, possibly Berwick-upon-Tweed.

MAURICE
GB 1987 Cinecom/Merchant Ivory DVD
Dir: James Ivory
James Wilby, Hugh Grant

The life of a Cambridge homosexual

Features a shot filmed on Horsted Keynes station, Bluebell Railway, although no locos are seen.

MEETINGS WITH REMARKABLE MEN
GB 1979 Enterprise/Remar VHS
Dir: Peter Brook
Dragan Maksimovic, Colin Blakely

The life of Asian mystic G. I. Gurdjieff

Includes a scene set in a railway works. This was filmed at Didcot Railway Centre with actors and some GWS members working on the frames of 'Castle' 4-6-0 No 5051.

MELBA
GB 1953 Horizon
Dir: Lewis Milestone
Patrice Munsel, Robert Morley

The life of the Victorian opera singer

Includes a scene filmed on the Longmoor Military Railway.

MELODY
GB 1971 British Lion VHS
Dir: Waris Hussein
Mark Lester, Jack Wild

An 11-year-old boy falls in love with a girl

There are a few railway shots throughout this film. When the characters go to the seaside there are a few good shots of a Class 33/1 diesel arriving at Weymouth Town station with a 4-TC set. Most of the film is set in South London with the viaduct section around Nine Elms/Clapham Junction being prominent – in one scene a 4-SUB EMU is passing. The two main characters make their escape at the end of the film on a hand-pump trolley, mostly shot in the abandoned sidings around Nine Elms although the location of the final aerial shot of the trolley heading along a rural single-track branch line is unknown.

METROLAND
GB/Germany 1997 Pandora/BBC VHS
Dir: Philip Saville
Christian Bale, Emily Watson

When his friend returns from Paris, an advertising executive questions his life

As its title suggests this film has the Metropolitan Railway very much as a backcloth to the action, despite part of it being set in Paris. Amersham station was used for some scenes, particularly a flashback sequence set in the 1960s for which vintage Metropolitan electric locomotive No 12 *Sarah Siddons* was used, as well as run-by shots. For contemporary scenes the film-makers used 'C'-type and 'A60' stock for lineside scenes on the Metropolitan Line. An interesting moment in the story involves Bale meeting a retired commuter who, during their conversation, gives a potted history of the Metropolitan & Great Central Railway, a very accurate one considering that this is a feature film not a documentary.

MICHAEL COLLINS
US 1996 Warner DVD
Dir: Neil Jordan
Liam Neeson, Aidan Quinn

The life of Irish republican leader Michael Collins

This biopic features a number of shots of preserved CIE 'K' Class 2-6-0 No 461 and train. Locations include Dublin Pearse

station (with coaches painted in period livery on one side only for filming) and Wicklow.

MILLIONS
GB 2005 Pathé/BBC DVD
Dir: Danny Boyle
Alex Etel, James Nesbitt

Two young boys find a mailbag full of money

The two lads live with their family close to a railway line (they later learn that the mailbag had been thrown off a passing mail train while a robbery was taking place), and there are a number of time-lapsed abstract shots of passing traffic on the West Coast Main Line, including Class 90 and 87 electrics, an HST and a 'Pendolino'. The mail train sequence features a rake of GUV parcels vans top-and-tailed by Class 37 diesels Nos 37 669 and 37 695 filmed at Liverpool Lime Street station and the East Lancashire Railway.

MILLIONS LIKE US
GB 1943 GFD DVD
Dirs: Frank Launder, Sidney Gilliat
Patricia Roc, Gordon Jackson

Experiences of a family in wartime

This classic wartime propaganda piece contains a number of railway shots throughout the story. There are two LMS shots – a 'Royal Scot' 4-6-0 is seen arriving at an unknown station with an express and a real shot of wartime workers making their way along the platform of what is believed to be Cold Meece station, with Fowler 2-6-4T No 2309 reversing. Also included are shots of a passing LNER 'B17' 4-6-0 with an express and an SR 2-6-0, with scenes at Waterloo station.

THE MIND BENDERS
GB 1963 Anglo-Amalgamated VHS
Dir: Basil Dearden
Dirk Bogarde, Mary Ure

A scientist undergoes sensory deprivation experiments that work too well

The beginning of the film features some shots filmed on Paddington station with a 'Castle' 4-6-0 leaving on an express. This is followed by a scene where a scientist throws himself out of the train. This involves some excellent night photography of 'Castle' No 5056 making an emergency break application at an unknown location. The train's journey in the film also uses some stock footage from *Brief Encounter* (qv) with 'Royal Scot' 4-6-0s.

THE MIND OF MR SOAMES
GB 1970 Columbia
Dir: Alan Cooke
Terence Stamp, Robert Vaughn

A man who has been in a coma for 30 years is revived

Features some lineside and on-board scenes with WR London area Class 117 DMUs (including one of Stamp jumping from the train). One scene was filmed on Bourne End station.

THE MINIVER STORY
GB 1950 MGM
Dir: H. C. Potter
Greer Garson, Walter Pidgeon

The sequel to Mrs Miniver (qv), now in post-war Britain

Features some shots of Waterloo station with SR 3-SUB EMUs. When Garson makes a studio-set railway journey, the back projection through the 'window' depicts scenes on the Euston-Watford section of the WCML, and a rake of 1924-built tube stock passes at one point. There are also scenes on the WR's Marlow branch.

MIRANDA
GB 1947 GFD
Dir: Ken Annakin
Glynis Johns, Griffith Jones

A doctor on holiday in Cornwall catches a mermaid

Includes a rare shot of a GWR '5400' 0-6-0PT with auto-coach calling at Golant station on the Lostwithiel-Fowey branch. A GWR 4-6-0 also features as Johns and Jones make their way to London, as well as some Paddington scenes. Extra unused Paddington and Fowey branch footage appears in Video 125's *Steam on 35mm Vol 3*.

MISS POTTER
US/GB 2007 Phoenix DVD
Dir: Chris Noonan
Renee Zellweger, Ewan McGregor

The life of Beatrix Potter

There is one scene filmed at Horsted Keynes station on the Bluebell Railway with a train departing hauled by SR 'U' Class 2-6-0 No 1638 with 'Northern' lettering on its tender.

MRS BROWN YOU'VE GOT A LOVELY DAUGHTER
GB 1968 MGM
Dir: Saul Swimmer
Herman's Hermits, Stanley Holloway

A pop group train a pet greyhound

Herman's Hermits take a train journey to London from Manchester midway through the film. There are some platform scenes on what is believed to be Manchester Piccadilly, with maroon and blue/grey-liveried Mk 1 coaches on view. The train's journey to London is depicted by an 'over the camera' shot of a Class 86 electric (possibly stock footage from British Transport Films). Later there are scenes at St Pancras and King's Cross stations, with a departing train of maroon Mk 1s – we don't see the loco but a view of the stabling point in the background reveals green Class 31s and a Class 47.

MRS MINIVER
US 1942 MGM DVD
Dir: William Wyler
Greer Garson, Walter Pidgeon

An English housewife's experiences during the Second World War

In this Hollywood depiction of the 'home front' in wartime Britain, amid all the studio sets there is one genuine shot of a British train – footage of a GWR large 2-6-2T arriving with a local passenger at an unknown station. See also *The Miniver Story*.

MISSION: IMPOSSIBLE
US 1996 Paramount DVD
Dir: Brian de Palma
Tom Cruise, Jon Voight

A secret agent is determined to find the killer of his colleagues

In this successful Hollywood blockbuster adaptation of the 1960s TV series, most of the filming was done in Britain and Europe. First there are some scenes filmed on Liverpool Street station with some Inter-City-liveried Mk 2s and an NSE EMU visible in the background. The main action occurs in the final half-hour where Cruise has to foil an attack on a French TGV heading for the Channel Tunnel. Viewers might notice something very strange about the TGV in that it is speeding along without any overhead wires or third rail! The real story is a fascinating one and illustrates just how movie-making techniques have progressed since the silent days. A pair of Class 33/1 diesels with rakes of 4-TC coaches were filmed on sections of the ex-GSWR Glasgow-Carlisle via Dumfries route from a helicopter, then a computerised image of a TGV was placed over it in production. A giveaway to the location is that at one point the train passes over Ballochmyle Viaduct. The 33s were also used for some 'phantom ride' shots with strategically placed cameras.

MR LOVE
GB 1986 Warner/Goldcrest VHS
Dir: Roy Battersby
Barry Jackson, Maurice Denham

A cinema projectionist develops a reputation as a ladies' man

Features a scene on the Southport miniature railway with a 'Western'-type loco and open-top coaches.

MR REEDER IN ROOM 13
GB 1938 British National
Dir: Norman Lee
Peter Murray-Hill, Sally Gray

Mr Reeder tracks down a master criminal

Features a night scene of an express on the Midland Main Line double-headed by an LMS 'Compound' 4-4-0 and a 'Jubilee' 4-6-0.

MONA LISA
GB 1986 HandMade DVD
Dir: Neil Jordan
Bob Hoskins, Cathy Tyson

An ex-con becomes chauffeur to a prostitute

Features a scene near the West London line's Chelsea Bridge over the Thames with a Class 119 DMU passing in the background.

A MONTH IN THE COUNTRY
GB 1987 Euston Films VHS
Dir: Pat O'Connor
Colin Firth, Kenneth Branagh

Two men recover from the First World War in rural England

The film is set in Yorkshire after the First World War and aptly makes use of the North Yorkshire Moors Railway for various scenes. Less aptly the motive power comprises preserved GWR '5600' Class 0-6-2T No 6619 (a type never seen in the area) in BR black livery and smokebox numberplate (ie 1950s guise) and LNER 'K1' Class 2-6-0 No 2005 (a type that didn't appear until the 1940s).

Some of the filming occurred at Levisham and Newtondale Halt.

MORGAN – A SUITABLE CASE FOR TREATMENT
GB 1966 British Lion DVD
Dir: Karel Reisz
David Warner, Vanessa Redgrave

A half-mad artist drives his wife to distraction

Includes some fantasy scenes filmed in the goods yards around Battersea – a number of BR mineral wagons can be seen, and in the background of a couple of shots there is a Class 08 diesel shunter.

THE MOTHER
GB 2003 BBC/Renaissance DVD
Dir: Roger Michell
Anne Reid, Daniel Craig

When widowed an older woman begins a relationship with a young builder

Features some scenes filmed inside Mk 2 air-conditioned coaches on the WCML and at London Euston station. Class 321 and Class 455 EMUs appear as well as LT Hammersmith & City Line C Underground stock with filming at Goldhawk Road station.

MURDER SHE SAID
GB 1961 MGM DVD
Dir: George Pollock
Margaret Rutherford, Charles Tingwell

Miss Marple investigates after seeing a murder from a train

The first of a series of films featuring Rutherford as Agatha Christie's sleuth made by MGM in the early 1960s, this is an adaptation of *4.50 from Paddington* and naturally contains a lot of railway scenes – a mixture of contemporary filming and stock footage. The opening scenes were filmed at Paddington with a general scene of the platforms from the footbridge and a '9400' 0-6-0PT and

large 2-6-2T visible. Then there is a close-up of a '9400' at the buffer stops before Rutherford gets on the train. There then follow a number of stock shots originally taken for 1948's *Train of Events* (qv):
- an LMS 'Jubilee' leaves Euston – a low-angle shot of engine and coach bogies
- an LMS 'Jubilee' leaves Euston – medium shot
- an LMS 'Jubilee' leaves Euston – medium shot, passing under a bridge
- another 'Jubilee' – medium shot – passes with a train on Bushey troughs
- a 1960s WCML shot – a BR Standard 2-6-4T on a passenger being overtaken by an LMS 4-6-0 behind; the overtaking train is depicted by a mixture of studio filming and back projection footage screened through Rutherford's carriage window. The loco is an unknown GWR type.
- one shot of a 'Black Five' on an express on the WCML – medium shot

Other railway shots appear throughout the film, filmed on the WR near Taplow:
- a 'King' (?) 4-6-0 passing while Rutherford searches the line for clues
- two pairs of three-car DMUs and a 'Castle' 4-6-0 passing over a bridge as she arrives at the hall
- a 'King' 4-6-0 in long shot passes as Rutherford pretends to play golf near a railway embankment
- NB D600-type 'Warship' diesel No D603 passes on an express – medium shot. This is the best shot of a train in the film and so far the only known appearance of one of these short-lived diesels in a feature film
- final scene – 'King' 4-6-0 passing with express

MY BEAUTIFUL LAUNDRETTE
GB 1985 Channel 4/Working Title VHS
Dir: Stephen Frears
Daniel Day Lewis, Saeed Jaffrey

A young Asian forms a relationship with a white racist in London

Features some shots of SR EMUs at Queenstown Road Battersea station in South London – Class 455 units and slam-door express sets.

MY BROTHER JONATHAN
GB 1947 ABP
Dir: Harold French
Michael Denison, Dulcie Gray

The life of a small-town doctor

Includes a scene filmed at Aston Rowant station on the Watlington branch from Princes Risborough.

MY BROTHER'S KEEPER
GB 1948 GFD
Dirs: Alfred Roome, Roy Rich
Jack Warner, George Cole

Two convicts escape handcuffed together, but one is innocent

Features some good action scenes filmed on the Watlington branch and at Aston Rowant station with some GWR '5700' Class 0-6-0PTs (including a '36XX' example).

MY SUMMER OF LOVE
GB 2004 BBC Films/Apocalypso
  Pictures DVD
Dir: Pawel Pawlikowski
Nathalie Press, Emily Blunt

Two lonely young girls have a relationship in a Northern town

Filmed in and around Todmorden in Yorkshire, a couple of 'Trans-Pennine' Class 158 'Sprinters' appear in shot, one two-car, the other a three-car set.

N

THE NAKED RUNNER
GB 1967 Warner VHS
Dir: Sidney J. Furie
Frank Sinatra, Peter Vaughan

A businessman is unwittingly influenced to become a spy killer

The background story to this spy thriller features a defecting spy making his way to Russia across Europe, although the rail travel is clearly filmed in Britain. A railway journey from France to Frankfurt uses a mix of scenes filmed on the Bluebell Railway (with one of the 'A1X' 'Terriers' and ex-GWR 'Dukedog' 4-4-0 No 3217) and on the Southern Region of BR, including a shot of a train hauled by one of the Bulleid 'Pacifics' in their last year of service.

NEAREST AND DEAREST
GB 1972 EMI/Hammer DVD
Dir: John Robins
Jimmy Jewel, Hylda Baker

Film spin-off of the television sitcom about brother and sister pickle-factory owners

A lot of the film is set in Blackpool and there are a few tram shots – one each of a Boat type, double-deck Balloon and a Brush single car.

NEARLY A NASTY ACCIDENT
GB 1961 British Lion
Dir: Don Chaffey
Kenneth Connor, Jimmy Edwards

Adventures of an accident-prone aircraftman

Features a railway journey sequence filmed on the Marlow branch where Connor attempts to fix the train's faulty steam heat supply and succeeds in flooding the carriages in steam! Marlow station appears in the early shots, although the locomotive is not visible. There is one stock shot of a 'Castle'-hauled express on the WR main line and a scene of the train arriving at Gerrards Cross station on the GW&GC Joint line.

NEVER LET GO
GB 1960 Rank DVD
Dir: John Guillermin
Richard Todd, Peter Sellers

A travelling salesman seeks his stolen car and the gangland boss responsible

Features a shot of a transfer freight heading along the West London line behind an ex-SR 'W' Class 2-6-4T and one of an Oerlikon EMU passing on a viaduct above a garage on the North London line.

NEVER LOOK BACK
GB 1952 Exclusive/Hammer
Dir: Francis Searle
Rosamund John, Guy Middleton

A lady barrister defends an old flame on a murder charge

Near the end of the film there are some

scenes on London Victoria station – frontage and concourse.

THE NEXT OF KIN
GB 1942 Ealing DVD
Dir: Thorold Dickinson
Mervyn Johns, Nova Pilbeam

A commando raid is jeopardised by careless talk

Features a number of railway journey sequences, virtually all filmed in the studio, but there is one stock shot of a 'Royal Scot' 4-6-0 on an express in the Lune Gorge.

A NICE GIRL LIKE ME
GB 1969 Anglo Embassy/Partisan
Dir: Desmond Davis
Barbara Ferris, Harry Andrews

A young girl sets off to see the world but keeps getting pregnant

Includes scenes filmed at St Pancras station with a Class 45 and Mk 1 coaches visible. Later in the film there is a scene at Bourne End station with Ferris on a departing Class 117 DMU.

NIGHT AND THE CITY
GB 1950 TCF
Dir: Jules Dassin
Richard Widmark, Gene Tierney

A crooked promoter is pursued by an underworld gang

Features some night shots of London trams.

NIGHT BOAT TO DUBLIN
GB 1946 ABP
Dir: Lawrence Huntington
Robert Newton, Muriel Pavlow

British Intelligence tracks down a missing German scientist

The Euston station scenes are studio sets but there are real shots of Waterloo station with a departing SR train and an 0-4-4T, partially obscured by crowds on the platform.

NIGHT OF THE DEMON
GB 1957 Columbia DVD
Dir: Jacques Tourneur
Dana Andrews, Peggy Cummins

A reporter finds himself cursed by an occultist who can summon a demon

Classic early horror film famous for its final sequence aboard an express train when the occultist, having had the curse thrown back at him, leaps from the train and is attacked by the demon before another express runs him down. These scenes were filmed on the Watford-St Albans Abbey branch, particularly around Brickett Wood station, although it is believed that Watford Junction station was also used. The giveaway is when Dana Andrews races into the station to catch the Southampton train (!) and there is a timetable behind giving details of stopping trains to St Albans. A couple of 'Black Five' 4-6-0s were used and there are some excellent shots of these in the final moments.

A NIGHT TO REMEMBER
GB 1958 Rank DVD
Dir: Roy Baker
Kenneth More, Honor Blackman

The story of the sinking of the Titanic

Near the start of the film a train journey from Liverpool to Southampton is quite accurately depicted by a vintage stock shot of an LNWR train hauled by a 3P 4-4-0 on the West Coast Main Line. The shot also appears in *Trains from the Arc* Vol 2 'The Edwardian Years' from Video 125.

NIGHT TRAIN
GB 1999 Alternative/Subotica DVD
Dir: John Lynch
John Hurt, Brenda Blethyn

An ex-convict forms a relationship with a lonely woman at a Dublin boarding house

Part of the plot involves Hurt building a

giant model railway layout in his room, depicting the route of the 'Orient Express' – this uses European loco models and rolling-stock. Earlier in the film there are scenes on board CIE 'Dart' EMUs and there is a shot of a 'Dart' unit crossing a bridge just outside Dublin Connolly station, together with a shot on Connolly itself. Later there are scenes on the 'Orient Express' filmed on Italian State Railways.

NIGHT TRAIN FOR INVERNESS
GB 1959 Danziger
Dir: Ernest Morris
Jane Hylton, Dennis Waterman

An estranged husband kidnaps his son and heads for Scotland, but the boy is diabetic

This neglected B-movie from the 1950s contains a number of railway shots. There are good scenes of Euston station before modernisation with shots of the frontage and the platforms. Many of the express train shots seem to have been filmed on the WCML and the Midland Main Line. Locomotives featured (in order of appearance) are a 'Black Five', 'V2' 2-6-2 No 60890, two shots of 'Royal Scot' 4-6-0s, 'Black Five', 'Black Five' No 45003 arriving at an unknown station, and another 'Black Five' on a parcels train.

NIGHT TRAIN TO PARIS
GB 1964 Lippert
Dir: Robert Douglas
Leslie Nielsen, Alizia Gur

A secret agent has to prevent a vital tape falling into the hands of the enemy

Features good scenes on Victoria station of the 'Night Ferry' Wagon-Lit stock (coach No 3792 is prominent), although sadly not the motive power. There is a stock shot of a passing train behind a rebuilt 'Royal Scot' 4-6-0 and a close-up of the cab of an LNER loco, again from stock material.

THE NIGHT WE GOT THE BIRD
GB 1960 British Lion
Dir: Darcy Conyers
Brian Rix, Ronald Shiner

A husband believes a talking parrot is a reincarnation of his predecessor

Features a scene where Rix pursues the parrot to a railway station where it boards a leaving train. Despite the name ('Brighton North') the station is actually Chessington North and the train is made up of a formation of SR pre-war EMUs.

NIGHTMARE
GB 1964 U-I/Hammer
Dir: Freddie Francis
Moira Redmond, David Knight

A traumatised young girl returns home but witnesses frightening visions

This Hammer horror film features a scene at Wargrave station on the Twyford-Henley-on-Thames branch.

NIL BY MOUTH
GB 1997 TCF DVD
Dir: Gary Oldman
Ray Winstone, Kathy Burke

A violent alcoholic terrorises his family in South London

This bleak 'kitchen-sink' drama features a scene on board 1960 Bakerloo Line stock and at Elephant & Castle Underground station.

1984
GB 1984 Umbrella/Rosenblum/Virgin VHS
Dir: Michael Radford
John Hurt, Richard Burton

Adaptation of George Orwell's novel about a fascist dehumanised future

Features a scene filmed on the Kent & East Sussex Railway with preserved 'USA' 0-6-0T No 22 and suitably bleak-looking coaching stock including a Pullman car. The locomotive is weathered in a dull grey livery with state plaques on the smokebox and tank sides. Filming took place in April 1984.

NO BLADE OF GRASS
GB 1970 MGM
Dir: Cornel Wilde
Nigel Davenport, Jean Wallace

Industrial pollution destroys the crops of the world and a family flees anarchy in the city

An ambush scene takes place at a level crossing and signal box, filmed at Park South box between Barrow-in-Furness and Dalton in Cumbria. Later in the film there is a scene filmed below Ribblehead Viaduct on the Settle & Carlisle line.

NO LIMIT
GB 1935 ATP VHS
Dir: Monty Banks
George Formby, Florence Desmond

A motor mechanic enters the TT Races

Most of the film was shot on the Isle of Man and in a couple of scenes there are Douglas horse-drawn trams.

NO LOVE FOR JOHNNIE
GB 1960 Rank
Dir: Ralph Thomas
Peter Finch, Mary Peach

A Labour MP faces political and personal problems

Features scenes filmed at Euston station with shots of trains hauled by 'Royal Scot' 4-6-0 No 46126 and a 'Black Five'. There is also a shot of a Northern railway station, believed to be Halifax.

NO MY DARLING DAUGHTER
GB 1961 Rank
Dir: Ralph Thomas
Michael Redgrave, Juliet Mills

A tycoon's daughter is believed to be eloping with an American

Features a scene filmed at Marylebone station with ex-LMS coaches visible but no locomotive.

NO PLACE FOR JENNIFER
GB 1949 ABPC
Dir: J. Lee Thompson
Leo Genn, Janette Scott

Divorcing parents cause their daughter to run away

Includes a couple of shots of passing LMR expresses, hauled by 'Black Five' and 'Jubilee' 4-6-0s respectively.

NO SMOKING
GB 1955 Tempean
Dir: Henry Cass
Reg Dixon, Belinda Lee

A village chemist invents an anti-smoking pill

This includes a scene in which Belinda Lee gets off a train at the village station, closely followed by male admirers. This was filmed at Denham station with an 'L1' 2-6-4T on suburban stock.

NO TRACE
GB 1950 Eros
Dir: John Gilling
Hugh Sinclair, Dinah Sheridan

A crime writer helps police to investigate a murder he has committed

Includes a scene where a couple of characters race to a railway station in a car. This involves a shot taken from the footbridge at Taplow station of the car heading for the station entrance, and what looks like a '4300' 2-6-0 approaching with a train in the background.

NORTH SEA HIJACK
GB 1979 Universal VHS
Dir: Andrew V. McLaglen
Roger Moore, Anthony Perkins

Terrorists take over a British oil rig and hold it for ransom

Features a shot of a Class 117 DMU arriving at an unknown WR station in the Home Counties.

NOTHING BUT THE BEST
GB 1964 Anglo-Amalgamated VHS
Dir: Clive Donner
Alan Bates, Denholm Elliott

An ambitious clerk fights his way to the top despite the class barrier

Features a number of shots around London main-line station entrances, namely Paddington, Waterloo and Marylebone, but no shots of any trains themselves.

NOWHERE TO GO
GB 1958 Ealing
Dir: Seth Holt
George Nader, Maggie Smith

A thief escapes from prison but gets no help from the underworld

The opening scenes were filmed at the old LMR platforms of Kew Bridge station on the Kew Bridge-Willesden Junction line, with a freight train hauled by an Ivatt 4MT 2-6-0 No 43019. Later there are scenes filmed at Marylebone with a 'K2' 2-6-0 visible on a GC-line service.

NUMBER ONE
GB 1984 Videoform VHS
Dir: Les Blair
Bob Geldof, Mel Smith

The life of a snooker hall hustler

In one scene the action is close to a Southern Region railway line and an SR slam-door express EMU passes by in the background, somewhere in South London.

NUMBER SEVENTEEN
GB 1932 BIP DVD
Dir: Alfred Hitchcock
Leon M. Lion, Anne Grey

A jewel thief reforms and helps police track down her gang

This early Hitchcock film starts slowly but features an excellent railway chase sequence in the latter half. Hitchcock

himself said in a later interview that it was the railway scenes that he really got his teeth into. In the story, the jewel thieves board a night ferry goods bound for Harwich with the intention of getting across to the Continent. The initial scenes feature some good floodlit shots of King's Cross yard, close to Copenhagen Tunnels, with Gresley 'A1' 'Pacific' No 2547 *Doncaster* on a freight and a 'J52' 0-6-0T in the background. We stay with No 2547 for most of the chase sequence with the hero in hot pursuit on a Green Line bus! This was filmed at night on the Hertford loop with plenty of action involving actors jumping from wagon to wagon, filmed from an adjacent train fitted with great banks of lights to illuminate the entire scene, as well as good shots of No 2547 itself. Eventually the crooks get to the engine cab, dispose of the crew and take over the train itself to gain time. This ends disastrously as they lose control and end up smashing into the ferry. This involved building a massive O-gauge model of the train, ferry and terminal at the Shepherds Bush studios, and using Bassett-Lowke and Bond equipment, resulting in one of most spectacular crash scenes for a film of its time. The train speeds onto the ferry and smashes into wagons already stabled there, causing wagons to go everywhere and resulting in the ferry breaking its moorings and beginning to sink, dropping some wagons into the sea. Although it looks a bit basic now, it does not distract from the excitement of the last half-hour of this rather neglected film.

NUNS ON THE RUN
GB 1990 Palace/HandMade VHS
Dir: Jonathan Lynn
Eric Idle, Robbie Coltrane

Two criminals hide as nuns to avoid capture

This successful British comedy features a scene with a passing London Underground train made up of 1960 tube stock.

O LUCKY MAN!

GB 1973 Warner VHS
Dir: Lindsay Anderson
Malcolm McDowell, Ralph Richardson

The surreal life and adventures of a trainee salesman

Features a shot of the approaches to Paddington around the Royal Oak area with LT Metropolitan 'C'-type stock and some scenes near the Borough Market area in South London with SR suburban EMUs.

THE OCTOBER MAN

GB 1947 GFD VHS
Dir: Roy Baker
John Mills, Joan Greenwood

A man recovering from a traumatic accident is suspected of murder

This post-war drama features a number of railway scenes – however, the scene where Mills is chased at a railway station is shot in a studio and the final scene of Mills contemplating suicide on a railway bridge is a combination of studio and model reconstruction. There is a real shot of the platforms of Paddington station, however, and a shot of an LMS 'Compound' 4-4-0 on an express on the Midland Main Line in the Elstree area – this view also appears in Video 125's *Steam on 35mm* Vol 3.

OCTOPUSSY

GB 1983 Eon/Danjaq DVD
Dir: John Glen
Roger Moore, Maud Adams

James Bond pursues an Afghan prince who plans to steal Tsarist treasure

This typically action-packed James Bond film has a good railway sequence as its climax, with 007 getting on board an East German circus train, which is actually a cover for the bad guys. The sequence was filmed in Britain on the Nene Valley Railway – an intensive operation that took place over a number of weeks during September/October 1982. DSB 2-6-4T No 740 was used as the train engine, numbered DR 62.015, with a number of Continental carriages and five ex-LMS CCT vans, painted pink and with circus 'embellishments'. The scenes where these are being marshalled into the train were filmed at Wansford station (renamed 'Karl-Marx-Stadt') and in Wansford Tunnel, and used RSH 0-6-0 diesel shunter *Horsa*. Ferry Meadows station was renamed 'Gutenfurst' and appeared as the East German border post.

One of the most spectacular scenes involves a specially adapted Mercedes car running along a line adjacent to the circus train, then being hit by a passenger train travelling in the opposite direction. The passenger train was hauled by 4-6-0 No 1697 disguised as DR 38.243, and the collision effect was caused by the Mercedes being catapulted away by a specially built 'air-gun' launch close to the line just outside Wansford. This take had to be filmed a number of times and was a bit close for comfort – on at least one take the car's front end found itself wrapped around the loco's chimney. As well as No 740 and No 1697, Swedish 2-6-2T No 1178 was also used for filming.

ODD MAN OUT
GB 1946 GFD DVD
Dir: Carol Reed
James Mason, Robert Newton

The final days of a wounded IRA man in Belfast

Filmed mainly on location on the streets of Belfast, there are good views of Belfast tram No 179 during a riot scene outside a pub, together with a couple more in the background in other scenes.

OF HUMAN BONDAGE
GB 1964 MGM
Dir: Henry Hathaway, Ken Hughes
Laurence Harvey, Kim Novak

A doctor is brought low due to his relationship with a waitress

This version of the classic novel was filmed in Ireland and features some scenes of trains hauled by CIE steam in its final years. Ex-GSR 'J15' 0-6-0s dominate, with some nice shots in Dublin Connolly station, and class member No 187 identifiable. Another 'J15'-hauled train appears near the end of the film, passing by on an embankment during the funeral scene.

THE OFFENCE
GB 1972 United Artists VHS
Dir: Sidney Lumet
Sean Connery, Trevor Howard

A tough police inspector loses control with a child murder suspect

Filmed around South London, with some shots around the Nine Elms/Clapham area, this drama features some Southern Region EMUs – a 4-SUB, 4-EPB and a South Western Division semi-fast slam-door set.

OH DADDY!
GB 1935 Gaumont-British
Dirs: Graham Cutts, Austin Melford
Leslie Henson, Frances Day

Members of the League of Purity are changed by a trip to London

The trip to London involves shots of King's Cross and Waterloo stations and a number of steam locos are visible – an LNER 'A3' 'Pacific', 'K2' 2-6-0 No 4664, SR 'N15' 'King Arthur' 4-6-0 No 780 (with another 'N15' in the background), and 'A3' 'Pacific' No 4472 *Flying Scotsman*.

OH MR PORTER
GB 1937 GFD/Gainsborough DVD
Dir: Marcel Varnel
Will Hay, Moore Marriott

A station master at an Irish halt catches gun-runners

Together with *The Titfield Thunderbolt*, this timeless classic has become everyone's favourite railway film, with many film historians regarding it as the best of all the Will Hay comedies. However, while 'Titfield' represents the Ealing tradition of gentle, nostalgic comedy with rural England cast in a warm summer glow, *Oh Mr Porter* is closer to music-hall knockabout humour. In 'Titfield', when the train is destroyed by being sent down an embankment it is seen as a tragedy. In 'Porter' wagons are sent crashing into quarries, coaches are destroyed by passing expresses and even the star engine, *Gladstone*, ends up exploding. Genteel comedy this ain't!

The facts surrounding the making of the film have become well-known. Most of the film was shot on the recently abandoned Basingstoke & Alton Light Railway; Gainsborough had made *The Wrecker* there eight years previously and it seems likely that when 'Porter' was announced someone at the studio remembered the B&ALR. Cliddesden station became the centre-point as 'Buggleskelly', with demolition work taking place just out of shot behind the cameras and a wooden building encasing the original corrugated iron one. Filming taking place over a hot summer, and it looks it. Star of the film is *Gladstone*, actually Kent & East Sussex Railway 2-4-0T No 2 *Northiam*, which was modified with a tall chimney and part of its cab cut away to allow better filming of the actors. Two Southern locomotives appear as express engines – the engine of the train that Will Hay halts at the station on his first day as station master is Adams '0395' Class 0-6-0 No 3509, and the express that is let through after the 'special' has gone is hauled by Adams 'X2' 4-4-0 No 657; both have 'Southern Railway of Northern Ireland' on their sides. The escape scene with the gun-runners on board uses shots filmed on the B&ALR and on the LSWR main line – a 'Lord Nelson' 4-6-0 is glimpsed, and there is a run through an engine yard with another Adams 4-4-0 prominent (this run-through appears twice in these scenes, but shot from different angles). The final crash uses the milk dock in the yard at Basingstoke.

There are some other points of interest from the film:

- It's not all on the Southern: the first scene has Hay wheel-tapping and there is a very good shot of LNER 'A4' 4-6-2 No 2509 *Silver Link* in the platform of an LNER suburban station. The 'A4s' were very new at this time and obviously someone thought their appearance in a film was good publicity.

- The opening title sequence uses reversed 'phantom ride' shots taken a train on the Southern, thought to be around the Southampton area.

- The tunnel on the 'loop line' was created by the film-makers in a cutting on the B&ALR. In one take the crew of *Northiam* were unable to stop in time and the locomotive crashed through the wooden door at its entrance. This incident is incorporated in the finished film. This and other stories of the filming are included in Edward Griffith's book about the line, *The Basingstoke & Alton Light Railway* – out of print but well worth reading.

OH WHAT A LOVELY WAR
GB 1969 Paramount DVD
Dir: Richard Attenborough
Ralph Richardson, John Mills

A musical fantasia on the First World War

This famous film features a musical scene involving a miniature train on Brighton Pier and an elaborate sequence filmed on Brighton station (masquerading as Waterloo) involving departing troops. Preserved 'M7' 0-4-4T No 245 appears in these scenes. Look closely in the background of some shots and you can see a 1930s-built 2-BIL EMU, clearly not meant to be seen but with no one apparently going to great lengths to hide it!

ON APPROVAL
GB 1944 GFD
Dir: Clive Brook
Clive Brook, Beatrice Lillie

A couple plan a trial marriage on a remote Scottish island

The station scenes are studio sets, but there is one real shot taken from the cab of an LMS 2-6-4T on the Midland Main Line, believed to be entering Luton.

ON THE BEAT
GB 1962 Rank DVD
Dir: Robert Asher
Norman Wisdom, Jennifer Jayne

A Scotland Yard car park attendant dreams of becoming a policeman

Features a sequence where Wisdom ends up handcuffed to a suspect on the wrong side of the doors of a tube train. A lot of this sequence uses a mix of studio filming and back projection, but the platform scenes are real – filmed on the Waterloo & City Line at Bank and Waterloo stations with Class 487 EMUs.

ON THE BLACK HILL
GB 1988 BFI/Channel 4
Dir: Andrew Grieve
Mike Gwilym, Robert Gwilym

Twin brothers grow up on a Welsh hill farm

Features a scene filmed at Arley station on the Severn Valley Railway with one of the preserved GWR '4500' 2-6-2Ts on a train.

ON THE FIDDLE
GB 1961 Anglo-Amalgamated
Dir: Cyril Frankel
Alfred Lynch, Sean Connery

Two soldiers in the RAF use their service to help themselves

This wartime comedy includes a scene filmed at Shepperton station with some SR Bulleid coaches in the background, and a stock shot from *Brief Encounter* (qv) of a 'Royal Scot' on an express (at Watford Junction).

ON THE NIGHT OF THE FIRE
GB 1939 GFD VHS
Dir: Brian Desmond Hurst
Ralph Richardson, Diana Wynyard

A barber murders the blackmailer of his wife

Filmed on location in Newcastle, the High Level Bridge appears in a few scenes and a distant LNER 0-6-2T can be seen passing over it on a train.

THE ONE AND ONLY
GB 2003 Pathé DVD
Dir: Simon Cellan Jones
Richard Roxburgh, Justine Waddell

A married man falls in love with a footballer's wife

Includes an aerial shot of a GNER-liveried Class 91-hauled express filmed from a helicopter, and a scene filmed at Newcastle Central station with Mk 4 coaches and two Class 158s visible.

ONE BRIEF SUMMER
GB 1969 TCF
Dir: John Mackenzie
Clifford Evans, Felicity Gibson

A wealthy man has an affair with his daughter's friend

Features a scene of a train departure from a station with maroon Mk 1 stock but no loco visible. This is believed to be a section of footage taken by ITC of a 'Warship'-hauled express at Chippenham station. The full take appears in Video 125's *Diesels and Electrics on 35mm*.

ONE GOOD TURN
GB 1954 GFD DVD
Dir: John Paddy Carstairs
Norman Wisdom, Joan Rice

An odd-job man fights to save an orphanage

This comedy features a typical Norman Wisdom slapstick sequence on a train journey to Brighton, with Wisdom managing to lose his trousers by hanging them out of a carriage window to dry; they end up getting wrapped around the chimney of a passing SR 'C' Class 0-6-0 on a freight! Quite a few EMUs appear in these scenes, although bizarrely for a Brighton trip the first type we see is an LMR Oerlikon set. When Wisdom is hanging out of the window the scene uses a mix of studio set and back projection from the window of a 4-SUB set. SR 6-PUL sets also appear (one of which has the leading car No 11014). Station locations are Brighton and Crawley (where Wisdom is chased by staff due to his lack of trousers).

ONE MORE KISS
GB 1999 Metrodome
Dir: Vadim Jean
Valerie Edmond, Gerard Butler

A terminally ill woman returns home to see an old boyfriend

Early on in the film there are some shots of Berwick-upon-Tweed station and the Royal Border Bridge with an arriving GNER service, which includes shots of Mk 4 stock and the DVT.

ONE OF OUR AIRCRAFT IS MISSING
GB 1941 British National DVD
Dirs: Michael Powell, Emeric Pressburger
Godfrey Tearle, Eric Portman

A bomber is grounded after a raid and its crew are helped by the Dutch Resistance

Although the story is set in Holland, as with many British wartime productions filming obviously took place in this country – the scene by a railway swing bridge was filmed at the LNER swing bridge on the Boston Docks branch, Lincolnshire.

ONE OF OUR DINOSAURS IS MISSING
GB 1975 Walt Disney VHS
Dir: Robert Stevenson
Peter Ustinov, Derek Nimmo

A secret service agent hides a secret formula in a dinosaur skeleton

Includes a scene filmed at Marylebone station, given a 1920s make-over to suit the period of the story. Preserved GWR '4300' Class 2-6-0 No 5322 and stock were used from the Didcot Railway Centre, but in the completed film they can barely be seen. Later in the film the dinosaur, loaded on a steam lorry, is driven onto a goods train at night, which

then sets off; the train is made up of a rake of GWR wagons, although the loco is not visible. This is believed to have been filmed at Didcot itself.

ONE PLUS ONE
GB 1969 Connoisseur/Cupid DVD
Dir: Jean-Luc Godard
The Rolling Stones, Anne Wiazemsky

Various scenes of revolutionary action mixed in with the Rolling Stones recording

A typical abstract film from this famous French director, some scenes are located in a scrapyard below the West London line's Chelsea Bridge and a green Class 33 passes over with a mixed freight.

THE ONE THAT GOT AWAY
GB 1957 Rank DVD
Dir: Roy Baker
Hardy Kruger, Michael Goodliffe

A German POW never gives up trying to escape

Includes a shot of a passing LNER express hauled by a 'B1' 4-6-0, and a scene where Kruger, attempting escape, converses with staff at a railway station. This was filmed at Gerrards Cross on the GW&GC Joint line.

ONE WAY PENDULUM
GB 1964 UA/Woodfall
Dir: Peter Yates
Eric Sykes, Jonathan Miller

An office clerk recreates the Old Bailey in his house and puts his son on trial

This surreal comedy features scenes with Miller studying a 'speak your weight' machine (he steals them with the intention of teaching them to sing!) on the Metropolitan Line platforms of Baker Street Underground station. There is a good shot of 'A60' stock arriving.

ONE WILD OAT
GB 1951 Coronet/Eros
Dir: Charles Saunders
Robertson Hare, Stanley Holloway

A solicitor is blackmailed by an old flame

Features one stock shot of a 'Black Five' 4-6-0 on a WCML express at Bushey troughs.

ONLY WHEN I LARF
GB 1968 Paramount
Dir: Basil Dearden
Richard Attenborough, David Hemmings

Adventures of three confidence tricksters

Features a scene at a goods yard at an unknown location with BR mineral wagons being loaded and a green-liveried Class 08 shunter moving in the background.

OOH YOU ARE AWFUL
GB 1972 British Lion DVD
Dir: Cliff Owen
Dick Emery, Derren Nesbitt

A con-man seeks clues to a fortune tattooed on the behinds of several girls

This comedy film has an amusing scene involving the train announcer at Waterloo station – this sequence uses various shots with actors on the concourse of the station, and suburban EMUs can be seen in the background. When Emery flees London later in the film, in one of his disguises, it involves a scene at Waterloo with him boarding a slam-door express EMU (leading coach No 75584) – as it pulls out a Class 33 diesel is revealed at the buffer stops. En route Emery is menaced by gangsters who end up being thrown out in the middle of a tunnel – as the train enters the tunnel it has become a 'Hastings' DEMU, then as it leaves it is a 4-CEP EMU!

OPERATION BULLSHINE
GB 1959 ABPC
Dir: Gilbert Gunn
Donald Sinden, Barbara Murray

During the Second World War a private suspects her husband of infidelity

Features a railway journey scene with a 'J15' 0-6-0 arriving at Braughing station with old GER stock, repainted in LNER livery for the filming.

THE OPTIMISTS OF NINE ELMS
GB 1973 Cheetah/Sagittarius VHS
Dir: Anthony Simmons
Peter Sellers, Donna Mullane

London slum children befriend an old busker

Filmed around Nine Elms, Battersea and Chelsea, there are various shots of Southern lines and the West London line as a backcloth to the action – a Class 25 and a Class 73 can be seen on cross-London freights, and a Class 33 on another freight crossing the Thames at Chelsea Bridge. SR Class 412/413-type two-car suburban EMUs are also seen, as well as 4-CEP EMUs passing in a scene where the children are running alongside a fence.

THE ORACLE
GB 1952 Group Three
Dir: C. M. Pennington-Richards
Robert Beatty, Virginia McKenna

A reporter discovers that a well in Ireland contains an oracle

Includes a shot of a Southern express hauled by an unrebuilt 'West Country' 4-6-2.

ORLANDO
GB/Russia/France/Italy/Netherlands 1992
    Electric/Adventure Pictures DVD
Dir: Sally Potter
Tilda Swinton, Billy Zane

An English lord lives for centuries as a man and a woman

Close to the end of the film there are scenes around Canary Wharf and some passing Docklands Light Railway units are seen.

ORPHANS
GB 1999 Downtown/Channel 4 DVD
Dir: Peter Mullan
Gary Lewis, Douglas Henshall

Four adults mourn the death of their mother in different ways

Filmed entirely in Glasgow, this includes a scene on the Glasgow Underground with Henshall on one of the units.

OTLEY
GB 1968 Columbia VHS
Dir: Dick Clement
Tom Courtenay, Romy Schneider

A London drifter gets involved with spies and murderers

This Swinging Sixties comedy involves a few railway locations in its story. In one scene Courtenay is interrogated at an old railway station – this was filmed at Quainton Road on the ex-Metropolitan & Great Central line (you can see a poster giving train times to Aylesbury in the background in some shots). Later in the film there is a scene involving a suitcase switch at a London Underground station – this is meant to take place at Notting Hill Gate, and while that location was probably used in some shots, it is believed that the Waterloo & City Line's Bank station was used for the platform scenes, disguised as a LT station.

OUR MOTHER'S HOUSE
GB 1967 MGM
Dir: Jack Clayton
Dirk Bogarde, Pamela Franklin

Seven children keep the death of their mother quiet until their father turns up

Includes a scene where Bogarde is playing with the children in the garden and a formation of SR 4-SUB EMUs passes on an embankment in the background, somewhere in South London.

OUT OF SEASON
GB 1975 EMI
Dir: Alan Bridges
Cliff Robertson, Vanessa Redgrave

A woman at an English seaside resort is visited by an old flame

Near the end of the film there are some good shots of trains at Weymouth Town station: a Class 33/1 with a 4-TC set at the buffer stops and Class 47 No 47 074 leaving with a Mk 1 formation, probably a Bristol service.

OVER THE MOON
GB 1938 London Films VHS
Dir: Thornton Freeland
Rex Harrison, Merle Oberon

A poor girl receives a fortune and woos a doctor

This is an early Technicolor film so we get a good colour shot of a passing LNER express hauled by a 'B17' 4-6-0 in apple-green livery.

OVERLORD
GB 1975 EMI/Jowsend
Dir: Stuart Cooper
Brian Stirner, Davyd Harries

A teenager is called up in 1944 and is killed in the D-Day landings

This drama was filmed in black and white to allow inclusion of a large proportion of wartime newsreel footage. Some of this footage includes railway scenes: an unrebuilt LMS 'Royal Scot' on an express, a 'Super D' 0-8-0 passing on a goods (filmed from a train heading in the opposite direction), a pair of LNER 'J20' 0-6-0s on an ammunition train, and a particularly good shot of 'D16' 'Claud Hamilton' 4-4-0 No 8797 leaving what is believed to be Aldeburgh station with a troop special. Some scenes filmed on the Kent & East Sussex Railway form part of the dramatised footage.

P

PAINTED BOATS
GB 1945 Ealing VHS
Dir: Charles Crichton
Jenny Laird, Bill Blewett

Two canal workers fall in love on the Grand Union Canal

This excellent outdoor drama is a must for narrowboat enthusiasts. There is one shot of a '1400'-hauled 'auto-train' on the GWR's Stroud Valley line, originally filmed for *The Proud Valley* (1940) (qv). Some steam-hauled freight trains can be seen distantly crossing the canals in some shots, but are too far away for any positive identification.

THE PAINTED SMILE
GB 1961 Planet/Mancunian
Dir: Lance Comfort
Liz Fraser, Kenneth Griffith

A student on a night out gets involved in murder

Includes a scene at St Pancras station, where a 'Black Five' 4-6-0 is seen propelling out a rake of coaches.

PAPER MASK
GB 1990 Enterprise/FilmFour VHS
Dir: Christopher Morahan
Paul McGann, Amanda Donohoe

A hospital porter poses as a doctor

Includes some shots of HSTs, one of which is a station scene at Bristol Temple Meads.

PAPERHOUSE
GB 1988 Vestron/Working Title VHS
Dir: Bernard Rose
Charlotte Burke, Ben Cross

A young girl has fits that take her into a fantasy world of her drawings

Includes a scene on the closed Highgate High Level station on the ex-LNER Finsbury Park-Alexandra Palace line.

THE PARADINE CASE
US 1947 Selznick DVD
Dir: Alfred Hitchcock
Gregory Peck, Ann Todd

A barrister falls in love with his client, on trial for murder

A Hollywood film using English locations, it includes a good shot of a train arriving at Keswick station in the Lake District behind an LNWR 'Cauliflower' 0-6-0, and a distant shot of a similar train in the Lakeland scenery.

THE PAROLE OFFICER
GB 2001 Universal DVD
Dir: John Duigan
Steve Coogan, Lena Headey

A parole officer clears his name after being framed by a corrupt cop

Filmed in Manchester, there is one shot of Manchester 'Metrolink tram' No 8001 passing. There are also distant shots of a Class 142 'Pacer' unit crossing a bridge in the city, and a Brush single-deck tram in Blackpool.

PARTING SHOTS
GB 1998 UIP/Scimitar VHS
Dir: Michael Winner
Chris Rea, Felicity Kendal

A terminally ill man decides to kill his enemies

Features scenes at London Victoria station with a 4-CEP EMU and overlooking Hungerford Bridge with a Class 465 EMU. There are also scenes at Latimer Road Underground station on the Hammersmith & City Line with 'C'-type LT stock.

THE PASSIONATE FRIENDS
GB 1948 GFD
Dir: David Lean
Ann Todd, Trevor Howard

A married woman meets her former young lover

Includes a scene in which Ann Todd attempts suicide by jumping in front of a London tube train. The scene is a mix of studio reconstruction and models with an obvious model of a 1938 Underground train.

PASSPORT TO PIMLICO
GB 1949 Ealing DVD
Dir: Henry Cornelius
Stanley Holloway, Margaret Rutherford

The London district is found to belong to Burgundy and is therefore free of rationing

This classic Ealing comedy includes a famous sequence where, with Pimlico now an independent state, London Underground travellers find themselves subject to passport control! The train interior scenes are studio recreations but there are a couple of shots of LT District Line trains. Above ground, there are a few scenes where Southern pre-war EMUs can be seen crossing bridges over

the main locations in the film (in one sequence food parcels are being thrown by passengers to members of the beleaguered state). These bridges were over Lambeth Road and Hercules Road in Pimlico.

THE PASSWORD IS COURAGE
GB 1962 MGM
Dir: Andrew L. Stone
Dirk Bogarde, Alfred Lynch

In occupied Europe, a British officer POW constantly sabotages the Nazis

This film contains some excellent railway sequences, elaborate and spectacular for their day. The entire film is set in Nazi-occupied Europe, yet all the railway scenes are British. For the sake of clarity it is easier to list them in order of appearance.

- Bogarde and his comrades are being taken to a camp on a POW train. As they pass a munitions train they throw some lighted rags, which cause the ensuing explosion. The POW train is hauled by an ex-LMS Fairburn 2-6-4T, and the munitions train by a Fowler 2-6-4T (possibly No 42325). It appears that some real wooden plank wagons were destroyed in this scene, which was filmed at Scratchwood sidings, Mill Hill.
- Bogarde is sent to work in a railway depot and marshalling yard. These scenes were filmed at Cricklewood motive power depot and a number of ex-LMS locos are seen – some Fairburn 2-6-4Ts, a Fowler 2-6-4T, a 4F, a 'Black Five' and an Ivatt 4MT 2-6-0. Wagons visible in the yard include vans, an LMS brake-van, an SR parcels van and some anachronistic BR container vehicles.
- Bogarde sabotages a goods train, which results in one of the most astonishingly destructive scenes ever to involve railway stock in a film. The locomotive

is Fowler tank No 42325, already withdrawn from service but in steam, fitted with smoke deflectors and German 'iron cross' insignia on its tank sides. Hauling a trainload of wooden-bodied wagons it is driven over an embankment at full steam with the wagons piling up around it. From the editing it is obvious that when the dust had settled the remaining wagons still left on the track were pushed forward by an unseen loco, to add to the scene of destruction. When the train starts out at the beginning of the scene there is a lot of smoke in the background at the train's tail, so it seems likely that a banker was used to ensure the train went over the edge. Rumour has it that No 42325 was cut up where she came to rest after filming had been completed. Again, it was filmed at Scratchwood sidings.

- Bogarde makes an attempted escape across Europe by train. This involves a scene boarding a train at Radlett station on the Midland Main Line with a 'Black Five' at the helm. The arrival scenes were filmed at Brighton station with relatively undisguised BR Standard 4-6-0 No 75075.

PATRIOT GAMES
US 1992 UIP DVD
Dir: Phillip Noyce
Harrison Ford, Anne Archer

A former CIA agent in London shoots an IRA terrorist and becomes a target for their revenge

Features a scene on the London Underground with 1972 Piccadilly Line stock, filmed at Aldwych station.

PERFECT FRIDAY
GB 1970 London Screenplays
Dir: Peter Hall
Stanley Baker, Ursula Andress

A bank manager decides to rob his own bank

Features a scene on Paddington station with a few blue/grey-liveried Mk 1 coaches but no locos visible.

PERFECT STRANGERS
GB 1945 MGM
Dir: Alexander Korda
Robert Donat, Deborah Kerr

A quiet, unadventurous married couple become revitalised during the war

Features various shots of passing express trains – many of the scenes take place at night, so it is impossible to see most of the motive power (there is a silhouetted shot of a double-headed express crossing a river bridge with possibly a pair of 'Black Fives'). Loco types that are identifiable, however, are a GNR 'C1' 4-4-2 and an unrebuilt 'Royal Scot'.

THE PERFECT WOMAN
GB 1949 GFD VHS
Dir: Bernard Knowles
Patricia Roc, Nigel Patrick

A girl changes places with her uncle's robot woman

Features a scene on London Underground's Bakerloo Line with 1938-built stock.

PERFORMANCE
GB 1970 Warner DVD
Dirs: Nicolas Roeg, Donald Cammell
James Fox, Mick Jagger

A gangster on the run moves in with a rock star

This classic drama includes a couple of scenes with a railway background. Fox makes a phone call outside the entrance to Wandsworth Town station and there is a shot inside Paddington station from the footbridge, which gives a view of a 'Blue Pullman' and two Class 117 DMUs.

PERSONAL AFFAIR
GB 1953 Rank VHS
Dir: Anthony Pelissier
Leo Genn, Gene Tierney

A schoolmaster finds trouble when a besotted schoolgirl disappears

In a sequence where the police make enquiries about the missing girl, one scene appears to have been filmed on an LMR station with 'Jubilee' 4-6-0 No 45557 passing on an express.

PETER'S FRIENDS
GB 1992 Entertainment/Channel 4 VHS
Dir: Kenneth Branagh
Kenneth Branagh, Stephen Fry

A group of ex-university friends have a reunion at a country mansion

A couple of the characters make the journey to the mansion by train and, unusually for a film set in the present day, this involves a shot of a steam-hauled train with Hunslet 'Austerity' 0-6-0ST No 68081 filmed on the Nene Valley Railway.

THE PHANTOM LIGHT
GB 1935 Gaumont British
Dir: Michael Powell
Gordon Harker, Binnie Hale

A new keeper takes over a remote haunted lighthouse

The lighthouse is set in Wales and in keeping with the story the early part of the film features some excellent shots of the narrow-gauge Festiniog Railway in its original form. There are actual shots of Harker on board a passenger working and a scene at Tan-y-bwlch station. For all these shots the motive power is Double-Fairlie 0-4-4-0 *Taliesin II*.

PHOTOGRAPHING FAIRIES
GB 1997 Entertainment/Polygram/Starry
   Night VHS
Dir: Nick Willing
Toby Stephens, Ben Kingsley

A photographer investigates pictures of fairies taken by two young girls

Based on the Cottingley Fairies stories of the 1920s, and made at the same time as *Fairytale – a True Story* (qv), it features a scene filmed on the Chinnor & Princes Risborough Railway with Austerity 0-6-0ST No 8 on, bizarrely for a story of this period, a train of Mk 2 coaches.

PICCADILLY INCIDENT
GB 1946 ABP
Dir: Herbert Wilcox
Anna Neagle, Michael Wilding

After the Second World War, a woman believed dead returns to find her husband remarried

Despite some studio sets, the film includes a couple of scenes on the Southern Railway with shots of Waterloo station. Locos featured are 'Lord Nelson' 4-6-0 No 864 and a Drummond large-boilered 4-4-0 on an express passing West Weybridge. A number of takes were made at Weybridge of passing trains, and these feature in Video 125's *Steam on 35mm*, including some 'Lord Nelsons'.

PICCADILLY THIRD STOP
GB 1960 Rank
Dir: Wolf Rilla
Terence Morgan, William Hartnell

A criminal seduces an ambassador's daughter so as to rob the embassy in London

Part of the action of this crime film takes place on the London Underground (used as part of the robber's plan), with a final chase through the tunnels. It was filmed on the Piccadilly Line and is believed to have made use of the Holborn-Aldwych section, with one station given fictitious 'Belgravia' signs, and 1924-built tube stock.

PIMPERNEL SMITH
GB 1941 British National VHS
Dir: Leslie Howard
Leslie Howard, Mary Morris

A professor goes into occupied Europe to rescue refugees

A journey of escape by train across Europe uses a lot of studio sets, but there is one shot of a passing GWR express train made up of non-corridor stock but with no engine visible, which was filmed on the GW main line.

PINK FLOYD – THE WALL
GB 1982 MGM DVD
Dir: Alan Parker
Bob Geldof, Christine Hargreaves

A pop star has a nervous breakdown while looking back on his life

A fantasy rock film based around Pink Floyd's music, this includes scenes of the rock star looking back on his childhood in the Second World War and features a couple of re-created wartime railway sequences of troop trains. These were filmed at Keighley station on the Keighley & Worth Valley Railway with preserved LMS 8F 2-8-0 No 8431 in charge of the trains.

THE PINK PANTHER STRIKES AGAIN
GB 1976 United Artists DVD
Dir: Blake Edwards
Peter Sellers, Herbert Lom

Chief Inspector Dreyfus sets out to exterminate Inspector Clouseau

Features a scene where a criminal escapes the police on a train by being taken off by helicopter. This was filmed on the CIE with one shot of a Metro-Vick 'A' Class diesel.

PLAY IT COOL
GB 1962 Independent Artists VHS
Dir: Michael Winner
Billy Fury, Dennis Price

A rock group saves an heiress from an unscrupulous singer

Features a scene filmed at Euston station with good shots of ex-LMS 'Coronation' 4-6-2 No 46245.

PLEASE TURN OVER
GB 1959 Anglo-Amalgamated
Dir: Gerald Thomas
Ted Ray, Jean Kent

A teenager writes a steamy novel using her family as characters

Features a scene filmed at Gerrards Cross station on the GW&GC Joint line. No trains appear.

THE PLEASURE GIRLS
GB 1965 Compton Tekli
Dir: Gerry O'Hara
Ian McShane, Francesca Annis

Girl flatmates have boyfriend trouble

The film begins with some shots at London Victoria station. An SR 4-CEP and a pre-war suburban EMU are in view.

THE PLEASURE PRINCIPLE
GB 1991 Palace VHS
Dir: David Cohen
Peter Firth, Lynsey Baxter

A man tries to keep three affairs going at once

Includes a scene filmed outside St Pancras station with the frontage in shot.

POISON PEN
GB 1939 ABP
Dir: Paul Stein
Flora Robson, Robert Newton

A village is an uproar when people receive vindictive letters

Includes a good shot of LMS 3P 2-6-2T No 10 arriving at a station with a local passenger train, believed to be Brickett Wood on the Watford Junction-St Albans Abbey branch.

POOL OF LONDON
GB 1950 Ealing
Dir: Basil Dearden
Bonar Colleano, Susan Shaw

Events in the lives of sailors in London's dockland

Filmed on location around south-east central London, various railway locations feature in the background of some scenes, including Blackfriars Bridge. A 'Schools' Class 4-4-0 can be seen in one shot, and when Colleano struggles on to the shore later in the film he is close to an industrial 0-6-0ST with some stone tippler wagons. This is believed to have belonged to one of the cement works' railways on the Kentish side of the Thames estuary, possibly in the Gravesend area. There are also some nice views of London trams in their final years, with good shots of car No 599.

POOR COW
GB 1967 Anglo-Amalgamated VHS
Dir: Ken Loach
Carol White, Terence Stamp

The life of a young mother in London married to a criminal husband

Filmed on location in South London, there is one shot looking towards the railway bridge over Plough Road, Battersea, with SR 4-SUB EMUs passing.

PORRIDGE
GB 1979 Black Lion/Witzend DVD
Dir: Dick Clement
Ronnie Barker, Richard Beckinsale

Two inmates at Slade Prison become involved in a break-out

In this big-screen adaptation of the famous TV comedy, the first scene in the film includes a railway station, which is Wargrave on the Henley-on-Thames branch with a three-car Class 117 DMU leaving.

PORTRAIT FROM LIFE
GB 1948 GFD/Gainsborough
Dir: Terence Fisher
Mai Zetterling, Robert Beatty

A German professor searches for his daughter after the Second World War

Features a studio scene in the back of a moving car, but with a back-projected street scene that includes passing London trams.

PORTRAIT OF CLARE
GB 1950 ABPC
Dir: Lance Comfort
Margaret Johnston, Richard Todd

A Victorian woman looks back on her three marriages

Features a couple of railway scenes: a nice shot of Aston Rowant station on the GWR Watlington branch with a local passenger train hauled by a '5700' 0-6-0PT, and a sequence portraying a railway journey to London that involves a passing shot of an ex-LMS 2P 4-4-0 on the Midland Main Line.

POSSESSION
GB 2002 Warner DVD
Dir: Neil LaBute
Gwyneth Paltrow, Jeremy Northam

A researcher sets out to unearth a secret romance involving a Romantic poet

The story in the film is set in the present day and in the 19th century, and there are railway scenes in both. The modern-day story involves a rail journey to Lincoln, which includes a scene filmed on Lincoln Central station and a passing shot of a Class 91-hauled express at Welwyn North. The historical scenes use preserved Furness Railway 2-4-0 No 20, filmed with a rake of vintage coaches on the North Yorkshire Moors Railway, including Pickering station.

POSTMAN'S KNOCK
GB 1962 MGM
Dir: Robert Lynn
Spike Milligan, Barbara Shelley

A village postman is transferred to London and finds city life bewildering

Early in the film there are a number of railway scenes shot on the ex-GER Buntingford branch with a 'mail train' hauled by 'J15' 0-6-0 No 65460. The scenes with Milligan departing from the village on his way to London were shot at West Mill station on the same line, renamed 'Upper Fringly' for the story. No 65460 also appears in these scenes with a short rake of Gresley suburban coaches. The London scenes feature an aerial shot of a Fairburn 2-6-4T arriving at Marylebone with a local (this also appears in *Steam on 35mm* Vol 2) and a shot of 'Coronation' Class 4-6-2 No 46241, possibly at Camden shed. There is also a comedy sequence with Milligan on the London Underground, including 1960-built tube stock.

PRAISE MARX AND PASS THE AMMUNITION
GB 1970 Mithras
Dir: Maurice Hatton
John Thaw, Edina Ronay

A revolutionary tries to start a Marxist uprising in Britain

At the end of the film there is a scene where Thaw boards a train at Euston station; it is made up of Mk 1s, but the loco is not seen. There are various shots taken from the train as it heads along the WCML, including Rugby and the London suburbs with Class 310s and a Class 304 EMU.

A PRAYER FOR THE DYING
GB 1987 Peter Snell/Samuel Goldwyn
  Co VHS
Dir: Mike Hodges
Mickey Rourke, Bob Hoskins

An ex-IRA gunman is unable to silence a priest who witnesses a killing

Features one scene close to a London Underground line with a rake of 1960-built tube stock passing in the background.

PRESS FOR TIME
GB 1966 Rank DVD
Dir: Robert Asher
Norman Wisdom, Derek Bond

The Prime Minister's grandson is sent to a seaside town as a journalist

The last Rank-made Wisdom comedy features a memorable couple of sequences in which the star hitches a ride on a Class 117 DMU by sitting on the rear car's buffer beam. These scenes seem to have been filmed at West Drayton station (appearing as the seaside station 'Tinmouth') and what is believed to be the Staines West branch. The same station is used for a shot of Wisdom arriving on a short freight hauled by Class 08 shunter No D3762. Near the start of the film there is a scene at the entrance to Westminster Underground station.

THE PRIVATE LIFE OF SHERLOCK HOLMES
GB 1970 UA DVD
Dir: Billy Wilder
Robert Stephens, Colin Blakely

A secret Watson manuscript reveals Holmes's relationships with women

A sequence where Holmes and Watson make a journey to Scotland was actually filmed on the Keighley & Worth Valley Railway with a train hauled by L&YR 2F 0-6-0 No 52044 specially painted green and lettered 'LNWR' for filming. Another train of vintage Victorian coaches was also used, hauled by 'J72' 0-6-0T No 69023 *Joem*, but only No 52044 seems to have made it to the finished film.

PRIVATE'S PROGRESS

GB 1956 British Lion VHS
Dir: John Boulting
Ian Carmichael, Richard Attenborough

An innocent serviceman gets involved with his comrades' art theft

Features a railway journey scene with a brief shot of passing LMS 'blood and custard'-liveried coaches, but no loco is seen.

PROSTITUTE

GB 1980 Kestrel VHS
Dir: Tony Garnett
Eleanor Forsythe, Kate Crutchley

A Birmingham prostitute heads for London and has a difficult time

Features one scene in an office next to a railway line and a Class 47 diesel passes by, running light, filmed somewhere in Birmingham.

THE PROUD VALLEY

GB 1940 Ealing
Dir: Pen Tennyson
Paul Robeson, Edward Chapman

A black stoker helps unemployed Welsh miners re-open their pits

This famous Robeson film features some railway scenes in its early stages with a good shot of a GWR '4500' 2-6-2T with a mineral train on an unidentified country branch line. Following this is a shot of an industrial 0-6-0ST entering a colliery. A couple of shots of GWR 'auto-trains' on the Stroud Valley line were filmed but not used for the completed production. One, however, turns up in *Painted Boats* (1945) (qv) and both appear in Video 125's *Steam on 35mm* Vol 1.

PUCKOON

GB/Ireland/Germany 2003 Guerilla Films DVD
Dir: Terence Ryan
Sean Hughes, Elliot Gould

The line between Northern Ireland and Eire is drawn through a small village

Based on Spike Milligan's comic novel, there is one railway scene as troops arrive at Puckoon station. This was filmed at Downpatrick station on the Downpatrick & County Down Railway with preserved Orenstein & Koppel 0-4-0T No 3 featured.

PURELY BELTER

GB 2000 FilmFour DVD
Dir: Mark Herman
Chris Beattie, Greg McLane

Two youths try every trick to get a Newcastle United season ticket

Filmed in and around Newcastle, there are appearances of a couple of Tyne & Wear Metro units crossing the Tyne and a Class 156 'Sprinter' DMU.

QUADROPHENIA
GB 1979 Brent-Walker/Polytel DVD
Dir: Franc Roddam
Phil Daniels, Sting

A Mod gets involved in the Brighton riots in 1964

This popular rock musical of the late 1970s includes some alarming anachronisms – mainly the fact that, despite being set in 1964, all the trains featured are in 1970s blue and yellow. Jimmy's house overlooks the lines at Old Oak Common, at the point where the High Wycombe route leaves the Reading main line. A pair of Class 117 DMUs pass on the High Wycombe line in one shot, while in others another pair of Class 117s and an HST (1976 design!) pass on the Reading line. A later scene at Paddington station reveals a Class 50 diesel (1967 design!) at the buffer stops. There are also scenes on the London Underground with 'C'-type stock on the Hammersmith line and a shot of Goldhawk Road station.

QUARTET
GB 1948 GFD/Gainsborough VHS
Dirs: Arthur Crabtree and others
George Cole, Dirk Bogarde

Compendium of four W. Somerset Maugham stories

In one story ('The Kite') there is a scene filmed at Wimbledon station with an arriving pre-war SR 3-SUB EMU.

QUATERMASS AND THE PIT
GB 1967 Hammer DVD
Dir: Roy Ward Baker
Andrew Keir, James Donald

During London Underground excavations an alien force is unleashed

Most of the action in this famous Hammer horror takes place at an Underground station closed for building work, although no trains are seen. Most of it is a studio set, but some shots are believed to have been filmed at Aldwych station.

QUEEN OF HEARTS
GB 1936 ATP VHS
Dir: Monty Banks
Gracie Fields, John Loder

A shop-worker becomes a big stage star

Features one scene where Fields is boarding a London tram – a night shot with an E1 type passing by.

QUEEN OF HEARTS
GB 1989 Enterprise/FilmFour/Nelson
Dir: Jon Amiel
Stefano Spagnoli, Vittorio Duse

Experiences of a ten-year-old growing up in a London-based Italian family

Includes a scene filmed at Victoria station with a 'Jaffa cake'-liveried Class 411 EMU.

THE QUIET MAN
US 1952 Republic DVD
Dir: John Ford
John Wayne, Maureen O'Hara

A disgraced American boxer returns to Ireland

A classic Hollywood comedy-drama with possibly the most famous (and endearing) depiction of old Ireland. There are a couple of good railway scenes at 'Castletown' station, which is actually Ballyglunin on the west-coast route from Limerick to Claremorris and Sligo. The station survives although it no longer sees passenger services. Motive power featured is veteran CIE-liveried ex-GS&WR 'D17' Class 4-4-0 No 59 on non-corridor stock. As John Wayne makes for the village in a horse and trap No 59 and train appear again, crossing a bridge over the road; this was filmed near Ballyglunin.

QUIET WEDDING
GB 1941 Paramount
Dir: Anthony Asquith
Margaret Lockwood, Derek Farr

A couple plan a quiet wedding but relatives make things complicated

Features a standard stock shot of a 'Royal Scot' 4-6-0 on an express in the Lune Gorge. When Lockwood returns from London there is a shot of an LNER 'K2' 2-6-0 arriving at a station on the West Highland line, but Lockwood gets out of GWR coaches! (This is a studio set.)

THE QUIET WOMAN
GB 1950 Eros
Dir: John Gilling
Derek Bond, Jane Hylton

A smuggler helps a publican's husband who is an escaped convict

Set mainly around the Romney Marsh area, the film features a scene at Lydd Town station on the New Romney branch with an arriving branch train hauled by an SR 'D3' 0-6-2T.

R

THE RACHEL PAPERS
GB 1989 Virgin/Longfellow Pictures VHS
Dir: Damian Harris
Dexter Fletcher, Ione Skye

An Oxford student has an affair with an American girl

Features a scene at Heathrow Airport LT station on the Piccadilly Line with 1972 tube stock.

THE RAGMAN'S DAUGHTER
GB 1972 TCF VHS
Dir: Harold Becker
Simon Rouse, Victoria Tennant

A petty thief and his girlfriend steal for kicks

Features a scene near the end of the film on Nottingham Midland station with an arriving Class 45 'Peak'-hauled express. An added bonus is that on-board filming as the train leaves reveals a passing pair of Class 20s, one of which is No 8016.

THE RAILWAY CHILDREN
GB 1970 EMI DVD
Dir: Lionel Jeffries
Jenny Agutter, Dinah Sheridan

When their father is arrested three children go to a country house with their mother

The famous story was given the big-budget treatment by EMI although there had already been some television productions, the most recent being by the BBC and shown only the previous year.

Like the BBC production, the film used the Keighley & Worth Valley Railway as its setting. The K&WVR, fairly recently established at that time, provided a ready-made steam railway for the film-makers with the added advantage of a range of motive power and rolling-stock. The two main locomotive stars are L&YR 'Ironclad' 0-6-0 No 957 in 'green dragon' livery and GWR '5700' 0-6-0PT No 5775. No 957 is the first K&WVR loco that the children wave to and features in the scenes where the children rescue a young runner from Mytholmes Tunnel, whereas No 5775 is the locomotive that hauls the train carrying the 'Old Gentleman', and also features when the children save a train from a landslide and in the end credits scene. Also central to the film is the setting of Oakworth station, with porter Perks played by Bernard Cribbins. Two other K&WVR locos appear in these scenes – Manchester Ship Canal 0-6-0T No 67 (which brings the family to Oakworth and hauls the train carrying the returning father) and 'N2' 0-6-2T No 4744 (on the 'Scotch express').

An interesting fact regarding the film is that, contrary to popular belief, not all the railway footage is on the K&WVR! When the family make their way from London to the North there is a stock silhouette shot of a train crossing

Barmouth Bridge in North Wales. Another feature of this classic, perhaps revealing the innocence of the story and the film, is that it includes the most nonchalant amount of line trespass you will ever see in a family film! No sooner have the children seen No 957 pass than they are on the track and use it as a way to get to the station. Perks barely raises an eyebrow. Similarly, a school paper-chase casually heads into a tunnel as two platelayers walk out. One makes some comment, but his mate couldn't care less. Then there is the landslide scene, and the end credits, where half the village seems to be on the line – and all this on a supposed main route to Scotland! The film enjoyed considerable box office success and remains a perennial Bank Holiday TV favourite, as well as a great permanent advertisement for the K&WVR, which feels justly proud of its contribution to this day.

A RAILWAY TRAGEDY
GB 1904 Gaumont DVD
Dir: Unknown
Actors unknown

A woman is attacked on a train journey

This early crime film uses real railway locations, although the 'attack' scene is obviously in a mock-up compartment (filmed on a cricket ground, of all places). There is one scene with an SECR well tank arriving at North Dulwich station, then a dramatic shot of the woman's body being removed from the track moments before LB&SCR 'A1' Class 0-6-0T *Deepdene* speeds past with a rake of four-wheelers. The scene of the villain's arrest is also at North Dulwich, with a train arriving behind an 0-6-2T.

THE RAINBOW JACKET
GB 1954 Ealing
Dir: Basil Dearden
Bill Owen, Kay Walsh

A banned jockey helps train a gifted newcomer

Features a scene at Liverpool Street station with a going-away shot of an express hauled by one of Stratford's 'Britannia' 4-6-2s, and an arrival scene at Newmarket station with 'blood and custard'-liveried stock. Video 125's *Steam on 35mm* Vol 2 includes an alternative departure shot of a Britannia from Liverpool Street and a more complete take of the arrival at Newmarket, which reveals the motive power to be an ex-LNER 'B1' 4-6-0.

RAISING THE WIND
GB 1961 GHW/Anglo-Amalgamated
Dir: Gerald Thomas
Leslie Phillips, Kenneth Williams

Adventures of students at a musical academy

Includes a brief shot of an express hauled by an ex-LNER 'A4' 'Pacific' somewhere in Scotland. This is from stock footage originally taken for *The Thirty Nine Steps* (1959) and also turns up in *Carry on Regardless* (1960) (both qv).

THE RAKE'S PROGRESS
GB 1945 GFD VHS
Dir: Sidney Gilliat
Rex Harrison, Lilli Palmer

The life of a playboy in the 1930s

Includes two shots of passing trains, one on the Southern with a 'King Arthur' 4-6-0 at the head of an express and one on the GWR with a '4100' Class 2-6-2T.

THE REBEL
GB 1960 Associated British DVD
Dir: Robert Day
Tony Hancock, George Sanders

A suburban clerk goes to Paris to be an artist

In this popular comedy vehicle for Hancock there is a famous scene where, making the journey to Paris by train with one of his sculptures attached to a flat wagon at the rear, the sculpture has its head unceremoniously knocked off as the train passes under a bridge. There is a good shot of a Bulleid 'Pacific' passing with the 'Golden Arrow' service on the SR, while the decapitation scene was filmed at East Grinstead Low Level, the sculpture hitting the bridge carrying the tracks of the High Level station.

REMEMBER ME?
GB 1997 FilmFour VHS
Dir: Nick Hurran
Robert Lindsay, Rik Mayall

A suburban couple's life is turned upside down by the arrival of an old flame

Filmed in South Western London, there are some mid-distant shots of passing Class 455 EMUs.

RETURN TO YESTERDAY
GB 1940 Ealing
Dir: Robert Stevenson
Clive Brook, Anna Lee

A Hollywood star joins a seaside theatre company

This early Ealing film includes quite a few railway shots filmed on the GWR. First there are scenes inside and overlooking Paddington station with a couple of 'Castles' and a '5700' 0-6-0PT visible on trains. A staged shot was filmed on the sea wall near Dawlish Warren to allow Clive Brook (or a stunt double!) to leave the train after pulling the communication cord. 'King' 4-6-0 No 6004 was filmed a bit further along the sea wall between Dawlish and Teignmouth. The final scenes where Brook leaves the seaside town by train were actually filmed at Ealing Broadway station, with a passenger train complete with milk tank departing (loco unseen). A substantial amount of out-take material appears in Video 125's *Steam on 35mm*.

RICHARD III
GB 1995 UA/British Screen VHS
Dir: Richard Loncraine
Ian McKellen, Annette Bening

The Shakespearean play set in a fascist Britain in the 1930s

The film features a number of railway scenes. The run-by shots of Richard's Royal Train were filmed on the Bluebell Railway, and it is hauled by preserved 9F 2-10-0 No 92240, although the arrival scenes in London are shot at St Pancras. Richard's military headquarters are actually at Steamtown, Carnforth, with preserved L&YR 0-6-0 No 1300, an 8F 2-8-0 and a German 'Austerity' 2-10-0 visible in one scene.

RING OF SPIES
GB 1963 British Lion
Dir: Robert Tronson
Bernard Lee, David Kossoff

A drama of how the Portland spy ring was broken

Features some good scenes filmed on the London Underground, including Baker Street and Ruislip stations with Metropolitan Line 'A60' stock. There is also a shot of a passing express on the ECML behind a 'V2' 2-6-2.

THE RISING OF THE MOON
Ireland 1957 Warner
Dir: John Ford
Maureen Connell, Frank Lawton

Three short Irish stories

The first story centres around a railway, and was filmed on the West Clare Railway with 0-6-2T No 5 appearing in a fictional livery.

ROBBERY
GB 1967 Joseph E. Levine/Oakhurst VHS
Dir: Peter Yates
Stanley Baker, James Booth

A criminal gang plot to rob the Glasgow to London night mail train

Although using fictional characters and plot situations, the actual robbery sequence is plainly based on the real Great Train Robbery of 1963, with the train being stopped at a signal at Danger, driven forward by the gang with the mail van, then plundered of £3 million (apparently a team of 20 lawyers assisted on the script to prevent any libel action). The film even uses the same type of diesel that hauled the actual train – a Class 40 – with the slight difference that the film uses disc-headcode example No D318; split-box No D326 was involved in the real robbery (see *Buster*). Most of the train scenes take place at night for the actual robbery, although there are a couple of day shots as the police examine the loco and stock. These were filmed near Theddingworth on the Rugby-Market Harborough (closed in June 1966) over a total of 29 hours. There are some excellent shots of D318 during the robbery scenes and in the opening credit sequence, with run-bys and a tracking shot filmed from the rear of a preceding train used by the film-makers. Look closely at the scenes as the robbers lie in wait for the night mail and you can see a Class 24 diesel ambling past in the distance on a freight train. The scene of the mail leaving Glasgow is believed to have been filmed at Euston. The Video 125 production *Diesels and Electrics on 35mm* Vol 1 contains a lot of footage of passing trains on the WCML hauled by Class 40s, 24s and 20s for a production with the provisional title of *Jack Mills* (the name of the train driver involved in the robbery) – possibly this might have been intended for this film.

ROOKERY NOOK
GB 1930 British and Dominions
Dir: Tom Walls
Ralph Lynn, Tom Walls

A husband on holiday has to protect a runaway girl from her stepfather

Features a scene filmed at Smallford station on the St Albans Abbey-Hatfield branch line.

ROOM AT THE TOP
GB 1958 Remus VHS
Dir: Jack Clayton
Laurence Harvey, Simone Signoret

An ambitious young clerk eventually marries into a rich family

This famous gritty drama began the Northern England-based 'kitchen sink' cycle of the 1960s. There is a scene at the beginning with Harvey arriving at Halifax station on a local hauled by Stanier 2-6-4T No 42477. Later in the film he makes a journey to the coast, which includes a shot of SR 'M7' 0-4-4T No 30027 on push-pull set No 431, exact location unknown.

A ROOM FOR ROMEO BRASS
GB 1999 Alliance Atlantis/BBC DVD
Dir: Shane Meadows
Andrew Shim, Ben Marshall

A relationship between two teenagers is threatened by an unbalanced adult

Set in the Nottingham suburbs, there is a shot near the start of the film with a Class 156 'Sprinter' passing in the middle distance.

A ROOM WITH A VIEW
GB 1985 Merchant Ivory/Goldcrest DVD
Dir: James Ivory
Helena Bonham Carter, Maggie Smith

In Edwardian times an innocent girl has her eyes opened to life and romance

This very successful period drama features a scene filmed at Horsted Keynes station on the Bluebell Railway with a train hauled by one of the preserved 'A1X' 'Terrier' 0-6-0Ts.

ROTTEN TO THE CORE
GB 1965 British Lion
Dir: John Boulting
Anton Rodgers, Charlotte Rampling

Crooks plan an Army payroll robbery

The robbery of the payroll train was filmed on the Guildford-Christ's Hospital branch, with Baynards and Christ's Hospital stations (renamed 'Longhampton') both appearing. The train itself was hauled by a Class 33 diesel on a short rake of Bulleid coaches, although interestingly an 'N' Class 2-6-0 is known to have also been used, but does not appear in the released print. Two Class 33s were used – Nos D6584 and D6550 (the latter numbered D6584 for continuity). Marylebone station provides the setting in the final scenes and there is a sequence with Eric Sykes on the London Underground that involves 1960 tube stock.

ROUGH SHOOT
GB 1953 Raymond Stross
Dir: Robert Parrish
Joel McCrea, Evelyn Keyes

A retired US officer believes he has shot a poacher but there is more to it than meets the eye

Features a railway journey to London that arrives at Waterloo station behind an unrebuilt 'West Country' 4-6-2. A Hornby model train set also makes an appearance in the film.

THE RULING CLASS
GB 1972 Keep Films DVD
Dir: Potor Modak
Peter O'Toole, Harry Andrews

The new Earl of Gurney is a madman who believes he is God

Features a scene at the entrance to a WR Home Counties station, possibly Denham.

A RUN FOR YOUR MONEY
GB 1949 Ealing VHS
Dir: Charles Frend
Donald Houston, Alec Guinness

A group of Welshmen go up to London to see a rugby match

This Ealing comedy includes a memorable sequence featuring Hugh Griffith travelling with a harp on the London Underground. This involves real scenes on the tube with 1920s-built stock. There is also a rare scene filmed at Nantymoel station, terminus of the branch from Tondu and Bridgend in the Welsh Valleys, with a '5700' 0-6-0PT arriving with the local train (this also appears in Video 125's *Steam on 35mm Vol 2*). There are some good scenes at Paddington station that include a 'Castle' 4-6-0 arriving.

RUNAWAY RAILWAY
GB 1965 CFF DVD
Dir: Jan Darnley-Smith
Sydney Tafler, Ronnie Barker

A group of children save their branch line and foil train robbers

This excellent children's film was shot entirely on the Longmoor Military Railway and, together with *The Great St Trinian's Train Robbery* (qv), stands as a great reminder of this long-gone system. The theme of crooks using a railway for their activities and the final mad dash along the main line to London is reminiscent of *Oh Mr Porter* (qv), whereas the actual filming and cross-cutting to the dashing locomotives reminds one of *The Last Journey* (qv). Most of the film takes place at 'Barming', which is actually Bordon station, the northerly terminus of the LMR and the end of the branch from Bentley (which had closed in 1957). The star of the film is *Matilda* – a disguised LMR Hunslet 'Austerity' 0-6-0ST with fake outside cylinders, an extended chimney and lined livery – which hauls the branch train made up of a single ex-SR 'birdcage' coach. The crooks plan to use the locomotive to steal a mail van from the morning express, and there is a scene where they use an OO-gauge railway layout to plan the robbery with a Hornby 'Jinty' and 'West Country' 'Pacific'. The robbery sequence and the children's attempt to foil it make great use of railway footage, particularly at Borden, the Hollywater loop and around Longmoor yard, with both *Matilda* and the mail train being filmed actually travelling in the same block. The mail train is hauled by the now preserved 'WD' 2-10-0 No 600 *Gordon*, although there is a stock shot of a train leaving Paddington behind 'Castle' Class 4-6-0 No 7020. Note also that the stock of the express varies in some shots – in one there is a small inspection coach that suddenly appears behind *Gordon*. The final scenes where the train reaches London feature a cleverly disguised Longmoor Downs station with an art department 'overlay' to give it the look of a modern 1960s station (similar to the then newly modernised WCML stations), although again there is stock footage cut in – a view from the platforms at Victoria

with a distant train approaching, and cab-view scenes from the front of an EMU arriving at Brighton.

RUNNERS

GB 1983 Goldcrest VHS
Dir: Charles Sturridge
James Fox, Jane Asher

A distraught parent looks for his missing daughter in London

The London scenes feature quite a few railway sequences, with a lot of the action taking place on the platforms and concourse of Victoria station. In one scene Fox and Asher board a Class 411 4-CEP EMU (with a Class 419 luggage single-car unit at the buffer stops behind), and there are some more shots on board another 411 unit. Fox later meets his wife at Liverpool Street station off a train hauled by Class 47 No 47 576 (with another 47 in a platform in the background). While searching Fox crosses a bridge in the Ladbroke Grove area and a Class 117 DMU passes under on the Paddington line. Near the end Fox talks with his daughter on Victoria and there is a suburban 2-HAP-type EMU in shot. There are a couple of scenes at Underground stations, including Paddington (Praed Street entrance).

SABOTAGE
GB 1937 Gaumont British DVD
Dir: Alfred Hitchcock
Oscar Homolka, Sylvia Sidney

The proprietor of a London cinema is really a dangerous foreign agent

Features some shots involving London trams and a scene that takes place on the London Underground – actually a studio set with mock-ups of 1924 tube stock.

SAILOR BEWARE!
GB 1956 Romulus DVD
Dir: Gordon Parry
Peggy Mount, Ronald Lewis

A young sailor has trouble with his mother-in-law-to-be

Features a night scene at an SR level crossing, probably on the South Western Division, with a passing pre-war EMU.

THE SAINT'S GIRL FRIDAY
GB 1953 RKO/Hammer
Dir: Seymour Friedman
Louis Hayward, Diana Dors

The Saint goes after a gang that has murdered a former girlfriend

Features a scene filmed on London Victoria station.

SALLY IN OUR ALLEY
GB 1931 ATP VHS
Dir: Maurice Elvey
Gracie Fields, Ian Hunter

A poor girl loves a wounded soldier

In the background to one scene outside a shop two London trams can be seen passing.

SATURDAY NIGHT AND SUNDAY MORNING
GB 1960 Bryanston/Woodfall VHS
Dir: Karel Reisz
Albert Finney, Shirley Anne Field

A factory worker is dissatisfied with his lot, which manifests itself over a weekend

Thus classic Northern drama was filmed in Nottingham. In one night scene near a pub an ex-LNER 'J6' 0-6-0 passes over a bridge on the GC line with a freight. Later in the film there is a scene near a playground with railway sidings nearby (believed to be at Basford), and an LNER tank loco is very briefly seen.

SAY HELLO TO YESTERDAY
GB 1970 Josef Shaftel
Dir: Alvin Rakoff
Jean Simmons, Leonard Whiting

A young man pursues a older woman on a shopping trip in London

The journeys to and from London are made by train with some good shots of SR EMUs. Early on there are scenes filmed at 'Cobham' station, although the actual location is believed to be Ascot, with express slam-door units (including set No 7805) and a couple of 2-BIL sets in an adjacent platform. There are also scenes filmed at Victoria station with suburban two-car units making an appearance.

SCHOOL FOR SCOUNDRELS
GB 1960 ABP VHS
Dir: Robert Hamer
Ian Carmichael, Alastair Sim

A failure takes a course in Oneupmanship and transforms his life

In this famous British comedy in the Ealing tradition, the railway station near the start of the film, purporting to be 'Yeovil', is actually Hertford East, with a local train arriving behind an 'F5' 2-4-2T. Carmichael makes his way out of the station past the yard outside, where 'J15' and 'J19' 0-6-0 types can be seen. A number of passing trains were filmed at Salisbury Tunnel Junction but did not make the final cut – these appear in Video 125's *Steam on 35mm* and feature Standard 4-6-0s and a Bulleid 'Pacific'.

THE SEA SHALL NOT HAVE THEM
GB 1954 Eros/Daniel M. Angel VHS
Dir: Lewis Gilbert
Dirk Bogarde, Michael Redgrave

A crashed plane's crew wait in a dinghy to be rescued from the sea

Some good shots filmed at Felixstowe Town station appear with a local passenger train arriving behind an 'F6' 2-4-2T.

SÉANCE ON A WET AFTERNOON
GB 1964 Rank DVD
Dir: Bryan Forbes
Richard Attenborough, Kim Stanley

A bogus medium persuades her husband to kidnap a child so she can become famous by 'finding' them

Features some scenes filmed on the London Underground including Leicester Square and Piccadilly Circus stations. There are good shots of 1960-built Piccadilly Line stock (with one car identifiable, No 9165).

THE SECRET AGENT
GB 1936 Gaumont British DVD
Dir: Alfred Hitchcock
John Gielgud, Peter Lorre

A reluctant spy is ordered to kill a man

This Hitchcock thriller is mainly set on the Continent, but one night railway scene was filmed on the Longmoor Military Railway, believed to be on the northern section, but with no locos visible.

THE SECRET AGENT
GB 1996 Fox/Capitol DVD
Dir: Christopher Hampton
Bob Hoskins, Patricia Arquette

In Victorian London a double agent becomes involved in a terrorist act

Features sequences filmed on two preserved railways. 'Maize Hill' station is actually Wansford on the Nene Valley Railway and is used in a scene with Hoskins, though no locos appear. The scenes where Hoskins and Arquette flee London for the coast were filmed on the Great Central Railway using Loughborough Central station and a train hauled by preserved L&YR 0-6-0 No 1300.

SECRET FRIENDS
GB 1991 FilmFour VHS
Dir: Dennis Potter
Alan Bates, Frances Barber

An artist goes through a breakdown while on a train journey

The entire journey is filmed inside a mock-up of a Mk 3 coach on a studio set, but there are a couple of real shots filmed out of the window of a train on the WR main line. Foxhall Junction, west of Didcot, is recognisable in one of them.

THE SECRET GARDEN
US 1949 MGM
Dir: Fred M. Wilcox
Margaret O'Brien, Herbert Marshall

An orphan girl goes to stay with her uncle and revitalises his family's life

This Hollywood version of the classic story includes a stock shot of a 'Dean Goods' 0-6-0 on a local passenger train on a rural part of the GWR.

THE SECRET PEOPLE
GB 1952 Ealing
Dir: Thorold Dickinson
Valentina Cortese, Audrey Hepburn

Refugees in London become embroiled with anarchists

The anarchists meet in a flat in the Paddington area that overlooks the WR main line and, through a window, a 'Hall' 4-6-0, '5700' 0-6-0PT and '5100' tank can be seen passing.

SECRET PLACES
GB 1984 Rank
Dir: Zelda Barron
Jenny Agutter, Tara MacGowran

During the Second World War a schoolgirl becomes friends with a German refugee

Features a scene filmed on the Bluebell Railway with BR suburban coaches visible but no loco, although there is a stock shot of a 'Royal Scot' 4-6-0. Also there are a couple of twin-deck electric trams, probably filmed at Beamish.

SECRETS AND LIES
GB 1995 FilmFour DVD
Dir: Mike Leigh
Timothy Spall, Phyllis Logan

A successful black woman discovers that her real mother is white

Features a scene outside Holborn Underground station.

SEPARATE LIES
GB 2005 TCF DVD
Dir: Julian Fellowes
Tom Wilkinson, Emily Watson

A solicitor's wife is involved in a hit-and-run and they have to cover up the killing

Features scenes at Marylebone station, with Wilkinson boarding a Class 165/166 unit, and at Denham station. In a night scene at Denham later in the film the unit disappearing into the distance out of the station is actually a digitally added image!

SERENA
GB 1962 Butchers
Dir: Peter Maxwell
Patrick Holt, Honor Blackman

A detective on a murder case unearths surprising information on the victim

Includes a scene filmed in Paddington station.

THE SERVANT
GB 1963 Elstree/Springbok DVD
Dir: Joseph Losey
Dirk Bogarde, James Fox

A rich young man is gradually overruled by his sinister manservant

Includes a scene filmed at St Pancras station with Bogarde on the platform as a Class 45 'Peak' arrives with an express.

SEVEN DAYS TO NOON
GB 1950 London Films
Dir: John Boulting
Barry Jones, André Morrell

An atomic scientist threatens to blow up London unless nuclear research stops

The first section of the film depicts the approaches to Waterloo and the station itself. A variety of ex-SR traction can be seen, including a 'Lord Nelson' 4-6-0, 4-COR 'Nelson' EMUs, 4-SUB unit No 4162, and 2-HAL No 2647, together with other EMUs. There are some scenes on the Underground at Piccadilly Circus station with 1938 Bakerloo Line stock, and a brief scene where some railway workers find a clue at Stewarts Lane shed with SR coaches on view.

THE SEVEN PER CENT SOLUTION
US 1976 Universal
Dir: Herbert Ross
Nicol Williamson, Robert Duvall

Dr Watson lures Sherlock Holmes to Vienna to be treated by Sigmund Freud

The high-point of this entertaining film is a spectacular chase sequence where Holmes and Watson pursue a villain (the Pasha) on a steam train. The whole sequence was filmed on the Severn Valley Railway with four locomotives used, all vaguely disguised as Austrian locomotives: the Pasha's train is hauled by No 90.160 ('Black Five' No 45110 in northbound shots, 8F 2-8-0 No 8233 southbound), with Holmes's train hauled by No 60.116 (Ivatt 2MT 2-6-0s Nos 46443 and 46521 northbound and southbound respectively). Most of the Severn Valley was used and a scene where the two trains converge onto the same section of track necessitated the relaying of part of the old Wyre Valley line at Bewdley for aerial shots. The Pasha's train was made up of two bogie-bolster underframes with studio-built plywood bodies on top. Holmes's train featured a similar carriage, which in the story gets chopped up to supply fuel for the loco! Northwood Halt can be seen in one scene, made up as an Austrian station, and the Austrian-Italian border checkpoint is located at the Bewdley end of Victoria Bridge.

SEVEN SINNERS
GB 1936 Gaumont
Dir: Albert de Courville
Edmund Lowe, Constance Cummings

Gun-runners cause train crashes to cover traces of murder

This is a remake of the earlier 1929 film *The Wrecker* (qv), and one of the major crash scenes uses almost all the footage from a staged crash from that earlier film (shot on the Basingstoke & Alton Light Railway with a Stirling 4-4-0). Apart from that there is not a huge amount of material of British trains – one crash uses model shots of a French locomotive and coaches (although one coach has LNER motifs on it) and another, which takes place in a tunnel, uses a combination of studio mock-up interiors and real footage, although it is too distant and indistinct to identify any engines. There is, however, one close-up shot of the cab and motion of an LMS 'Royal Scot' 4-6-0 and a scene filmed at Waterloo station.

THE SEVENTH VEIL
GB 1945 Theatrecraft/Sydney Box VHS
Dir: Compton Bennett
James Mason, Ann Todd

A concert pianist is torn between her psychiatrist and her mentor

This famous melodrama features a shot of the concourse of Waterloo station.

A SEVERED HEAD
GB 1970 Columbia
Dir: Dick Clement
Ian Holm, Lee Remick

A wine merchant having an affair finds his wife is playing the same game

Features a scene at Paddington station with blue/grey Mk 1 coaches on view, but we don't see the loco.

SHADEY
GB 1985 Larkspur/Otto Plashkes
Dir: Philip Saville
Anthony Sher, Billie Whitelaw

A car mechanic raises money for his sex-change operation

This odd drama features a scene with some of the characters on board an SR express slam-door EMU, together with other similar units appearing around these scenes, believed to have been filmed around the Clapham Junction area.

SHADOW OF A MAN
GB 1954 New Realm
Dir: Michael McCarthy
Paul Carpenter, Rona Anderson

An author proves that a friend was killed by a diabetic

Features a scene filmed at the frontage of Hastings station.

SHADOWLANDS
GB 1993 UIP DVD
Dir: Richard Attenborough
Anthony Hopkins, Debra Winger

The story of writer C. S. Lewis and his relationship with an American woman

The film used footage shot on the Great Central Railway, with Loughborough Central standing in for Oxford. Preserved 'Black Five' 4-6-0 No 45231 was commendably weathered to look like a typical work-stained 1950s loco, as well as 'Castle' 4-6-0 No 7029.

SHE'LL HAVE TO GO
GB 1962 Anglo-Amalgamated
Dir: Robert Asher
Bob Monkhouse, Alfred Marks

Two brothers plan to murder the woman who has inherited their home

Features some good shots filmed on the Watford Junction-St Albans Abbey branch at Brickett Wood station with a train hauled by an Ivatt 2-6-2T.

SHERLOCK HOLMES AND THE VOICE OF TERROR
US 1942 Universal DVD
Dir: John Rawlins
Basil Rathbone, Nigel Bruce

Sherlock Holmes unmasks a traitorous radio broadcaster

Features stock footage of Westminster Bridge with a London tram passing.

SHINER
GB 2001 Geoff Reeve/VisionView/
    Wisecroft DVD
Dir: John Irvin
Michael Caine, Martin Landau

A ruthless boxing promoter fixes a fight his son is appearing in

Features a night scene near Stratford locomotive depot in East London, with refurbished Class 37 and Class 58 diesel types outside. Also there are some distant SR EMUs visible in the South London scenes.

SHIRLEY VALENTINE
GB 1989 UIP/Paramount DVD
Dir: Lewis Gilbert
Pauline Collins, Tom Conti

A housewife leaves her husband and takes a romantic holiday in Greece

Features a scene where Collins gets her passport photos done on a London main-line station. This was filmed on St Pancras station with an HST and DMU visible in the background.

SHOOTING FISH
GB 1997 Entertainment/Fox VHS
Dir: Stefan Schwartz
Dan Futterman, Kate Beckinsale

Two con-men find love instead of the stately home they desire

One scene takes place in a modern office next to a railway in South London and an express slam-door EMU passes by outside.

SHOPPING
GB 1994 Rank/Channel 4/Polygram
    DVD
Dir: Paul Anderson
Jude Law, Sadie Frost

A young thief leaves prison and reverts to his old crime of ram-raiding

In one scene the thieves seek refuge in a railway shed – this is the old Southall shed, which was then occupied by the

Southall Railway Centre, and a lot of their stock can be seen, including unrestored GWR '2800' Class 2-8-0 No 2885.

THE SHOW GOES ON
GB 1936 ATP VHS
Dir: Basil Dean
Gracie Fields, Owen Nares

A mill girl becomes a star singer

Includes some good shots filmed on the LMS – expresses hauled by a 'Royal Scot' 4-6-0 in the Lune Gorge and a 'Claughton' 4-6-0, together with a scene at an unknown station with a local train hauled by Stanier 2-6-4T No 2616.

THE SILENT PASSENGER
GB 1935 Phoenix
Dir: Reginald Denham
Peter Haddon, John Loder

Lord Peter Wimsey clears a man on a murder charge

This is another forgotten little film from the 1930s that includes some great railway scenes. Wimsey follows the murderer by train to Stratford and corners him in the locomotive works where a fight ensues. First we see scenes filmed on Liverpool Street station with a departing train, which then arrives at a different platform at the same station, pretending to be Stratford! 'B12' 4-6-0 No 8542 features, together with a couple of 'N7' 0-6-2Ts on 'Jazz' local train. The excellent fight scene was actually shot at night in Stratford Works with powerful arc lights highlighting the various locos. Star of the show is 'N7' No 2616, which is in steam when Wimsey waylays the villain. The loco is in gear and as pressure builds up it moves slowly forward, forcing the two men into an inspection pit as it passes over them, before crashing through the shed doors. Other locos visible in this sequence include a 'Claud Hamilton' 4-4-0 and a 'J17' 0-6-0 without tender aloft on a crane hoist.

SILENT SCREAM
GB 1989 BFI/FilmFour
Dir: David Hayman
Iain Glen, Paul Samson

A dying murderer recalls his past life

A childhood flashback features scenes filmed on the Strathspey Railway in Scotland at Boat of Garten station, with preserved 'Black Five' 4-6-0 No 5025 making an appearance.

SILVER BLAZE
GB 1937 Twickenham DVD
Dir: Thomas Bentley
Arthur Wontner, Ian Fleming

Sherlock Holmes clears a racehorse of having killed its trainer

This early Holmes film features real scenes of races at Newbury racecourse, and there are a couple of shots of excursions at the Racecourse station. No locos are visible, but there are some fine GWR coaches.

SILVER DREAM RACER
GB 1980 Rank DVD
Dir: David Wickes
David Essex, Beau Bridges

A garage mechanic becomes a racing motorcyclist

Features a scene with Essex at an Underground station talking to his father on a motorised PW trolley, believed to have been filmed on the Waterloo & City Line.

SIMON AND LAURA
GB 1955 GFD DVD
Dir: Muriel Box
Peter Finch, Kay Kendall

A married acting couple hate each other but must appear happy for a television series

Features some scenes filmed at St Pancras station with no locos but good colour shots of 'blood and custard'-liveried ex-LMS coaches.

SIMON MAGUS

GB/France/Germany/Italy 1999 Channel
  4 Films DVD
Dir: Ben Hopkins
Noah Taylor, Rutger Hauer

*A simple-minded man is instrumental in
deciding a village's future*

Set in Silesia in the 19th century, the
dramatic railway scenes in the film were
actually filmed on the Severn Valley
Railway close to Country Park Halt. GWR
'5700' 0-6-0PT No 7714 was partially
disguised as a Polish locomotive with
Polish eagle emblems and masking tape
over the smokebox numbers. However, it
hauls some obviously British LNER Gresley
teak coaches and an SR bogie brake-van!

SING AS WE GO

GB 1934 ATP VHS
Dir: Basil Dean
Gracie Fields, John Loder

*An unemployed mill girl has experiences in
Blackpool*

Filmed on location in Lancashire. there
are a myriad of shots of various Blackpool
excursion trains near the start of the film
with headboards proclaiming them as
from places such as Leeds and Edinburgh.
Motive power respectively is provided by
a 'Lanky' 'Dreadnought' 4-6-0, a Fowler
2-6-4T, an L&YR 2-4-2T and an LNWR
4-4-0. Another 'Lanky' 2-4-2 tank, No
10953, appears later in the film, and there
are scenes at Blackpool Central station.
Some of the trams make an appearance –
Gracie Fields almost rides her bike under
a Brush single-decker and there are some
of the earlier open-platform double-deck
examples. Scenes filmed at the Pleasure
Beach include rare views of the miniature
railway with its steam-profile tank loco.

SINGLE HANDED

GB/US 1953 TCF
Dir: Roy Boulting
Jeffrey Hunter, Michael Rennie

*A Canadian seaman causes the destruction
of a German battleship*

A railway journey, supposedly set in the
First World War, includes a number of ex-
Southern locos. Some early scenes in the
film are believed to have been filmed at
Portsmouth, and shortly after departure
the back projection scenes through the
carriage window depict a yard with an
'E4' 0-6-2T in attendance. Other locos
that appear include 'T9' 4-4-0 No 30119
(note the BR number!), a stock shot of
'U1' 2-6-0 No 1901 from SR days, and a
rare type in 'L12' 4-4-0 No 30420 in
mock LSWR livery arriving with a train
at Liss station – again with a BR number.

THE SINISTER MAN

GB 1961 Anglo-Amalgamated
Dir: Clive Donner
Patrick Allen, John Bentley

*The murder of an Oxford scholar is linked to
ancient relics*

This adaptation of an Edgar Wallace story
features a scene at a level crossing with an
ex-GWR large 2-6-2T passing with a
passenger train, believed to have been
filmed at Cookham.

SITTING TARGET

GB 1972 MGM
Dir: Douglas Hickox
Oliver Reed, Jill St John

*A killer escapes from jail to take revenge on
those who shopped him*

Includes a lot of scenes shot in and
around Clapham Junction, featuring the
station and yards. Suburban units of the
2-EPB and 4-EPB type appear, as well as
four-car express units, and a Class 73
electro-diesel can be seen in the distance
of one shot. The final scenes take place
around the Nine Elms goods yards and
some wagons can be seen, including
parcels vans.

6-5 SPECIAL
GB 1957 Anglo-Amalgamated VHS
Dir: Alfred Shaughnessy
Petula Clark, Pete Murray

A number of pop acts head to London by train to put on a show

This film version of the famous 1950s pop show is basically a number of pop acts with a loose story linking them together. The title shots are similar to those of the TV show, with stock footage – an aerial shot from the 1930s of the streamlined 'Coronation Scot', a 'Royal Scot', a couple of 'A2' 'Pacifics' and footage taken out of the window of a train passing Twyford station. The rest of the film is basically studio sets with stock railway shots inserted at certain moments – various night shots of LMS expresses, including an out-take from *Brief Encounter* (qv) of a 'Royal Scot' passing Watford Junction, and a scene with a 'King' 4-6-0 arriving at Paddington.

SLAYGROUND
GB 1983 EMI VHS
Dir: Terry Bedford
Peter Coyote, Mel Smith

An assassin is hired by a rich man to track a criminal who killed his daughter

Some of the film is set in Blackpool and there are shots of trams – single-deck Brush and double-deck Balloon types.

SLEEPING CAR
GB 1933 Gaumont
Dir: Anatole Litvak
Ivor Novello, Madeleine Carroll

A woman on the run marries a sleeping-car attendant

Mainly filmed on the French railway system, there is one British scene at the end where an SR 'H' Class 0-4-4T hauling a parcels van passes over Carroll's dog, which is sat in the four-foot. (Animal lovers take note – it's a dummy!)

SLIDING DOORS
GB/US 1998 Paramount/Miramax DVD
Dir: Peter Howitt
Gwyneth Paltrow, John Hannah

When an executive misses a train we see how life would have unfolded if she had caught it

This successful romantic drama has its pivotal scene on the Waterloo & City Line, with Bank and Waterloo stations appearing, and Paltrow just missing a departing 1990s-built unit. Also in the film are a couple of scenes on the London Underground, including Embankment station (entrance only).

THE SMALL BACK ROOM
GB 1948 London Films VHS
Dirs: Michael Powell, Emeric Pressburger
David Farrar, Kathleen Byron

A bomb disposal expert battles disability and a drink problem

Includes a rare scene filmed at Abbotsbury station, terminus of the branch from Upwey in Dorset, with a GWR '1400' 0-4-2T entering on an 'auto-train'.

THE SMALLEST SHOW ON EARTH
GB 1957 British Lion DVD
Dir: Basil Dearden
Peter Sellers, Bill Travers

A young married couple take over a dilapidated cinema

This classic comedy was not made by Ealing, but is very much in its tradition. The 'cinema' was a specially built frontage constructed by the railway bridges between Kilburn (now Jubilee Line) station and the adjacent ex-GC lines in North West London. A number of train shots appear in the film, exact locations unknown, but loco types include an 'A3' 'Pacific', a couple of ex-LMS 2-6-4Ts and an 'L1' 2-6-4T. The station scenes near the end, where Bill Travers and Virginia McKenna leave the town, were shot at Uxbridge Vine Street station, five years before closure – we see ex-GWR coaches but not the locomotive.

SMASH AND GRAB
GB 1937 GFD VHS
Dir: Tim Whelan
Jack Buchanan, Elsie Randolph

A detective and his wife track down a master criminal

Buchanan's character in the film is a train buff, which brings some nice touches to the story. One of the first scenes in which he appears shows him climbing along the front end of LMS 'Royal Scot' 4-6-0 No 6152, station unknown. Later in the story there is a comedy sequence where Buchanan and his manservant operate an OO-gauge model railway and at the climax the criminal is foiled by a gun disguised as a model 0-6-0 tank loco!

THE SMASHING BIRD I USED TO KNOW
GB 1969 Titan
Dir: Robert Hartford-Davis
Madeline Hinde, Dennis Waterman

A schoolgirl is sent to a remand home after stabbing her mother's lover

One scene involving a sports car travelling along a main road was filmed close to the WCML and a Class 310 EMU can be seen passing in the background. The final scenes involve the car driving off an old railway viaduct in a rural setting – the location is unknown, but it is believed to be on one of the abandoned GWR lines in the West Country.

SMASHING TIME
GB 1967 Paramount
Dir: Desmond Davis
Rita Tushingham, Lynn Redgrave

Two Northern girls have experiences in Swinging London

Features a brief scene with Tushingham tied to a track 'Perils of Pauline'-style in a siding near St Pancras station with a green Class 45 diesel on an express in the background.

SMOKESCREEN
GB 1964 Butchers
Dir: Jim O'Connolly
Peter Vaughan, John Carson

An insurance agent solves a murder

Features a scene outside Brighton station and at Hellingley station on the line from Shoreham. There is also a distant view of an SR 2-BIL EMU.

SO WELL REMEMBERED
GB 1947 RKO
Dir: Edward Dmytryk
John Mills, Trevor Howard

A mill-owner's daughter marries a local politician and ruins his life

A Northern drama using real locations filmed around Macclesfield. A couple of railway shots are included near the start of the film, one with a local passenger train hauled by an LMS 2-6-4T and a distant steamy shot of another 2-6-4T with an 0-6-0 running light.

SOLITAIRE FOR TWO
GB 1994 Entertainment VHS
Dir: Gary Sinyor
Mark Frankel, Amanda Pays

A woman is able to read the minds of men around her

Features a scene on the London Underground with an interior view on board a Northern Line 1972 unit.

SOME VOICES
GB 2000 FilmFour DVD
Dir: Simon Cellan
Daniel Craig, David Morrissey

A released schizophrenic causes problems for his brother and a woman he meets

Features some scenes around West London with Hammersmith & City Line 'C'-type stock passing. There are some on-board train scenes that were filmed on the Bluebell Railway.

SOMETHING IN THE CITY
GB 1950 Nettlefold
Dir: Maclean Rogers
Richard Hearne, Betty Sinclair

An out-of-work businessman pretends to his wife that he still works in the City

One scene was filmed on Shepperton station on the SR.

SOMEWHERE IN CAMP
GB 1942 Mancunian
Dir: John E. Blakeley
Frank Randle, Harry Korris

Misadventures of a motley group of Army soldiers

Features a montage journey sequence with a number of distant shots of GWR 4-6-0s on expresses on the GWR main line.

SOMEWHERE IN ENGLAND
GB 1940 Mancunian
Dir: John E. Blakeley
Frank Randle, Harry Korris

New Army recruits stage a show

A low-budget comedy that features a scene with a couple of the characters boarding a train at a Southern station. No loco is visible, but there is a good view of SR corridor stock (complete with fare-paying passengers staring at the camera). There is also a shot of a passing LNER express behind one of the rare Gresley 'P2' 2-8-2s (possibly an out-take from the 'lost' 1935 film *Cock o' the North*).

SOMEWHERE ON LEAVE
GB 1942 Mancunian
Dir: John E. Blakeley
Frank Randle, Harry Korris

Army soldiers spend a weekend in a stately home

Features a scene filmed in Victoria station and a suburban SR station, believed to be Barnes, with a pre-war 3-SUB EMU (one coach numbered 9720).

SONG OF FREEDOM
GB 1936 Hammer
Dir: J. Elder Wills
Paul Robeson, Elizabeth Welch

A docker becomes an opera singer and goes to Africa to free his tribe

As Robeson tours the country on his opera tour there is a montage sequence of 'travelling' shots that includes close-ups of locomotive wheels and motion, and a shot of an SR train hauled by an LSWR 4-4-0.

SONS AND LOVERS
GB 1960 TCF
Dir: Jack Cardiff
Dean Stockwell, Trevor Howard

A Nottingham miner's son learns about life and love

'Bestwood' station in the film is Longmoor Downs on the Longmoor Military Railway, and there are good shots of LMR coaches hauled by an 0-6-0ST (distantly seen). Some other scenes were actually filmed in Nottinghamshire – there is a distant view of a colliery coal train hauled by an unidentified industrial tank loco and night scenes filmed by Weekday Cross Junction on the GC main line, with a passing local hauled by a 'J6' 0-6-0.

SORTED
GB 2000 Metrodome/Jovy Junior DVD
Dir: Alex Jovy
Matthew Rhys, Tim Curry

A lawyer tries to find the truth behind his brother's death in London's clubland

Features a scene at Green Park

Underground station with 1990s tube stock.

SOUTH RIDING
GB 1937 London Films
Dir: Victor Saville
Ralph Richardson, Edna Best

A schoolmistress in Yorkshire exposes crooked councillors

Includes a shot of a 'Castle' 4-6-0 on an express on the GWR. A horse-riding scene was shot in the grounds of Denham Studios and eagle-eyed viewers will see a brief glimpse of one of the 'J15' 0-6-0s owned by the studio, which had been used for *Knights Without Armour* (qv).

SPARE THE ROD
GB 1961 British Lion
Dir: Leslie Norman
Max Bygraves, Geoffrey Keen

A young schoolmaster wins over tough kids at an East End school

Includes a shot of a District/Metropolitan Underground train made up of 'R'-type stock. During one of his lessons Bygraves has some photos of trains fixed to the blackboard, which include Trevithick's Penydarren loco, an LMS 'Duchess' and Class 40 and 'Peak' diesels.

SPARROWS CAN'T SING
GB 1962 Elstree/Carthage
Dir: Joan Littlewood
James Booth, Barbara Windsor

A sailor searches for his wife and threatens vengeance on her lover

Filmed in the East End of London around the Stepney area, there is a shot of a pair of Class 302 EMUs passing open ground by a housing estate.

SPICEWORLD – THE MOVIE
GB 1997 Polygram DVD
Dir: Bob Spiers
The Spice Girls, Richard E. Grant

The Spice Girls encounter problems preparing a concert at the Albert Hall

Features a shot of a Docklands Light Railway unit near Canary Wharf and a distant view of a Class 319 EMU on Blackfriars Bridge.

SPIDER
Canada/GB 2003 Redbus/Capitol DVD
Dir: David Cronenberg
Ralph Fiennes, Miranda Richardson

A mentally disturbed man is released but gets visions from his past

There is a good opening shot of Class 47 diesel No 47 774 *Poste Restante* arriving at St Pancras station with a rake of blue and grey Mk 1 coaches, with a Class 170 DMU in the background. Later in the film a pair of Class 317 EMUs can be seen crossing a bridge in the background to a scene.

THE SPY WHO CAME IN FROM THE COLD
GB 1966 Paramount VHS
Dir: Martin Ritt
Richard Burton, Claire Bloom

A British agent is apparently sacked by the secret service so he can be recruited by the Russians

Features a shot with Burton outside South Kensington Underground station.

THE SQUARE PEG
GB 1958 Rank DVD
Dir: John Paddy Carstairs
Norman Wisdom, Edward Chapman

A council worker is called up into the Army

Includes a comedy scene with Wisdom filmed on Wooburn Green station on the Maidenhead-High Wycombe line with an ex-GWR '5100' 2-6-2T on a passenger train.

THE SQUEEZE
GB 1977 Warner
Dir: Michael Apted
Stacy Keach, David Hemmings

An ex-cop rescues his wife from kidnappers

Includes a scene on the London Underground with 1960-built Northern Line tube stock.

STAR!
GB 1968 TCF DVD
Dir: Robert Wise
Julie Andrews, Richard Crenna

The life of stage star Gertrude Lawrence

Includes a flashback scene filmed at Marylebone station with borrowed SR suburban coaches to give the right period feel.

THE STARS LOOK DOWN
GB 1939 Grafton VHS
Dir: Carol Reed
Michael Redgrave, Margaret Lockwood

The son of a coal-miner enters politics to improve their conditions

Features a station scene in the coal-mining town with an ex-LNWR tender loco (obscured but possibly a 'Cauliflower') arriving with a single-coach train. Shot at Workington Central station on the ex-C&WJR.

STARTER FOR TEN
GB 2006 Icon/HBO Films DVD
Dir: Tom Vaughan
James McAvoy, Rebecca Hall

A college student trains to go on TV's University Challenge

Features a snowy scene filmed at Sheffield Park station on the Bluebell Railway, but with no locos visible. There are also a couple of brief shots on the platform at Bristol Temple Meads.

STELLA DOES TRICKS
GB 1996 BFI/Channel 4 DVD
Dir: Coky Giedroyc
Kelly Macdonald, James Bolam

A Scottish prostitute in London tries to escape her pimp

Features a scene on the WCML in North London with a pair of passing Class 321 EMUs.

STEVIE
GB/US 1978 First Artists/Grand
   Metropolitan VHS
Dir: Robert Enders
Glenda Jackson, Mona Washbourne

The life of suburban poet Stevie Smith

Features some shots of 1938 tube stock filmed on the Northern Line with passing shots and cab views, particularly on a section entering and exiting a tunnel. There is also a scene with Jackson walking out of Southgate Underground station and a shot of Trevor Howard crossing a footbridge over the Midland Main Line under which a formation of Class 127 DMUs is passing.

THE STICK UP
GB 1977 Backstage
Dir: Jeffrey Bloom
David Soul, Pamela McMyler

An American meets up with a café waitress in Devon and finds that she's a thief

One scene in the film involves an armoured car stuck on a level crossing as a steam train approaches. This was filmed at Nappers Crossing on the Dart Valley (now South Devon) Railway with a train of six coaches hauled by '4500' 2-6-2T No 4555; it was filmed over three days in May 1977.

STIFF UPPER LIPS
GB 1997 Cavalier/Impact/Chrysalis VHS
Dir: Gary Sinyor
Peter Ustinov, Sean Pertwee

An upper-class girl falls for a working-class boy

The early part of the film includes some scenes filmed on the Isle of Man Steam Railway with a train hauled by 2-4-0T No 15 *Caledonia* at Castletown station. Some Indian railway scenes feature later in the film.

STOLEN FACE
GB 1952 Exclusive/Hammer DVD
Dir: Terence Fisher
Paul Henreid, Lizabeth Scott

A girl criminal is given a new face by plastic surgery but she resembles the doctor's old girlfriend

The film ends with a death as a character falls out of a railway carriage. Includes a scene at Surbiton station and shots of SR expresses hauled by a 'Lord Nelson' 4-6-0 and a Bulleid 'Pacific' (on the 'Bournemouth Belle').

STORMBREAKER
GB 2006 Entertainment/Samuelson DVD
Dir: Geoffrey Sax
Alex Pettyfer, Bill Nighy

A teenager is recruited as a spy

Includes an aerial shot of Grosvenor Bridge with a Class 465 EMU crossing, and a scene near Battersea with another Class 465 set passing. Later in the film there is a scene on Liverpool Street station where government agents access headquarters via a photo booth.

STORMY MONDAY
GB 1987 Palace/FilmFour/Atlantic DVD
Dir: Mike Figgis
Melanie Griffith, Tommy Lee Jones

An American gangster tangles with a Newcastle club-owner

Filmed on location in Newcastle, railway scenes include a high-rise shot of an HST crossing the King Edward Bridge, Class 143 'Pacer' units and a scene on the Tyne

& Wear Metro with one of the line's units.

THE STRANGE AFFAIR
GB 1968 Paramount
Dir: David Greene
Michael York, Susan George

A young policeman finds his superiors almost as corrupt as the villains

Includes a night scene with a passing London Underground train made up of 1960-built tube stock.

STRICTLY SINATRA
GB 2001 UIP/DNA Films
Dir: Peter Capaldi
Ian Hart, Kelly Macdonald

A night-club singer gets involved with criminals

Filmed around Glasgow, a couple of Class 314 Strathclyde EMUs appear in the background of one scene, and there is a scene on Glasgow Queen Street station with an arriving Class 158 'Sprinter'.

A SUMMER STORY
GB 1987 Warner/ITC
Dir: Piers Haggard
James Wilby, Imogen Stubbs

A lawyer recalls his love affair with a country girl

Features scenes filmed on the Dart Valley Railway and the Torbay & Dartmouth Railway, including Kingswear station with a period train hauled by GWR '4500' 2-6-2T No 4555.

SUPERMAN IV – THE QUEST FOR PEACE
GB 1987 Cannon DVD
Dir: Sidney J. Furie
Christopher Reeve, Gene Hackman

Superman is determined that the world will lay down nuclear weapons

Features a scene supposedly on the New York subway but actually filmed at

Aldwych station on the London Underground with Piccadilly Line 1972-built tube stock. In other scenes Milton Keynes Central station was used as the setting for the United Nations building!

SUSPENDED ALIBI
GB 1957 Rank
Dir: Alfred Shaughnessy
Honor Blackman, Patrick Holt

A businessman is framed for the murder of his mistress

Features a scene at Liverpool Street station with a rake of 'blood and custard'-liveried coaches, and another at Harwich Parkeston Quay. No locos are seen.

SWALLOWS AND AMAZONS
GB 1974 EMI DVD
Dir: Claude Whatham
Virginia McKenna, Ronald Fraser

Four children have adventures in the Lake District

The start of the film depicts railway journey scenes filmed on the Lakeside & Haverthwaite Railway, with a train hauled by one of the preserved Fairburn 2-6-4Ts. There is also a shot of the frontage of Haverthwaite station.

SWEENEY 2
GB 1978 Euston Films VHS
Dir: Tom Clegg
John Thaw, Dennis Waterman

The Flying Squad investigates a series of armed robberies

In this film version of the TV series there is a scene where Thaw and Waterman cross a footbridge over an SR line under which an express slam-door EMU is passing. It was situated between Barnes and Mortlake stations.

SWEET WILLIAM
GB 1980 Kendon
Dir: Claude Whatham
Jenny Agutter, Sam Waterston

A London girl has a relationship with an American but finds that he strays

Features a scene where two of the characters leap from a train of Mk 1 coaches down an embankment, exact location unknown but probably on the WR. Another scene was filmed at Finchley Road Underground station.

SWIMMING POOL
France/GB 2003 Fidelite/Canal+ DVD
Dir: Francois Ozon
Charlotte Rampling, Ludivine Saguier

A writer takes a place in France to gain inspiration, and witnesses a murder

Features a scene on the London Underground with Central Line 1972-built tube stock.

THE SYSTEM
GB 1964 British Lion
Dir: Michael Winner
Oliver Reed, Barbara Ferris

Seaside youths enjoy chasing rich young girl visitors

The opening part of the film depicts a railway journey in the West Country, which is interesting despite being 'all at sea' in terms of geography and continuity. First some young men join the train at Churston station, which can be made out to be a Class 120 Cross-Country DMU. As the train continues there are a number of shots of 'Warship' diesels on expresses passing Dawlish. The journey finally ends at Brixham station, with a rare shot of a disc-headcode Class 22 diesel-hydraulic. These scenes were filmed after the Brixham branch had closed and the station was specially spruced up for the film.

Above THE SECRET AGENT (1996): Lancashire & Yorkshire Railway 0-6-0
No 52322 (also known as 1300) is prepared for night filming at Loughborough Central station,
Great Central Railway. *Paul Holroyd*

Below THE SECRET AGENT (1996): Finishing touches are given to Vintage Carriage Trust
stock at Loughborough Central in readiness for filming. *Paul Holroyd*

Above THE SEVEN PER CENT SOLUTION (1976): A German lobby-card
showing Ivatt 2MT No 46521 masquerading as No 60.116 for this Sherlock Holmes adventure,
filmed on the Severn Valley Railway. *Universal*

Below TIME BOMB (1952): Victor Maddern as the mad train bomber.
The film was also released as *Terror on a Train*. MGM

THE TITFIELD THUNDERBOLT (1952): One of the famous scenes in this legendary film. '1400' Class 0-4-2T No 1401 battles its way into screen immortality. *Canal + Image*

THE TITFIELD
THUNDERBOLT (1952):
An unusual rear shot of *Lion.*
Canal + Image

Above TRAIN OF EVENTS (1948): The elaborate train wreck
scene created at Wolverton by Ealing Studios. *BFI*

Below TURN THE KEY SOFTLY (1953): Yvonne Mitchell and
Kathleen Harrison on the platform of Holborn Underground station. *Rank*

Above THE VIRGIN AND THE GYPSY (1970): Peckett 0-4-0ST No 1999 runs into Cromford station on the Matlock branch for the cameras. *Martin Welch*

Below THE WRONG BOX (1966): The spectacular crash scene – the locomotives are actually well-constructed dummies, and the scene is believed to have been filmed on the Longmoor Military Railway. *Columbia*

Above YANKS (1979): BR Standard Class 5 4-6-0 No 75078 makes a surprise appearance as an LMS locomotive at Keighley station in this Second World War-based film. *Martin Welch*

Below YANKS (1979): American GIs arrive at Keighley goods yard while mobilising for D-Day. 'USA' 2-8-0 No 28201 awaits its next duty. *Martin Welch*

Above YOUNG WINSTON (1972): An armoured train comes under attack
in the African hills during the Boer War. Actually, it's heavily disguised GWR '1400' Class 0-4-2T
No 1466 in the Welsh hills! *Great Western Society*

Below YOUNG WINSTON (1972): No 1466 is prepared for its next take during filming.
Note the Class 08 shunter behind, which was used as motive power for a 'supply train' during filming
near Craig-y-Nos on the Neath & Brecon line. *Great Western Society*

T

TAKE A GIRL LIKE YOU
GB 1970 Columbia VHS
Dir: Jonathan Miller
Hayley Mills, Oliver Reed

A Northern girl comes to teach in London

The opening scenes depict Hayley Mills travelling by train – there is a distant shot of a Class 47 on an express on the WR main line and a scene in which Mills arrives at 'Henge' station – actually Slough – with a 'Hymek' bringing a train into the Windsor branch bay platform. Slough appears later on in the film, and there is a shot of Reed waiting in his car at a level crossing on the SR with a formation of four 2-BIL EMUs passing.

TAKE MY LIFE
GB 1947 GFD VHS
Dir: Ronald Neame
Hugh Williams, Greta Gynt

A woman journeys to Scotland to prove her husband innocent of murder

Includes a couple of stock shots from *Brief Encounter* (qv), with expresses hauled by an unrebuilt 'Royal Scot' 4-6-0 and a streamlined 'Duchess' passing Watford Junction. Later there is a shot of an 'A4' 'Pacific' on an express on the LNER main line. Stations at Edinburgh, York and King's Cross are all studio sets.

TALK OF THE DEVIL
GB 1936 B and D
Dir: Carol Reed
Ricardo Cortez, Sally Eilers

An impersonator pins a crooked deal on a shipping magnate

Features SR 'Lord Nelson' 4-6-0 No 859 passing with a Pullman express, and a scene at London Victoria station with 'King Arthur' 4-6-0 No 772 awaiting departure.

A TASTE OF HONEY
GB 1961 British Lion DVD
Dir: Tony Richardson
Rita Tushingham, Dora Bryan

A Salford teenager becomes pregnant by her black lover

Most of the film is set in Salford with some shots around the Manchester Ship Canal, with MSC wagons visible in the background. A Cravens Class 105 DMU also just makes it into the background of one scene. In the Blackpool scenes some trams can be seen passing by in the middle distance.

TAWNY PIPIT
GB 1944 GFD VHS
Dirs: Bernard Miles, Charles Saunders
Bernard Miles, Rosamund John

The discovery of a rare bird in a country village at wartime causes disruption

Features a scene at an unknown GWR country station with a local arriving behind '4575' 2-6-2T No 5518.

TEMPTATION HARBOUR
GB 1946 ABP
Dir: Lance Comfort
Robert Newton, Simone Simon

A railway signalman finds stolen money but also trouble when he decides to keep it

The signalman scenes were filmed at Folkestone Harbour with 'R1' Class 0-6-0Ts. Out-takes appear in Video 125's *Steam on 35mm* Vol 1.

TEN RILLINGTON PLACE
GB 1971 Columbia DVD
Dir: Richard Fleischer
Richard Attenborough, John Hurt

The story of the Christie murders in London in the 1940s

The sequence where Evans, played by Hurt, returns to Wales involves a scene at Merthyr Vale station on the Pontypridd-Merthyr line.

THE TENTH MAN
GB 1936 BIP
Dir: Brian Desmond Hurst
John Lodge, Antoinette Cellier

A crooked businessman tries every trick to get re-elected as an MP

The film opens with a shot looking up Ludgate Hill in London with an SR suburban EMU crossing the railway bridge heading for Holborn Viaduct. At the end there is a death scene with crowds filmed at King's Cross with an LNER Gresley 'A1' 'Pacific' at the buffer stops.

TERM OF TRIAL
GB 1962 Romulus
Dir: Peter Glenville
Laurence Olivier, Sarah Miles

A schoolteacher is accused of rape by a schoolgirl

Features a scene at an unknown terminus station with LMS and BR Mk 1 coaches visible.

TERROR
GB 1979 Entertainment/Bowergrange/ Crystal DVD
Dir: Norman J. Warren
John Nolan, Glynis Barber

An undead witch take revenge on her persecutor's descendants

Includes a scene on the London Underground on board 1972-built Bakerloo/Northern Line stock.

TERROR BY NIGHT
US 1946 Universal DVD
Dir: Roy William Neill
Basil Rathbone, Nigel Bruce

Sherlock Holmes recovers a stolen jewel on board the London-Edinburgh express

This Hollywood-made Sherlock Holmes mystery contains a pretty ramshackle collection of shots intended to depict the journey to Scotland. There are a couple of actual stock shots of British trains – one of a Royal Scot '4-6-0' leaving Euston and another of a passing rake of GWR coaches. The rest is studio, models (a replica of a GWR 4-6-0 and stock), some shots of American stock, and what seems to be a German loco, No 01-089!

TESS
France/GB 1979 Renn-Burrill DVD
Dir: Roman Polanski
Nastassja Kinski, Leigh Lawson

A peasant girl of noble heritage finds herself with an illegitimate child

This version of the famous Thomas Hardy novel features railway scenes filmed on the Bluebell Railway, including Horsted Keynes station. Trains that appear are hauled by preserved SECR 'H' Class 0-4-4T No 263.

THE TESTIMONY OF TALIESIN JONES
GB 2001 Snake River/CF1 Cyf
Dir: Martin Duffy
Griff Rhys Jones, Jonathan Pryce

A schoolboy thinks he has the power to heal

Features a scene at Pontypridd station (renamed 'Cwmderwen' for the film), with Class 150 'Sprinter' unit No 150 276 arriving, and Barry Town station as West Country resort 'West Haven', with a Class 142 'Pacer' set on screen.

THEATRE OF BLOOD
GB 1973 UA DVD
Dir: Douglas Hickox
Vincent Price, Diana Rigg

A Shakespearean actor murders the critics who have given him bad reviews

Features one shot filmed in South London with a passing SR 4-SUB EMU.

THESE FOOLISH THINGS
GB 2006 Outsider Pictures
Dir: Julian Taylor
Andrew Lincoln, Lauren Bacall

A actress in the 1930s tries to become a big stage star

A station scene near the end of the film is actually the transfer shed at Didcot Railway Centre. Preserved GWR '4575' Class 2-6-2T No 5572 can be seen in an adjacent platform.

THEY CAME TO A CITY
GB 1945 Ealing
Dir: Basil Dearden
Googie Withers, John Clements

Various people find themselves at the gate to a Utopian city

Two of the characters find themselves transported to the city while on a train journey. There is a rail-level shot of GWR '6100' 2-6-2T No 6108 passing on the GW&GC Joint line and an interesting shot of a double-headed parcels or milk working hauled by a 'Star' 4-6-0 and a 'Deans Goods' 0-6-0 entering a tunnel. An alternative tunnel scene appears in Video 125's *Steam on 35mm* Vol 2, with an LNER 'A5' entering.

THEY MET IN THE DARK
GB 1943 Rank VHS
Dir: Karel Lamac
Tom Walls, James Mason

A Blackpool theatre agent is actually a traitor and a spy

Includes some scenes filmed on the Midland Main Line with passing trains hauled by LMS 'Black Fives', a 'Jubilee' and a footplate shot from a 2-6-4T. There is also a Liverpool sequence with shots of Exchange station and Liverpool trams visible. A number of shots of GWR trains at Heyford were taken for this film, but none of them seem to have made it to the completed picture – these out-takes appear in *Steam on 35mm* Vols 3 and 4.

THEY WERE SISTERS
GB 1945 GFD/Gainsborough VHS
Dir: Arthur Crabtree
James Mason, Phyllis Calvert

The problems of three married sisters

Features a railway scene at Baynards station with a branch passenger train hauled by SR 'D3' 0-6-2T No 2372.

THINGS ARE LOOKING UP
GB 1935 Gaumont VHS
Dir: Albert de Courville
Cicely Courtneidge, Max Miller

A circus worker has to pose as her schoolmistress sister

Features a scene at an unknown SR station with a stationary train hauled by SR Maunsell 2-6-0.

13 EAST STREET
GB 1952 Eros/Tempean
Dir: Robert S. Baker
Patrick Holt, Sandra Dorne

An undercover policeman exposes a hijacking gang

Includes a scene where a couple of criminals escape from a speeding express. There is one shot of a GWR 'Castle' 4-6-0 on an embankment, probably on the GW&GC Joint line.

THIRTY IS A DANGEROUS AGE CYNTHIA

GB 1967 Columbia
Dir: Joe McGrath
Dudley Moore, Suzy Kendall

A night-club pianist has women trouble

Includes a couple of good shots of express trains on the LSWR main line hauled by Bulleid 'Pacifics', including 'West Country' No 34060. Later in the film there are some scenes filmed in a railway yard, with vans, a bolster wagon and a Pullman coach visible, location unknown.

THE 39 STEPS

GB 1935 Gaumont British DVD
Dir: Alfred Hitchcock
Robert Donat, Madeleine Carroll

A man wrongly pursued for murder flees to Scotland to find the real killer

The first and most famous adaptation of Buchan's story, this film is memorable for the sequence where Hannay makes his way to Scotland by train and jumps out on the Forth Bridge to avoid detectives. Ironically it is also the version that uses the least actual railway filming – most of the journey takes place in the studio; the shot where Donat (as Hannay) opens the carriage door and clings to the side of the carriage to enter the next door uses a section of wooden mock-up carriage and back projection from a train crossing the bridge, as well as the scenes of the train stopped on the bridge (which are believed to have been filmed on the roof of Islington Studios). There is a real shot,

however, taken from the bridge looking down at the Firth (with a small boat passing), and a general view of it as the police make a radio message looking for the wanted man. Earlier in the film, when Donat makes his journey, there are some real shots of King's Cross station with a couple of 'Gresley' 'A1' 4-6-2s (including No 2595). On the journey north we see a 'Castle' 4-6-0 (!) leaving a tunnel and trains hauled by a 'K2' 2-6-0 (possibly on the West Highland line) and an ex-NBR 'Atlantic' (entering the Forth Bridge). Some other LNER express shots taken for the film but not used appear in Video 125's *Steam on 35mm* Vol 3.

THE THIRTY NINE STEPS

GB 1959 Rank DVD
Dir: Ralph Thomas
Kenneth More, Taina Elg

A remake of the above

This colour version of the story follows the plot of the 1935 film and has some excellent railway shots. Two advantages this film has over the original is that the journey north to Scotland is a lot more accurate (we see real ECML expresses – no 'Castles' here!) and the film-makers clearly had full co-operation from BR Scottish Region to use the actual Forth Bridge. An 'A4' 'Pacific' on a rake of maroon Mk 1 coaches (used for Edinburgh-Aberdeen services) was run a number of times onto the bridge with a flat wagon on the back used by the film crew to film the back projection scenes where More hangs onto the side. A number of interesting out-takes survive, one revealing a 'J36' 0-6-0 in the background with an inspection saloon, thought to have been used by the film cast and crew. Back projection also appears where More is clinging to the girders of the bridge after he has made his escape, although he does use the actual inspection hatch between the tracks.

Earlier in the film there are shots of Edinburgh Waverley station – again, a number of out-takes survive that reveal 'V3' 2-6-2Ts and Metro-Cammell DMUs in the background; these all appear in *Steam on 35mm* Vol 3. 'A4' 'Pacifics' dominate the journey scenes – Nos 60012 and 60027 make appearances, not forgetting the 'A1' 'Pacifics' with which More has close encounters – Nos 60147 and 60162. Despite the accuracy and general excellence of the railway scenes, in terms of handling and style the film is seen as the worst of the three versions – c'est la vie!

THE THIRTY NINE STEPS
GB 1978 Rank DVD
Dir: Don Sharp
Robert Powell, Karen Dotrice

Another remake, but this time sticking closer to the original story

Clearly it was not possible to use steam trains on the Forth Bridge for this adaptation, so Rank used the Victoria Bridge on the Severn Valley Railway instead. Elegant as it is, it's not quite the same thing! This is also the worst of the three versions for accuracy. As Powell gets on the train bound for Scotland there are GWR-liveried coaches alongside – and note the BR-style 'First Class' totems in the windows. The location of the London scenes is supposed to be St Pancras but appears to have been filmed at Marylebone. The train is made up of Ivatt 2MT 2-6-0 No 644 (built after 1948!) in black livery with no lettering and a rake of LMS coaches with a 'MIDLAND' legend on their sides. As well as Victoria Bridge there are also shots of the train at Arley station. Later in the film, Powell's return from Scotland uses a stock shot of a night express hauled by a rebuilt 'Royal Scot' 4-6-0 and a brief cab-view scene from a train entering one of the Hadley Wood tunnels on the ECML (there is a brief glimpse of a very anachronistic colour light gantry as we enter!).

36 HOURS
GB 1954 Exclusive
Dir: Montgomery Tully
Dan Duryea, Kenneth Griffith

An American pilot on leave is framed for his estranged wife's murder

Features a shot of 'A1X' 'Terrier' No 3 on a branch train on the New Romney branch, taken from the earlier film *The Loves of Joanna Godden* (1947) (qv).

THIS HAPPY BREED
GB 1944 GFD VHS
Dir: David Lean
Robert Newton, Celia Johnson

Life between the wars with a London suburban family

Some railway shots appear in this minor classic – general shots of Paddington goods yard with various wagons on view, and the lines at Clapham Junction. There is a shot of a steam-shrouded GWR loco, possibly a 'Mogul'. Later there are scenes filmed on Clapham Common and a London tram can be seen passing.

THIS OTHER EDEN
GB 1960 Regal
Dir: Muriel Box
Leslie Phillips, Audrey Dalton

Passions stir when a statue of an IRA hero is unveiled in an Irish town

Made on location in Ireland, there is a shot of a branch-line train hauled by a Metro-Vick 'A' Class diesel.

THIS SPORTING LIFE
GB 1963 Rank VHS
Dir: Lindsay Anderson
Richard Harris, Rachel Roberts

A miner becomes a rugby player but cannot find contentment

Includes a scene where Harris wanders through a goods yard at night – mineral and van wagons are visible, together with a possible fruit van – location unknown.

THOMAS AND THE MAGIC RAILROAD
US/GB 2000 Icon/Destination/Gullane
   DVD
Dir: Britt Allcroft
Peter Fonda, Alec Baldwin

Thomas the Tank Engine's railway is threatened by an evil diesel

Rev Awdry's famous stories had already been adapted into a very popular television series and it was inevitable that they would eventually get the big-screen treatment. The result, however, is a transatlantic mish-mash incorporating characters from the US series 'The Magic Railroad'. The story has no relation to any of Awdry's but uses some of the loco characters – mainly centring on Thomas, Toby, James, Gordon and the villainous Diesel 10. 10 is a character made up for the film and seems to be based on a D800-series 'Warship' with a mechanical grab on the roof! His two henchmen are based on a pair of Class 08 shunters. Also in the film are some scenes filmed in the goods shed at Port St Mary on the Isle of Man Steam Railway with 0-6-0T No 15. The loco also appears later in the film in 'Isle of Sodor' form. Despite the negative critical reviews, the film was fairly popular and did the preservation movement, with its regular 'Thomas' events, no harm at all.

THOSE MAGNIFICENT MEN IN THEIR FLYING MACHINES
GB 1965 TCF DVD
Dir: Ken Annakin
Terry-Thomas, Stuart Whitman

A newspaper owner organises a London-Paris air race

This all-star spectacular has a memorable sequence in which Terry-Thomas lands his plane on a French steam train, but it is destroyed when the train enters a tunnel. These scenes were filmed on the now closed Bedford-Hitchin line around Shefford and Old Warden Tunnel with a train made up of preserved Highland Railway 'Jones Goods' 4-6-0 No 103 (with 'NORD' on its tender) and a rake of Caledonian coaches. Look to the right of Thomas as he walks along the carriage roofs in some shots and you can see a modern 1960s power station, even though the film is set in 1910!

THUNDER IN THE CITY
GB 1937 Atlantic
Dir: Marion Gering
Edward G. Robinson, Ralph Richardson

An American salesman helps a duke promote a non-existent metal

Features a shot of a passing LMS express – editing means that we don't see the engine, but there is a good view of the coaches, comprising compartment and non-corridor stock. There is also a studio scene with Robinson and the engine crew in a mock-up of a GWR tender loco cab.

THURSDAY'S CHILD
GB 1943 ABPC
Dir: Rodney Ackland
Stewart Granger, Sally Ann Howes

A child becomes a film star and success goes to her head

Features some scenes on the London Underground – a mixture of studio sets and real footage of 1938 tube stock arriving at Finchley Central on the Northern line. Later in the film there is a scene at King's Cross station with a close-up of the buffer-beam of 'A3' 4-6-2 No 4472 – probably taken from 1929's *The Flying Scotsman* (qv) – and a shot of an 'A3' with an express, probably on the GW&GC Joint line.

TIGER BAY
GB 1959 Rank DVD
Dir: J. Lee Thompson
Hayley Mills, Horst Buchholz

A Polish seaman in Cardiff kills his girlfriend and kidnaps a girl who witnesses it

The early scenes in this classic drama depict Buchholz using the Newport Transporter Bridge and walking past a GWR '5700' 0-6-0PT, close to Newport Pill sheds.

TIGER BY THE TAIL
GB 1955 Eros/Tempean
Dir: John Gilling
Larry Parks, Constance Smith

An American journalist uncovers a conspiracy in London

One scene in this film takes place near a railway line with a fight taking place, resulting in one of the villains being thrown under a train. Filmed somewhere next to the GW main line, a couple of 'Castle' 4-6-0s pass on expresses and a '5100' 2-6-2T can be seen on a freight train.

TIGER IN THE SMOKE
GB 1956 Rank
Dir: Roy Baker
Tony Wright, Donald Sinden

Ex-commando criminals search London for hidden loot

Features a scene believed to have been filmed at Fenchurch Street station with a train headed by BR Standard 2-6-4T No 80136.

TILL DEATH US DO PART
GB 1968 British Lion DVD
Dir: Norman Cohen
Warren Mitchell, Dandy Nichols

The life of Alf Garnett through the war years to the 1960s

A film spin-off from the successful TV sitcom, the war period sees the Garnett

family sleeping at an Underground station, believed to have been partly filmed at Aldwych station.

TIME BOMB (aka TERROR ON A TRAIN)
GB 1952 MGM
Dir: Ted Tetzlaff
Glenn Ford, Anne Vernon

A saboteur places a bomb on an ammunition train

Suspense drama that contains some excellent railway shots – one of those railway films that has become forgotten over the years. The terrorist smuggles the bomb aboard a night freight train carrying naval mines from the Midlands to Portsmouth and hides under a tarpaulin in one of wagons – there is a brief shot of a 'Black Five' 4-6-0 passing in the opposite direction. The motive power of the ammunition train is 8F 2-8-0 No 48600 – very much the star of these scenes, with some very good atmospheric shots of the loco passing back and forth as it reverses the train into sidings. The siding where the bomb is defused is believed to have been shot in the Willesden area. The terrorist is caught by police on Platform 1 at Portsmouth & Southsea station, and there are shots of trains arriving behind a 'T9' 4-4-0 and a 'U' Class 2-6-0.

TIME GENTLEMAN PLEASE
GB 1952 Group Three DVD
Dir: Lewis Gilbert
Eddie Byrne, Hermione Baddeley

A lazy tramp is a nuisance to a prize-winning village

Shot on location at Thaxted in East Anglia, there is a good overall view of Thaxted station near the start of the film, but with no trains present.

THE TITFIELD THUNDERBOLT

GB 1952 Ealing DVD
Dir: Charles Crichton
Stanley Holloway, John Gregson

Villagers take over a railway branch line to save it from closure

Probably the most famous railway film of all, and certainly one of the best-looking with the trains passing through the English countryside shot in loving Technicolor by a studio in its golden period. The railway details behind the film are well known. It was shot on the Limpley Stoke-Camerton branch with Monkton Coombe as 'Titfield' and Bristol Temple Meads as 'Mallingford'. *Lion* is, of course, the main star of the film as *Thunderbolt*, as well as two '1400' 0-4-2Ts, Nos 1401 and 1456 (both numbered 1401 for continuity reasons). Another '1400', No 1462, appears later in the film on the turntable at Oxford shed for a scene where it is driven off down a road (actually achieved with a very effectively disguised lorry). A '4500' 2-6-2T can be seen in the background during some of the shed scenes. The famous opening scene, filmed at Midford where the Somerset & Dorset line passed over the Camerton branch, features an S&D working hauled by 'West Country' 'Pacific' No 34043. A 'Hall' 4-6-0 passes with an express when *Lion* joins the main line near the climax at Fishers Crossing near Limpley Stoke, and, of course, there are the well-known final scenes at Bristol, with locomotives in the station and on Bath Road shed joining in for a chorus of whistles. A couple of 'Halls' are visible, as well as 'Star' 4-6-0 No 4056. A detailed book about the locations and filming of 'Titfield', *On the Trail of The Titfield Thunderbolt* by Simon Castens, published by Thunderbolt Books, is recommended.

Despite being well-loved by railway enthusiasts, the critical opinion of 'Titfield' has always been rather mixed. The main criticism voiced is that compared to other Ealing comedies it lacks bite, the satire is rather tame and it uses eccentric make-believe characters rather than anyone the audience can really identify with. Another criticism is that it is a retrograde film that celebrates an outdated railway for the sake of it, without moving on to the future, and the fact that the railway is saved because it is so slow typifies this. What is overlooked is that the film is actually rather ahead of its time in some of its attitudes:

- the idea of volunteers taking over and running a railway line with ancient stock predates what really began a decade later with the preservation movement. Actually, 'Titfield' was partly inspired by the Talyllyn Railway.
- additionally, the film predicts the move towards railway privatisation and local communities 'adopting' stations and branch lines.
- most tellingly, take note of the scene where an enquiry takes place regarding the closure of the Titfield line. The Squire, played by John Gregson, makes an impassioned speech about what might happen to the village if the railway closes and road transport is king. Seen today it is astonishingly far-sighted, with many villages and towns later being ruined by road-building schemes, as well as costs related to road deaths and the environment.

Aside from this it is important to enjoy the film on its own merits. Yes, it might seem a bit twee and unrealistic in places, but no other film captures the country branch line scene so romantically, and even if you get a bit tired of that the opening S&D and closing Bristol scenes are worth seeing on their own.

TOM AND VIV

GB/US 1994 Entertainment/Samuelson
Dir: Brian Gilbert
Willem Dafoe, Miranda Richardson

The story of poet T. S. Eliot's marriage and his wife's mental problems

Features a brief shot of a passing train filmed on the Bluebell Railway, hauled by Adams 4-4-2T No 488.

TOMMY
GB 1975 Hemdale VHS
Dir: Ken Russell
Roger Daltrey, Oliver Reed

A deaf, dumb and blind child is cured and becomes a rock star

The film version of The Who's rock opera includes a night scene filmed on the Bluebell Railway and a train hauled by preserved BR Standard 4MT No 75027.

TOMORROW WE LIVE
GB 1942 British Aviation
Dir: George King
John Clements, Greta Gynt

A spy in France is helped back to Britain by villagers

Features a scene where French Resistance fighters sabotage a railway line and cause the crash of a train, filmed in the studio with one night shot of a passing British train hauled by an unidentified loco.

TOP SECRET!
US 1984 Paramount DVD
Dir: Jim Abrahams, David Zucker, Jerry Zucker
Val Kilmer, Lucy Gutteridge

A rock star finds himself involved in espionage behind the Iron Curtain

Spoof comedy featuring sequences involving train journeys in East Germany. These scenes were filmed on the Nene Valley Railway with the Swedish 'B' Class 4-6-0 being used as motive power.

A TOUCH OF LARCENY
GB 1959 Paramount
Dir: Guy Hamilton
James Mason, Vera Miles

A naval commander deliberately disappears so he can be branded a traitor and sue for libel

Features a couple of shots of passing streamlined 'Duchess' 4-6-2s on expresses passing Watford Junction (stock shots originally filmed for *Brief Encounter* – qv).

A TOUCH OF LOVE
GB 1969 Amicus VHS
Dir: Waris Hussein
Sandy Dennis, Ian McKellan

A student tries to get an abortion but later decides against it

Includes a scene on the concourse of Marylebone station.

TOWN ON TRIAL
GB 1956 Columbia
Dir: John Guillermin
John Mills, Charles Coburn

A police inspector investigates the murder of a girl in a small town

Shot on location in and around the town of Weybridge, early in the film there is a scene looking down on the station with a couple of 2-BIL EMUs in the platform.

TRAIN OF EVENTS
GB 1948 Ealing VHS
Dirs: Basil Dearden, Charles Crichton, Sidney Cole
Jack Warner, Peter Finch

A number of stories climax with a train disaster

This was one of a series of 'portmanteau' films that appeared from various companies in post-war Britain in which a number of stories are all linked to a certain event, in this case a train disaster. A large amount of fascinating railway footage was filmed for the production on the LMR West Coast Main Line with a mixture of locomotives in both LMS and the new British Railways liveries. The bulk of the footage is split between departures from Euston station, the section between Euston and the top of Camden Bank (including Camden shed) and in the Home Counties around Bushey. Most of this footage was not used and a lot appeared hidden behind opening screen titles, although throughout the next two decades the odd shot would appear in other films that required a scene of a passing train. Indeed, this footage has since been released by Video 125 in their *Steam on 35mm* video.

The main loco in the film is rebuilt 'Royal Scot' 4-6-0 No 46126, which hauls the doomed train, but throughout the film other 'Royal Scots' (both rebuilt and unrebuilt) appear, together with 'Jubilees', 'Duchesses', 4F and 2F 0-6-0s, 2-6-4Ts, 'Patriot' 4-6-0 No 45588, 'Jubilee' 4-6-0 No 5613, two 'Jinty' tanks, Nos 47675 and 47327 (which Jack Warner refers to as 'Old Lizzie'), and ex-LNWR 'Super D' 0-8-0s. The crash scene itself uses model shots, with the aftermath of the wreckage filmed at Wolverton Carriage Works using old coach parts. An unintentionally amusing moment occurs earlier in the film where two of the characters go to a flat in 'Camden', which overlooks a line on which an express passes behind a Southern 'West Country' 'Pacific'! Another scene featuring the same characters occurs outside Strand Underground station (now Charing Cross).

Jack Warner was left with a painful reminder of this film when he overbalanced and fell in the cab during filming of the crash scene, causing an injury to his spine that stayed with him for the rest of his life – ironic, considering that it was all about a real train accident. Maybe concerns about a jinx prompted the blacking out of the last digit of No 46126's number in some scenes so it runs as '4612'. It is impossible to know, but an interesting postscript to the 'jinx' story

occurred years later in the late 1980s. Channel 4 was scheduled to screen the film one afternoon, but the Clapham rail disaster a couple of days before caused it to be cancelled at short notice, as it was deemed inappropriate to show the story so soon after a real crash. Rescheduled for a later date, a couple of days before screening the Purley rail disaster occurred, causing Channel 4 to change its schedule again. Channel 4 did eventually successfully show the film without incident, so perhaps it was all an unfortunate coincidence…

TRAINSPOTTING
GB 1996 Polygram/Channel 4 DVD
Dir: Danny Boyle
Ewan McGregor, Robert Carlyle

Four Scottish friends suffer the highs and lows of heroin addiction

This phenomenally successful British film of the 1990s includes a well-known scene filmed at Corrour station on the West Highland line (a Class 156 'Sprinter' can be seen departing). Later there is a shot of a Class 87 electric on an express on the WCML.

TREAD SOFTLY STRANGER
GB 1958 Alderdale VHS
Dir: Gordon Parry
Diana Dors, George Baker

Two brothers in a Northern town rob a steelworks

This gritty North Country drama has a number of atmospheric railway scenes. George Baker gets off a train at 'Rawborough', hauled by an LMS Compound 4-4-0 – the actual location is Parkgate & Rawmarsh station near Sheffield. Most of the action takes place around a steelworks, believed to be in Parkgate itself, with a number of industrial 0-4-0STs visible on coal and steel trains. There is one good shot of loco No 28 crossing a street with a rake of mineral wagons. A 'J11' 0-6-0 also appears in a night shot and there is one daytime scene, believed to have been shot in Rotherham, with a freight passing behind an 8F 2-8-0.

TREE OF HANDS
GB 1988 Pathé/Granada/FilmFour
Dir: Giles Foster
Helen Shaver, Lauren Bacall

An American writer provides a home for an abused boy

Features a scene filmed in East London with a Class 315 EMU passing on a viaduct.

THE TRIALS OF OSCAR WILDE
GB 1960 Warwick
Dir: Ken Hughes
Peter Finch, John Fraser

Oscar Wilde sues the Marquis of Queensberry for libel with disastrous results

The final scenes, where Wilde leaves Britain for France, take place on Marylebone station. A rake of suburban coaches are prominent but the loco that takes the train out is not seen, presumably to keep the period feel.

TRIO
GB 1950 Rank DVD
Dirs: Ken Annakin, Harold French
James Hayter, Kathleen Harrison

A collection of three stories by W. Somerset Maugham

The final story in the collection, 'Sanatorium', takes place in the Scottish Highlands and there are a couple of shots of a railway journey as one of the characters arrives there. A 'Black Five' 4-6-0 passes on a train on the West Highland and there is a rare shot of an ex-NBR 4-4-0 arriving at an unknown station. Some extra material was shot at Newcastle Central but was not used – this appears in *Steam on 35mm* Vol 4.

TROTTIE TRUE
GB 1949 GFD VHS
Dir: Brian Desmond Hurst
Jean Kent, James Donald

The life of a gaiety girl who married into nobility

Includes a scene with Kent boarding a departing train. We don't see the motive power, but there are some nice colour views of green-liveried SR suburban stock, location not known.

THE TRUTH ABOUT LOVE
GB 2004 Piccadilly Pictures
Dir: John Hay
Jennifer Love Hewitt, Dougray Scott

A man drunkenly sends a valentine card to his best friend's wife

The final scenes were filmed at Cardiff Central station (with one brief shot of Hewitt running up to the entrance of Bristol Temple Meads), with some good views of Arriva-liveried Class 158 'Sprinters' (including set No 158 818) in Platform 1.

TURN THE KEY SOFTLY
GB 1953 GFD
Dir: Jack Lee
Yvonne Mitchell, Joan Collins

Three women are released from prison with the chance to go straight

Includes some scenes filmed at Holborn Underground station (Piccadilly Line platform), with a couple of 1924-built tube trains, and a scene at the entrance to Leicester Square station.

TURTLE DIARY
GB 1985 CBS/United British Artists VHS
Dir: John Irvin
Glenda Jackson, Ben Kingsley

Two eccentrics decide to release turtles from London Zoo

Includes a scene on the London Underground with Kingsley on board a District Line 'D'-type unit.

24 HOUR PARTY PEOPLE
GB 2002 Pathé/FilmFour DVD
Dir: Michael Winterbottom
Steve Coogan, Sean Harris

The story of record producer Tony Wilson and the Factory Records label

This curiously surreal drama about the early Manchester music scene features a number of railway sequences: a train journey made by Coogan in the film is made from shots taken on board real Mk 2 coaches, a OO-gauge model of some Mk 2s, and a computer-generated scene where Coogan narrowly avoids being hit by an HST! There is also some brief stock footage of the Liverpool & Manchester Railway's *Lion*, probably taken from the 1930s, which crops up in an earlier part of the film.

TWENTYFOURSEVEN
GB 1997 Pathé/BBC/Scala VHS
Dir: Shane Meadows
Bob Hoskins, Mat Hand

A man tries to set up a boxing club for local youths

A couple of scenes feature Hoskins using an old wooden box wagon, possibly an ex-NE type, filmed at Rushcliffe Halt on the Great Central Railway (Nottingham) line to Ruddington.

28 DAYS LATER
GB 2002 TCF/DNA Films DVD
Dir: Danny Boyle
Cillian Murphy, Christopher Eccleston

A virus turns most of the population of Britain and Europe into vicious zombies

This doomsday science-fiction horror ingeniously used scenes of a deserted London to disturbing effect. In one sequence some of the characters hide out in the empty Canary Wharf Underground station, and later they can be seen walking along the Docklands Light Railway and leaving via South Quays station.

29 ACACIA AVENUE
GB 1945 Boca/Columbia
Dir: Henry Cass
Gordon Harker, Betty Balfour

Young people's fun is disrupted when their parents arrive unexpectedly from holiday

Features one going-away shot of an SR 3-SUB EMU, somewhere on the South Western Division.

TWICE ROUND THE DAFFODILS
GB 1962 Anglo-Amalgamated VHS
Dir: Gerald Thomas
Donald Sinden, Kenneth Williams

Comic and serious scenes of life in a TB sanatorium

There are good shots of Seer Green station on the GW&GC Joint line at the start of the film, with a Class 115 DMU arriving.

TWIN TOWN
GB 1997 Polygram DVD
Dir: Kevin Allen
Rhys Ifans, Dougray Scott

Two brothers take revenge on a local businessman for the death of their parents and sister

In this successful Welsh-based comedy of the 1990s there is one scene outside Swansea station with an HST visible at the buffer stops in the background.

TWO LEFT FEET
GB 1963 British Lion VHS
Dir: Roy Baker
Michael Crawford, Nyree Dawn Porter

A young man has woman trouble

Features a railway journey sequence where a party joins a train at Windsor & Eton Central station made up of a green Class 121 single-car unit and trailer. There is a good shot of a Class 121 en route along the branch, then a shot of the train arriving at its destination – Windsor & Eton Central again!

TWO MEN WENT TO WAR
GB 2002 Guerilla Films DVD
Dir: John Henderson
Kenneth Cranham, Leo Bill

During the second World War a couple of Army dentists decide to invade France on their own

Features some good railway scenes as the two soldiers head from Aldershot to Plymouth by train, filmed on the Bluebell Railway. Sheffield Park doubled as 'Aldershot' and Horsted Keynes as 'Plymouth', with preserved 'West Country' 4-6-2 No 21C123 *Blackmore Vale* hauling the train. When in France the two attempt to derail an ammunition train by getting into a signal box – these scenes were filmed on the Mid-Hants Railway at Ropley station with disguised 'N' Class 2-6-0 No 31874 (it had to be disguised as it was running as James the Red Engine at the time!). The shot of the wreckage after the train crash is a model.

TWO WAY STRETCH
GB 1960 British Lion DVD
Dir: Robert Day
Peter Sellers, Lionel Jeffries

Three convicts break jail to commit a robbery

The actual robbery takes place at an overbridge, with Sellers using a railway steam crane to lift the jewel van, location unknown. The final scenes feature a comedy sequence filmed at Windsor & Eton Central with Sellers and Co leaving on a departing train (Wilfred Hyde White gets left behind in an uncoupled coach), and a scene where Bernard Cribbins has to take the loot with him onto a carriage roof to avoid the police. This sequence was filmed on the then freight-only Pulborough-Midhurst branch with a short train hauled by a 'C2X' 0-6-0. The jewel bag is lost as the train passes through Fittleworth station.

U

UFO

GB 1993 Feature Film/Polygram DVD
Dir: Tony Dow
Roy 'Chubby' Brown, Sara Stockbridge

Female aliens kidnap Roy 'Chubby' Brown for telling offensive jokes

Features scenes filmed in Blackpool and a Boat-type tram makes an appearance.

ULYSSES

GB 1967 Walter Reade DVD
Dir: Joseph Strick
Milo O'Shea, Martin Dempsey

Life in Dublin with a Jewish newspaperman and a poet

This version of the James Joyce novel includes a scene at Dublin Pearse station with a departing CIE 1950s-built DMU.

UNCLE SILAS

GB 1947 GFD
Dir: Charles Frank
Jean Simmons, Derrick de Marney

A young Victorian girl is pursued by her uncle for her inheritance

A railway journey in the film is made up of the clever use of studio models with locomotives of various Victorian types including single-drivers.

UNDER SUSPICION

GB 1991 Rank VHS
Dir: Simon Moore
Liam Neeson, Kenneth Cranham

In the 1950s a private detective is suspected of murder

Includes a scene shot at the frontage of Brighton station.

UNDER THE SKIN

GB 1997 BFI/Channel 4 VHS
Dir: Carine Adler
Samantha Morton, Claire Rushbrook

Two women deal with the death of their mother in different ways

Features a scene filmed on the concourse of Liverpool Lime Street station.

UNDERCOVER

GB 1943 Ealing
Dir: Sergei Nolbandov
Tom Walls, Michael Wilding

In occupied Yugoslavia, partisans fight the Nazis

This obscure propaganda film was made by Ealing in the middle of the war, and part of the story involves the sabotage of Nazi supply trains. With filming in Yugoslavia obviously out of the question, British rolling-stock was used; a German 'Pacific' does appear in one shot, but this is thought to be a model. One, maybe two 'A3' 4-6-2s were modified with smoke deflectors and stovepipe chimneys to appear as Continental locos – in various shots the numbers appear to be '743' and '274'. Possibly it was one locomotive, No 2743, with one number blacked out in different scenes to give the impression of two locos. There are some shots that appear to be in some quarry sidings with a 'J52' 0-6-0ST in the background, and in a tunnel, possibly Welwyn, during the night. A later scene, where ammunition train wagons are blown up, was filmed at Ravenscourt Park coal sidings in West London.

UNDERGROUND
GB 1928 BIP
Dir: Anthony Asquith
Brian Aherne, Elissa Landi

Two Underground workers fight over the same girl

This silent melodrama uses many location shots filmed on the London Underground. Throughout the film there are scenes filmed at Waterloo station on the escalators, booking hall and Bakerloo Line platforms, and there are a couple of shots of 1920s-built tube stock. The final chase sequence was filmed inside and on the roof of Lots Road power station, and climaxes in a lift in Covent Garden station at night. Grosvenor Bridge can be seen in the background of one scene with distant SR steam-hauled services visible.

UP THE CREEK
GB 1958 Byron DVD
Dir: Val Guest
Peter Sellers, David Tomlinson

A naïve naval lieutenant is put in charge of a disreputable ship

Various wagons can be seen on the dockside in some early scenes in this film, and briefly what looks like a small privately owned 0-4-0 diesel shunter.

UP THE JUNCTION
GB 1967 Paramount/BHE
Dir: Peter Collinson
Suzy Kendall, Dennis Waterman

A well-off girl goes to live with the working class in Clapham

As the title suggests, various railway scenes appear filmed around Clapham Junction and Battersea. Electric units seen include a 4-SUB, 2-BIL, 4-EPBs and a Class 205 DEMU.

UPSTAIRS AND DOWNSTAIRS
GB 1959 Rank
Dir: Ralph Thomas
Michael Craig, Anne Heywood

Newlyweds have problems with maids and a French au pair girl

A railway journey in the film features shots of a 'Castle' 4-6-0 passing with 'blood and custard'-liveried stock (in later shots it changes to local passenger maroon stock!), and an 'A3' 4-6-2 on an express, possibly on the GW&GC Joint line. There is also a scene with maroon GWR stock at Windsor & Eton Central station. Near the end of the film there is a departure from what is supposed to be King's Cross, but this was actually made up of shots of Edinburgh Waverley station (taken from footage for the same year's *The Thirty Nine Steps* – qv); 'A4' 'Pacific' No 60012 is at the head of the train. Note the close-up shot of the engine whistle blowing – it's actually the whistle and firebox of an ex-LMS loco.

V FOR VENDETTA
GB/US 2005 Warner DVD
Dir: James McTeigue
Natalie Portman, Hugo Weaving

A totalitarian British government is opposed by a terrorist in a Guy Fawkes mask

The film's climax depicts a tube train loaded with explosives being driven under and destroying the Houses of Parliament. These scenes were filmed at the abandoned Aldwych station with 1972-built tube stock.

VALLEY OF SONG
GB 1953 ABPC
Dir: Gilbert Gunn
Mervyn Johns, Clifford Evans

Members of a Welsh town choir are split over an interpretation of Messiah

The opening title sequence of this Welsh comedy is taken from the front of a train on the Carmarthen-Aberystwyth line near Conwil. The entire footage, without titles, survives and appears in Video 125's *Steam on 35mm Vol 2*. Elsewhere there are shots of Collett '2251' Class 0-6-0-hauled trains on the Carmarthen-Llandeilo branch line, with scenes at Golden Grove and Drysllwyn stations.

VALUE FOR MONEY
GB 1955 Rank
Dir: Ken Annakin
John Gregson, Diana Dors

A Yorkshire businessman falls for a London showgirl

Features a scene filmed at Batley station, West Yorkshire, with a local train arriving hauled by an ex-LMS Fowler 2-6-4T.

THE VAN
Ireland/GB 1996 VHS
Dir: Stephen Frears
Colm Meaney, Donal O'Kelly

A redundant baker starts a mobile fish and chip business with a friend

Filmed in and around Dublin with one shot of a CIE 'Dart' unit passing in the background.

THE VERY EDGE
GB 1963 British Lion
Dir: Cyril Frankel
Richard Todd, Anne Heywood

A pregnant woman is menaced by an obsessive stalker

In one scene Heywood goes to a railway station to take a train to London, but the station is actually Broad Street, so she's already there! A 'Black Five' 4-6-0 is reversing a rake of stock out of one platform and one of the North London line's Oerlikon EMUs is in another.

VICTORIA THE GREAT
GB 1937 British Lion VHS
Dir: Herbert Wilcox
Anna Neagle, Anton Walbrook

The life of Queen Victoria

This all-stops-out expensive biopic for its time was a big box office success. The scenes where Victoria and Albert go away on honeymoon used a vintage train supplied by the LMS, comprising Liverpool & Manchester Railway 0-4-2 *Lion* with replica coaches and a mix of outdoor filming and studio sets. There are some good shots of the vintage train passing on the Watford Junction-St Albans Abbey branch at Brickett Wood.

A VIEW TO A KILL

GB 1985 MGM-UA DVD
Dir: John Glen
Roger Moore, Christopher Walken

James Bond fights a ruthless industrialist

The climax of the film takes place at a supposed silver mine in Silicon Valley. These scenes were filmed at Amberley Chalk Pits Museum in Sussex, and some of the narrow-gauge railway system can be seen.

VILLAIN

GB 1971 EMI VHS
Dir: Michael Tuchner
Richard Burton, Ian McShane

The rise and fall of a sadistic East End gangland boss

Features some scenes involving a train journey along the North London Line with Nigel Davenport boarding a Class 501 EMU at South Acton station and a shot outside Acton Central station. The back projection plate through the carriage window as he makes his journey clearly shows the freight yards around the Old Oak and Acton areas. The final scenes in the film are located near to the SR lines from Waterloo in the Battersea area, and 2-BIL and 4-SUB EMUs can be seen passing. A good out-take of a passing 4-SUB appears in Video 125's *Diesels and Electrics on 35mm* Vol 1.

VIOLENT PLAYGROUND

GB 1958 Rank
Dir: Basil Dearden
Stanley Baker, Anne Heywood

A junior liaison officer in Liverpool tries to solve fire-raising incidents

Filmed on location in Liverpool, there is one scene on the now vanished Liverpool Central station and a scene under the Liverpool Overhead Railway with one of the dock 0-6-0STs moving slowly past with some wagons.

THE VIRGIN AND THE GYPSY

GB 1970 Kenwood
Dir: Christopher Miles
Joanna Shimkus, Franco Nero

A clergyman's daughter falls in love with a gypsy fortune-teller

D. H. Lawrence set the opening scenes of his short story at Cromford station, close to where he lived, and this is the actual railway location that appears in the film, with a rare occurrence of a privately preserved steam train being filmed on BR metals during the steam ban. Peckett 0-4-0ST No 1999 was used with a Midland six-wheeler and Metropolitan Railway coach, all from the Keighley & Worth Valley Railway. The loco came by road with the coaches by rail; the train was steamed up and down the Matlock line with a BR crew during a couple of days in July 1969. The sight of the train on a normal running BR line caused some confusion, with at least one enquiry at Matlock station as to whether it was the train to Derby!

THE VIRGIN SOLDIERS

GB 1969 Columbia DVD
Dir: John Dexter
Hywel Bennett, Lynn Redgrave

Trials of British Army troops on active duty during the Malayan Emergency

Although many railway scenes from this

film were shot in Malaya itself, a train crash that occurs near the end was filmed in this country on the abandoned Audley End-Bartlow branch at Saffron Walden. Withdrawn 'Black Five' 4-6-0 No 44781 was bought by Columbia and 'modified' to look like a Far Eastern locomotive with cow-catcher, headlamp and large side tanks, then 'derailed' and positioned in a ditch alongside the wrecked track. Columbia offered the locomotive for sale to a local enthusiast after filming for £1,700, but the quoted cost of £5,000 for salvaging and transportation was prohibitive, so No 44781 was eventually sold for scrap and cut up where it lay, a circumstance that has caused controversy and speculation in the railway preservation circle ever since.

VIRTUAL SEXUALITY
GB 1999 Columbia TriStar DVD
Dir: Nick Hurran
Laura Fraser, Rupert Penry-Jones

When an experiment goes wrong a teenage girl is transformed into two people

Features a scene outside Earls Court Underground station.

WALTZ OF THE TOREADORS
GB 1962 Rank Wintle-Parkyn DVD
Dir: John Guillermin
Peter Sellers, Margaret Leighton

A retired general loses his mistress to his son

Features scenes filmed on the then newly formed Bluebell Railway with a train hauled by a preserved SECR 'P' Class 0-6-0T and Sheffield Park station.

THE WAR LOVER
GB 1962 Columbia VHS
Dir: Philip Leacock
Steve McQueen, Shirley Anne Field

An American Air Force commander in 1940s England causes problems at an East Anglian base

Features some fascinating scenes filmed at Liverpool Street with 'B1' 4-6-0 No 61378 entering with McQueen on the footplate. Some attempt has been made to give the loco a 1940s look (despite being a post-war design) with NE transfers on the tender and the BR '6' prefix removed from the cabside number. In the following shots another 'B1' can be seen in another platform in the background. There is also a stock shot of an ECML express hauled by a named 'V2' 2-6-2.

A WARM DECEMBER
GB/US 1973 First Artists/Verdon
Dir: Sidney Poitier
Sidney Poitier, Esther Anderson

A doctor in London falls for a dying girl

Features a scene at an unknown station with an SR 4-EPB EMU.

WATERFRONT
GB 1950 GFD
Dir: Michael Anderson
Robert Newton, Richard Burton

A drunken seaman returns to Liverpool and causes trouble

Filmed on location in Liverpool, there are scenes on the Liverpool Overhead Railway with some LOR sets, including original unit No 44 and refurbished No 16. There are also some Liverpool trams on view.

WATERLAND
GB 1992 Mayfair/Palace/Pandora/
    Channel 4 VHS
Dir: Stephen Gyllenhaal
Jeremy Irons, Sinead Cusack

A teacher tells his class of his life growing up in East Anglia

Includes some scenes filmed on the North Norfolk Railway with a train hauled by preserved LMS 'Jinty' 0-6-0T No 47383.

WATERLOO BRIDGE
US 1940 MGM DVD
Dir: Mervyn Le Roy
Vivien Leigh, Robert Taylor

An Army officer marries a ballerina but she becomes a prostitute when he is reported missing

Includes a shot of a passing GWR express hauled by a 'King' 4-6-0.

WATERLOO ROAD
GB 1944 GFD DVD
Dir: Sidney Gilliat
John Mills, Stewart Granger

A soldier goes AWOL to sort out his wife's relationship with a crook

As the title suggests this production was set in and around the confines of Waterloo station and includes some great scenes of trains passing into the terminus. In the opening credit sequence an 'M7' 0-4-4T passes and there are shots of trains leaving behind 'Schools' Class 4-4-0 No 932, 'Lord Nelson' 4-6-0 No 864, and a real rarity – 'N15X' 4-6-0 No 2332. John Mills escapes the military police by leaping from a departing Portsmouth line 4-COR EMU and runs across the tracks, narrowly missing a light 'H' Class 0-4-4T. Also visible at various points in the film are another 'Lord Nelson', a 'King Arthur' 4-6-0 and some suburban three-car and four-car EMUs, as well as London trams. Some extra footage appears in the Video 125 production *Steam on 35mm Vol 4*.

WEDDING REHEARSAL
GB 1932 Ideal/London Films VHS
Dir: Alexander Korda
Roland Young, Merle Oberon

An officer foils an attempt by his grandmother to get him married

Includes a train arriving at Cole Green station on the LNER's Hatfield-Hertford branch, with some good views of the locomotive, 'N7' 0-6-2T No 2655.

WE'LL MEET AGAIN
GB 1942 Columbia
Dir: Phil Brandon
Vera Lynn, Geraldo

A singer suffers when her boyfriend loves another

Features one shot taken from a signal box of a passing LMS express hauled by a 'Royal Scot' 4-6-0.

WHAT A CARVE UP
GB 1961 New World/Baker-Berman VHS
Dir: Pat Jackson
Sid James, Kenneth Connor

A madman plots to murder his relatives

This 'Carry On'-style farce includes a stock shot of a short LMS passenger arriving at an unknown station behind an ex-LNWR 0-6-0ST.

WHAT'S UP NURSE
GB 1978 Blackwater VHS
Dir: Derek Ford
Nicholas Field, Graham Stark

Sexual adventures of a new doctor at a provincial hospital

A train journey sequence features at the start of the film, and there is a shot of a Class 55 'Deltic' on an express on the ECML. Most of the film was shot in and around Southend, and there is a scene outside Westcliffe station.

WHEEL OF FATE
GB 1953 Rank/Kenilworth
Dir: Francis Searle
Patric Doonan, Bryan Forbes

A garage owner has problems with his black sheep brother

There are some good railway scenes near the end of this second feature with Forbes running across tracks in front of a train at night – the locomotive in question is slow-moving 'B1' 4-6-0 No 61106, probably filmed in sidings at King's Cross goods yard. Also making an appearance are 'L1' 2-6-4T No 67786 on a passenger train and stock footage from *Brief Encounter* (qv) of a streamlined 'Duchess' 'Pacific' with an express.

WHEN SATURDAY COMES
GB 1996 Guild/Capitol DVD
Dir: Maria Giese
Sean Bean, Emily Lloyd

A brewery worker dreams of becoming a professional footballer

Includes a scene where Bean walks along a railway track contemplating suicide and is almost run down by a Class 56 diesel on a short train of MGR wagons. This was filmed on a freight branch in the Sheffield area.

WHEN THE DEVIL DRIVES
GB 1907 Charles Urban DVD
Dir: W. R. Booth
Actors unknown

The Devil blights a family's day trip

This early special-effects film was designed to thrill audiences with the Devil taking the controls of a train, taking it through the sea and spinning it around the sky. Most of this makes use of a Bassett-Lowke O-gauge model and painted-on effects. Look closely at the scene where the train 'travels' along the sea-bed and you can see the cameraman reflected in the glass of the fish tank! There are also some real railway scenes: a shot outside a railway station believed to be Muswell Hill, an LNWR 4-4-0 arriving at Llandudno Junction station, a very rare shot of an express passing near Llandudno behind a Compound 2-2-2-2, and a shot of an LSWR 4-4-0 on an express taken from another train travelling in the opposite direction. All this footage also appears in Video 125's *Trains from the Arc*.

WHERE ANGELS FEAR TO TREAD
GB 1991 Rank VHS
Dir: Charles Sturridge
Helena Bonham Carter, Judy Davis

A brother and sister travel to Italy to bring back the baby of their dead sister-in-law

Features scenes filmed on the Bluebell Railway, with Horsted Keynes station posing as 'Sawton'. Preserved North London Railway 0-6-0T No 58850 was used to haul a period train.

WHERE THE BULLETS FLY
GB 1966 Golden Era/Alastair Films
Dir: John Gilling
Tom Adams, Dawn Addams

A secret agent is assigned to get a secret formula for nuclear energy

This spy drama, clearly imitating the James Bond style popular at the time, has action scenes filmed at Staines West station and along the branch with Mk 1 coaches used but unseen motive power. There are a couple of shots, however, of 'Hymek' diesels with expresses on the WR main line and a scene on Waterloo station concourse.

WHERE THERE'S A WILL
GB 1953 Film Locations/Eros
Dir: Vernon Sewell
Kathleen Harrison, George Cole

A London family inherits a derelict Devon farm

Features a nice shot of a Dart Valley branch train arriving at Staverton station, long before preservation was thought of, made up of '1400' Class 0-4-2T No 1439 and auto-coach No W244W.

WHISPERING SMITH HITS LONDON
GB 1951 Exclusive/Hammer
Dir: Francis Searle
Richard Carlson, Greta Gynt

An American detective investigates a London murder

Features scenes filmed at Paddington station at the conclusion of the film. No locos are seen, but there is a good view of Hawksworth-designed coaches.

WHISTLE DOWN THE WIND
GB 1961 Rank/Allied Film Makers DVD
Dir: Bryan Forbes
Hayley Mills, Alan Bates

Children think a murderer on the run is Christ

In one scene of this classic film set and filmed in Lancashire, Mills runs onto a railway track and into a tunnel, which is at Bacup, Lancs.

WHITE CARGO
GB 1973 Border/Negus-Fancey
Dir: Ray Selfe
David Jason, Hugh Lloyd

A civil servant rescues some strippers from a slave-trader

Features a scene with David Jason on the platform at an unknown SR station with an SR two-car suburban EMU departing.

THE WILDCATS OF ST TRINIAN'S
GB 1980 Wildcat
Dir: Frank Launder
Sheila Hancock, Michael Hordern

The schoolgirls form a union and kidnap an Arab's daughter

Features a number of railway shots: two of passing HSTs probably filmed on the WR, a scene at Windsor & Eton Central station with a refurbished Class 117 DMU, and a scene at London Victoria with 4-EPB and express EMUs.

THE WIND IN THE WILLOWS
GB 1996 Guild/Allied Film-makers DVD
Dir: Terry Jones
Terry Jones, Eric Idle

Weasel property developers threaten the homes of Mole and Toad

An adaptation of the famous Kenneth Grahame story, it includes a spectacular railway sequence filmed on the Bluebell Railway. Toad has escaped from prison with the police in pursuit and heads for the railway station. Getting on board the footplate of an arriving train he is forced to take the controls after losing the driver with the police shooting from the carriages. The highly complex scenes, with special equipment attached to the locomotive and rolling-stock to allow actors to move around, used preserved 'C' Class 0-6-0 No 592 and the K&ESR's vintage train rake. Horsted Keynes is the station where Toad and his friends board the train and much of the filming, where Toad drives the train up to 106mph (!), takes place between Monteswood Lane bridge and Waterworks bridge, with West Hoathly Tunnel in one scene. The final scene where the engine, by now uncoupled from its train, leaves the rails used a very realistic wooden and plastic replica of 592's tender placed next to the line in the trees as well as a lot of speeded-up photography.

A WINDOW IN LONDON
GB 1939 G and S/GFD
Dir: Herbert Mason
Michael Redgrave, Sally Gray

A construction worker thinks he sees a murder from a train

Includes scenes on the London Underground on the Piccadilly/District Lines shared section between Earls Court and Barons Court (the murder takes place in one of the tenement flats that overlooks the lines near Barons Court). There are good shots of District Line units with a couple of the older 1920s clerestory-type sets, a modern oval-window unit and a brief shot of 'R'-type stock with 1920s Piccadilly tube stock passing. There is also a scene at Earls Court station itself. The construction site where Redgrave works in the film has a narrow gauge line with a small petrol locomotive, possibly a Lister.

THE WINGS OF THE DOVE
GB/US 1997 Miramax/Renaissance Dove
   DVD
Dir: Iain Softley
Helena Bonham Carter, Linus Roache

A journalist has an affair with a dying heiress, prompted by his lover

Includes scenes shot at Aldwych station on the London Underground.

WINGS OF THE MORNING
GB 1937 New World
Dir: Harold Schuster
Henry Fonda, Annabella

Romance develops between the descendants of a nobleman and a gypsy princess

The first British feature film made in colour has a brief shot of a London tram crossing Westminster Bridge, partially obscured in traffic.

THE WINSLOW BOY
GB 1949 British Lion/London Films VHS
Dir: Anthony Asquith
Robert Donat, Margaret Leighton

A naval cadet's father is determined to prove his son innocent of stealing

Features a good shot of an LNER 'F6' 2-4-2T arriving at an unknown station, possibly Stratford, with a local passenger train. Elsewhere in the film there is a scene at Liverpool Street station.

THE WISDOM OF CROCODILES
GB 1998 Entertainment/Zenith/Goldwyn
   DVD
Dir: Po Chih Leong
Jude Law, Elina Lowensohn

A vampire in London survives by drinking the blood of women who love him

Includes scenes filmed at Waterloo Underground station on the Waterloo & City Line platforms with 1990s tube stock.

WITHOUT A CLUE
US 1988 Rank/ITC
Dir: Thom Eberhardt
Michael Caine, Ben Kingsley

In reality Sherlock Holmes is a mediocre detective and it is Watson who is the real sleuth

This interesting comedy based on the Holmes legend features scenes filmed on the Lakeside & Haverthwaite Railway, including Lakeside station itself with Hudswell-Clarke 0-6-0T No 31 from the Keighley & Worth Valley Railway and two Metropolitan coaches from the Vintage Carriage Trust.

WOMBLING FREE
GB 1977 Rank DVD
Dir: Lionel Jeffries
David Tomlinson, Bonnie Langford

The Wombles of Wimbledon make contact with humans

This big-screen version of the classic children's series has a number of railway scenes, with shots of passing Class 117 DMUs on WR London suburban services and a scene with Tomlinson filmed outside Marlow station.

WOMEN IN LOVE
GB 1969 UA/Brandywine VHS
Dir: Ken Russell
Glenda Jackson, Alan Bates

Two girls' sexual encounters in the 1920s

This famous adaptation of the D. H. Lawrence novel includes some dramatic scenes filmed with coal trains hauled by Hunslet 'Austerity' 0-6-0STs. The exact location for these scenes is unknown, but it is believed to be near a colliery in the Derbyshire/Nottinghamshire coalfield. There are also period scenes with restored double-deck trams filmed at Crich open-air museum.

WONDERLAND
GB 1999 Universal/BBC DVD
Dir: Michael Winterbottom
Shirley Henderson, Ian Hart

Three sisters have man trouble

A scene near the end of this London-set drama was filmed at Euston station with an HST and a rake of Mk 3 stock headed by DVT car No 82129 visible. Elsewhere there is a night shot of a passing electric-hauled express and some distant views of SR EMUs.

WORK IS A FOUR LETTER WORD
GB 1967 Universal
Dir: Peter Hall
David Warner, Cilla Black

A social misfit gets a job at a power station so he can grow mushrooms

Includes a scene at a railway carriage washing plant, which was filmed at Marylebone DMU depot with a couple of Class 115 sets passing through it – car Nos M59655 and M51879 are identifiable.

THE WORLD TEN TIMES OVER
GB 1962 Cyclops
Dir: Wolf Rilla
Sylvia Sims, June Ritchie

Life with two escort girls in London

Features a scene at Marylebone station with Class 115 DMUs in adjacent platforms. Rather bizarrely this sequence incorporates a brief shot of the characters walking across Waterloo station concourse! There is also a scene on the South Bank close to the Charing Cross-Waterloo East line, and a couple of BR-built EMUs can be seen in the background passing by.

THE WRECKER
GB 1929 Gainsborough
Dir: G. M. Bolvary
Carlyle Blackwell, Benita Hume

A crook wrecks trains to discredit the railway companies

An early Gainsborough film, one of the last made as a silent, it features a most elaborate crash scene for the time using a real locomotive and rolling-stock hitting a lorry on a level crossing. The footage was so spectacular that most of it was used for a crash in the 1936 film *Seven Sinners* as well as later films such as *The Earth Dies Screaming* (1964) (both qv). The location of the crash was Salter's Ash crossing near Lasham on the Basingstoke & Alton Light Railway. Gainsborough bought ex-SECR Stirling 4-4-0 No A148 with six ex-SECR coaches from the SR and painted the loco grey with 'United Coast Lines' lettering on the tender. After a number of rehearsals the train was set off by its crew who then jumped clear as it slowly accelerated down the gradient. An old Foden steam lorry was placed on the crossing with dynamite on board to create a good explosion for the cameras. Additionally the track beyond the crossing was undermined to cause the ensuing derailment. The end result was indeed spectacular, with all but the pair of wheels on the rear coach leaving the rails. After filming was completed the wreckage was cut up by contractors, although one coach underframe remained on site in the bushes until the 1950s, long after the line had closed. Even after this, when the land was cultivated, removing all trace of the trackbed, small pieces of wreckage turned up in the field from time to time. The crash sequence has rather overshadowed the other railway scenes in the film, which feature a variety of Southern motive power – 'D' Class 4-4-0, Maunsell 2-6-0, a rare 'H16' 4-6-2T, 'L' Class 4-4-0 No 756, Urie 4-6-0 No 452, 'U' Class 2-6-0 No 803, 'D15' Class 4-4-0 No 463 and 'King Arthur' 4-6-0 No 773. Locations include Waterloo station, Sevenoaks and Polhill Tunnel.

THE WRONG BOX

GB 1966 Columbia
Dir: Bryan Forbes
Michael Caine, Ralph Richardson

Two elderly brothers are the last survivors of a tontine lottery and try to stay alive

Part of the story involves a head-on crash between two Bournemouth expresses, which involved some clever editing and an elaborate set involving a couple of full-size replica locomotives placed in 'crash' position. The coaches in this scene look real, however, and it seems likely, judging from the scenery, that this footage was filmed on the Longmoor Military Railway. Interestingly, just before the crash there are a couple of shots of one of the approaching expresses and it seems to be hauled by a light-green-liveried 'Terrier' 0-6-0T, indicating that these shots were filmed on the Bluebell Railway. Later in the film there is a scene with Dudley Moore filmed at Bath Green Park station, not long before closure, with 'Jinty' 0-6-0T No 47676 painted light green to look like an LSWR locomotive at the buffer stops.

XYZ

A YANK AT OXFORD
GB/US 1938 MGM
Dir: Jack Conway
Robert Taylor, Maureen O'Sullivan

A cocky American goes to Oxford University

Features a view of a GWR 4-6-0 on an express, possibly on the Didcot-Oxford section of the GWR.

YANKS
GB 1979 United Artists DVD
Dir: John Schlesinger
Richard Gere, Vanessa Redgrave

American GIs find romance in a Lancashire town during the Second World War

This successful blockbuster of the late 1970s has some excellent scenes filmed on the Keighley & Worth Valley Railway, with Keighley station and yard dominating as troop trains send the American Army off to war. Locomotives prominent in these scenes include LMS 8F 2-8-0 No 8431, 'USA' 2-8-0 No 474 (as USA Transportation Corp 28201), BR Standard 5MT 4-6-0 No 75078 (as '5078') and SR 'West Country' 'Pacific' (!) No 34092. An interesting development during filming of the 'specials' was that K&WVR locomotives had to run along BR metals to Shipley to turn on the triangle there between takes. Filming took place in June/July 1978.

THE YELLOW BALLOON
GB 1952 ABP
Dir: J. Lee Thompson
Andrew Ray, William Sylvester

A small boy thinks he has killed a friend and is menaced by a real murderer

Features some suspense scenes on the London Underground with 1924-built tube stock appearing.

YELLOW CANARY
GB 1943 RKO
Dir: Herbert Wilcox
Anna Neagle, Richard Greene

A Nazi sympathiser is actually a British spy setting out to fool the Germans

Features a railway scene where a night train is caught in the middle of a bombing raid. This is mainly studio material, but includes a couple of shots of passing night expresses, one behind an unidentified Southern passenger loco and another behind an LNER 'C1' 4-4-2.

YESTERDAY'S HERO
GB 1979 Columbia VHS
Dir: Neil Leifer
Ian McShane, Suzanne Somers

A successful footballer goes off the rails but recovers

The opening scene features a freight train behind a 'skinhead' Class 31 diesel passing a football ground, location unknown.

THE YOUNG AMERICANS
GB 1993 Rank/Polygram VHS
Dir: Danny Cannon
Harvey Keitel, Iain Glen

An American cop helps London police solve drug-related killings

Features some shots of Southern EMUs passing in the Borough/Southwark area of South London, including 4-EPB and 4-CEP/VEP types. There is also a scene on the London Underground at Holborn station with 1972 Piccadilly Line tube stock.

YOUNG AND INNOCENT
GB 1937 GFD/Gainsborough DVD
Dir: Alfred Hitchcock
Nova Pilbeam, Derrick de Marney

A man is suspected of murder and goes on the run with his girlfriend

There are no real trains in this Hitchcock film, but there is a scene next to a railway line in which the trains that appear are obviously models – very good models, in fact, of Gresley 'Pacifics' on expresses (possibly Bassett-Lowke), but rather artificial-looking after *The Thirty Nine Steps*!

THE YOUNG LOVERS
GB 1954 GFD VHS
Dir: Anthony Asquith
Odile Versois, David Knight

A US Embassy man falls in love with the daughter of a Soviet minister

In the latter half of the film the two lovers flee to the coast by train and there are a couple of stock shots of LMS expresses hauled by a 'Duchess' 'Pacific' and a 'Royal Scot' 4-6-0. There are also scenes at Victoria and Newhaven Harbour stations with an SR 4-COR EMU (set No 3133) and a 2-BIL unit appearing.

YOUNG WINSTON
GB 1972 Columbia DVD
Dir: Richard Attenborough
Simon Ward, Robert Shaw

The early life of Winston Churchill, including his time in the Boer War

Much of this lavish epic deals with Churchill's time in the British Army during the Boer War, which called for a number of elaborate railway sequences. First in the film is a scene in which an armoured train comes under attack in the hills. This was shot in Wales on the Neath-Brecon line near Craig-y-Nos with heavily disguised GWR '1400' 0-4-2T No 1466 (borrowed from GWS Didcot), fitted with dummy armour plating and a large headlamp. Later in the film, when Churchill is making his escape after imprisonment, there are some scenes filmed on the Longmoor Military Railway with 'USA' 0-6-0T No 30064 and 9F 2-10-0 No 92203 both disguised as South African locomotives. No 30064 escapes fairly lightly with just a cow-catcher and 'SAR' on its side tanks, but 92203 has had its smoke deflectors removed, and a large fibreglass chimney and dome, cow-catcher and headlight added, together with an 'SAR' motif on its tender and the first and last digits blacked out on its smokebox numberplate, making it '220'.

ZEE AND CO
GB 1971 Columbia
Dir: Brian G. Hutton
Elizabeth Taylor, Michael Caine

An architect battles with his wife and seeks an affair

Features a scene at King's Cross station with Class 47 diesel No 1934 at the buffer stops together with a Class 125 suburban DMU.

Appendix 1
Preserved railways
in feature films

Bluebell Railway

The Innocents (1961)
Waltz of the Toreadors (1962)
Khartoum (1966)
I'll Never Forget Whatsisname (1967)
The Naked Runner (1967)
The Beast in the Cellar (1970)
Adolf Hitler – My Part in his Downfall
   (1972)
Savage Messiah (1972)
Mahler (1974)
Lisztomania (1975)
Tommy (1975)
Double Exposure (1976)
Dracula (1977)
Emily (1977)
Hardcore (1978)
Let's Get Laid (1978)
Tess (1979)
Bullshot (1983)
A Room with a View (1985)
Maurice (1987)
A Handful of Dust (1988)
Where Angels Fear to Tread (1990)
Tom and Viv (1991)
Black Beauty (1993)

Richard III (1995)
Haunted (1996)
The Wind in the Willows (1996)
102 Dalmatians (2000)
Charlotte Gray (2002)
The Importance of Being Earnest (2002)
Two Men Went to War (2002)
Starter for Ten (2006)
London to Brighton (2006)
Miss Potter (2007)

Bodmin & Wenford Railway

Half Light (2006)

Bo'ness Railway

Beautiful Creatures (1999)

Buckinghamshire Railway Centre

The Crucifer of Blood (1991)

Chinnor & Princes Risborough Railway

Photographing Fairies (1997)

Dean Forest Railway

Darklands (1995)

Didcot Railway Centre

One of Our Dinosaurs is Missing (1975)
The Incredible Sarah (1975)
Meetings with Remarkable Men (1979)
Distant Voices Still Lives (1988)
Funny Bones (1995)
These Foolish Things (2006)

Great Central Railway

Buster (1988)
Shadowlands (1993)
Enigma (2001)
The Hours (2003)

Keighley & Worth Valley Railway

The Railway Children (1970)
The Private Life of Sherlock Holmes
   (1970)
Escape from the Dark (1976)
It Shouldn't Happen to a Vet (1976)
Yanks (1979)
Pink Floyd – The Wall (1982)
Jude (1995)
Feast of July (1997)
Fairytale – A True Story (1997)
Amy Foster (1997)

Kent & East Sussex Railway

Flame (1973)
Dracula (1973)
1984 (1984)
Cold Comfort Farm (1995)

Lakeside & Haverthwaite Railway

Swallows and Amazons (1974)
Without a Clue (1988)

Mid-Hants Railway

Bullseye (1990)
Clockwork Mice (1995)
High Heels and Low Lifes (2001)
Two Men Went to War (2002)
Children of Men (2006)

Nene Valley Railway

Octopussy (1983)
Top Secret! (1984)
Biggles (1986)
Peter's Friends (1991)
Goldeneye (1996)
The Secret Agent (1996)
GMT – Greenwich Mean Time (1998)

North Norfolk Railway

Waterland (1992)

North Yorkshire Moors Railway

A Month in the Country (1987)
Amy Foster (1997)
Harry Potter and the Philosopher's Stone
   (2001)
Possession (2002)
Keeping Mum (2005)

Paignton & Dartmouth Railway

The French Lieutenant's Woman (1981)
A Summer Story (1987)
Churchill – the Hollywood Years (2004)

Severn Valley Railway

The Seven Per Cent Solution (1976)
Candleshoe (1977)
The Thirty Nine Steps (1978)
Howards End (1992)
Simon Magus (1998)
The Chronicles of Narnia (2005)

South Devon Railway

The Stick Up (1977)
A Summer Story (1987)
Churchill – the Hollywood Years (2004)

Strathspey Railway

Silent Scream (1989)

Wells & Walsingham Light Railway

Dad Savage (1997)

West Somerset Railway

The Land Girls (1997)

Appendix 2:
London termini in feature films

Broad Street

The Very Edge (1963)

Charing Cross

Mad Dogs (2002)

Euston

I See Ice (1938)
Terror by Night (1946)
Train of Events (1948)
Mandy (1952)
The Silken Affair (1956)
Indiscreet (1958)
Night Train for Inverness (1959)
No Love for Johnnie (1960)
Play it Cool (1962)
It Happened Here (1963)
Praise Marx and Pass the Ammunition (1968)
Lamb (1986)
Wonderland (1999)
The Mother (2003)

King's Cross

The Flying Scotsman (1929)
Friday the Thirteenth (1933)
Oh Daddy (1935)
The Thirty Nine Steps (1935)
The Tenth Man (1936)
Bank Holiday (1938)

Thursday's Child (1943)
The Ladykillers (1955)
Bachelor of Hearts (1958)
Mrs Brown You've Got a Lovely Daughter (1968)
Hoffman (1970)
Zee and Co (1971)
Tank Malling (1988)
Killing Dad (1989)
Career Girls (1997)
Born Romantic (2000)
Harry Potter and the Philosopher's Stone (2001)
Harry Potter and the Chamber of Secrets (2002)
Harry Potter and the Prisoner of Azkaban (2003)

Liverpool Street

The Silent Passenger (1935)
The Winslow Boy (1949)
The Holly and the Ivy (1952)
Rainbow Jacket (1954)
Suspended Alibi (1957)
I Was Monty's Double (1958)
The Inn of the Sixth Happiness (1958)
The War Lover (1962)
The Informers (1963)
The File on the Golden Goose (1969)
The Sex Express (1973)

The Dogs of War (1980)
Runners (1983)
A Prayer for the Dying (1987)
Mission Impossible (1991)
Stormbreaker (2006)

Marylebone

Lady Godiva Rides Again (1951)
Nowhere to Go (1958)
The Trials of Oscar Wilde (1960)
No My Darling Daughter (1961)
The World Ten Times Over (1962)
Day of the Triffids (1962)
Postman's Knock (1962)
Billy Liar (1963)
The Beauty Jungle (1964)
A Hard Day's Night (1964)
The Battle of the Villa Florita (1964)
Nothing But the Best (1964)
The Ipcress File (1965)
Rotten to the Core (1965)
Khartoum (1966)
The Brides of Fu Manchu (1966)
Star! (1968)
A Touch of Love (1969)
Young Winston (1972)
Carry on Girls (1973)
Mahler (1974)
The Internecine Project (1974)
One of Our Dinosaurs is Missing (1975)
Let's Get Laid (1978)
The Great Rock 'n' Roll Swindle (1979)
Separate Lies (2005)

Paddington

The Last Journey (1936)
Return to Yesterday (1940)
The Black Sheep of Whitehall (1941)
The Echo Murders (1943)
The October Man (1947)
Counterblast (1948)
The Astonished Heart (1949)
Dr Morelle (1949)
A Run for Your Money (1949)
Miranda (1949)
Whispering Smith Hits London (1951)
The Frightened Man (1952)

Mad About Men (1954)
Fast and Loose (1954)
The Belles of St Trinian's (1954)
The Man Who Never Was (1956)
The Flying Scot (1957)
6.5 Special (1957)
The Battle of the Sexes (1960)
Murder She Said (1961)
Selena (1962)
Bitter Harvest (1963)
The Mind Benders (1963)
Nothing but the Best (1964)
Dr Terror's House of Horrors (1965)
Joanna (1968)
Perfect Friday (1970)
Cool it Carol (1970)
Performance (1970)
A Severed Head (1970)
Quadrophenia (1979)
The Long Good Friday (1980)
Runners (1983)
Bellman and True (1987)
A Handful of Dust (1988)
Paper Mask (1990)
Chaplin (1992)
The Girl from Rio (2001)
The Chronicles of Narnia (2005)
Breakfast on Pluto (2006)

St Pancras

Appointment with Crime (1945)
Simon and Laura (1955)
The Painted Smile (1961)
The Servant (1963)
The Comedy Man (1963)
The Great British Train Robbery (1967)
A Nice Girl Like Me (1969)
Brannigan (1975)
McVicar (1980)
Just Ask for Diamond (1988)
High Hopes (1988)
Smiling Through (1991)
King Ralph (1991)
The Pleasure Principle (1991)
Howards End (1992)
Richard III (1995)
Five Seconds to Spare (2000)

102 Dalmatians (2000)
Spider (2003)

Victoria

Love Life and Laughter (1936)
The Divorce of Lady X (1938)
The Lady Vanishes (1938)
The Black Sheep of Whitehall (1941)
Somewhere on Leave (1942)
English Without Tears (1944)
Never Look Back (1952)
A Day to Remember (1953)
The Saint's Return (1953)
Father Brown (1954)
The Girl on the Pier (1954)
Forbidden Cargo (1954)
The Young Lovers (1954)
The Man from Tangiers (1958)
The End of the Line (1959)
Night Train to Paris (1964)
The Pleasure Girls (1964)
The Alphabet Murders (1965)
Say Hello to Yesterday (1970)
The Wildcats of St Trinian's (1980)
Runners (1983)
Bullseye (1990)
Parting Shots (1998)
High Heels and Low Lifes (2001)
London to Brighton (2006)

Waterloo

Dusty Ermine (1935)
Oh Daddy (1935)
Seven Sinners (1936)
Bank Holiday (1938)

The Girl in the News (1940)
The Gentle Sex (1943)
Millions Like Us (1943)
The Demi Paradise (1943)
Waterloo Road (1944)
The Brighton Strangler (1945)
The Seventh Veil (1945)
Night Boat to Dublin (1946)
Piccadilly Incident (1946)
The Miniver Story (1950)
Seven Days to Noon (1950)
The Long Memory (1951)
The Final Test (1953)
Rough Shoot (1953)
The Good Die Young (1954)
John and Julie (1955)
The Heart Within (1957)
The Hypnotist (1957)
The Rebel (1960)
The World Ten Times Over (1962)
Nothing But the Best (1964)
Arabesque (1966)
Where the Bullets Fly (1966)
Alfie (1966)
The Jokers (1966)
Inadmissible Evidence (1968)
Ooh You Are Awful (1972)
Horror Hospital (1973)
Juggernaut (1974)
Hennessey (1975)
B Monkey (1998)
Londinium (2001)
The Constant Gardener (2005)
London to Brighton (2006)